Middle East Today

Series Editors
Fawaz A. Gerges, Department of International Relations, London
School of Economics, London, UK
Nader Hashemi, Josef Korbel School of International Studies, Center for
Middle East Studies, University of Denver, Denver, CO, USA

The Iranian Revolution of 1979, the Iran-Iraq War, the Gulf War, and the US invasion and occupation of Iraq have dramatically altered the geopolitical landscape of the contemporary Middle East. The Arab Spring uprisings have complicated this picture. This series puts forward a critical body of first-rate scholarship that reflects the current political and social realities of the region, focusing on original research about contentious politics and social movements; political institutions; the role played by non-governmental organizations such as Hamas, Hezbollah, and the Muslim Brotherhood; and the Israeli-Palestine conflict. Other themes of interest include Iran and Turkey as emerging pre-eminent powers in the region, the former an 'Islamic Republic' and the latter an emerging democracy currently governed by a party with Islamic roots; the Gulf monarchies, their petrol economies and regional ambitions; potential problems of nuclear proliferation in the region; and the challenges confronting the United States, Europe, and the United Nations in the greater Middle East. The focus of the series is on general topics such as social turmoil, war and revolution, international relations, occupation, radicalism, democracy, human rights, and Islam as a political force in the context of the modern Middle East.

More information about this series at
http://www.palgrave.com/gp/series/14803

Saad N. Jawad

Iraq after the Invasion

From Fragmentation to Rebirth and Reintegration

Saad N. Jawad
London, UK

Middle East Today
ISBN 978-3-030-72105-3   ISBN 978-3-030-72106-0   (eBook)
https://doi.org/10.1007/978-3-030-72106-0

This Palgrave Macmillan imprint is published by the registered company Springer Nature Switzerland AG
The registered company address is: Gewerbestrasse 11, 6330 Cham, Switzerland

To Sawsan and Mariam

CONTENTS

Contents

CHAPTER 1

Introduction

In 2003, invading and occupying Iraq was neither a trivial or passing matter, nor an event that could be easily forgotten. This was primarily due to its catastrophic consequences which affected not only Iraq but the whole region, and the world at large. Instead of turning Iraq into a stable democratic country as the invaders claimed, in which human rights had to be respected, it turned it into a failed state. The other disastrous results were the prevalence and spread of terrorism not only in Iraq but also in the region, the end of Iraq as a united country, the spread of corruption, the deaths of more than one million people killed, as well as the immense financial cost that caused the United States itself a severe economic crisis.

It is true that the Iraqis, just like most peoples of the world, were expecting a major attack on their country, but they thought it was simply designed to overthrow the regime of the late Iraqi President Saddam Hussein. They did not think or anticipate the whole plan to end with direct occupation which was later approved by the United Nations, the organization that declared the end of the era of colonialism and direct rule in the sixties of the last century. The majority of Iraqis, including the political leadership, had imagined that the whole process was an attempt to overthrow a regime in the region hostile to the United States, replacing it with another one loyal to it and that that would comply with its idea of a new Middle East led by Israel.

© The Author(s), under exclusive license to Springer Nature Switzerland AG 2021
S. N. Jawad, *Iraq after the Invasion*, Middle East Today,
https://doi.org/10.1007/978-3-030-72106-0_1

1

It seems, however, that President Saddam Hussein himself was of the opinion that the main objective of the military operation was to inflict as much damage as possible to Iraqi's military power and infrastructure of Iraq. He may have thought that it would be difficult to remove him from power, and that the Iraqi military might at least hinder the advancement of the invaders, inflict heavy losses and force them to limit their military objectives. He realized as soon as the invasion began that his calculations were wrong. As it became clear at that time that the Iraqi forces were not a match to the huge coalition military strength that was prepared to invade Iraq.

On the other hand, some observers and analysts argued that what happened to Iraq was a result of the many political flaws committed by the Baath regime and its leader Saddam Hussein, which involved Iraq in many crises and wars that ended with the occupation of the country. Although, others believe that the emergence of a powerful Iraq in the region after 1968 (the Baath's party coming to power), that adamantly rejected the United States plans for a new Middle East, of which Israel would be a key factor, was the real reason behind all that happened. They also believe that all the fuss about the weapons of mass destruction (WMD), lack of respect for human rights and about Iraq being a threat to neighbouring countries, (especially after the massive destruction of the country's capabilities after the 1991 war), was nothing but fabricated lies to justify aggression and then occupation.

What supports the group's opinion that Iraq was able to find a peaceful solution to the Kurdish crisis based on autonomy in 1970 against all expectations. This agreement peacefully ended a long internal war, stopped a crisis that impoverished the country and drained its human and economic resources. The nationalization of the oil industry in 1972, which meant the end of foreign investment in this sector and a huge increase in oil revenues particularly after 1973 was more alarming to the West, the USA and Israel, who were keen to see the Kurdish problem continue and the internal fighting in Iraqi Kurdistan continued. It also meant a large hard currency surplus that allowed Iraq to implement ambitious programmes for development, especially in the field of military power. The well-drilled Iraqi army was clearly demonstrated in the 1973 war against Israel and the 1974–1975 war in Iraqi Kurdistan. It should also be noted the signing of the Treaty of Friendship between Iraq and the Soviet Union in (April 1972) was another cause for concern in the United States and the West. The USA, Britain, the West, Israel and Iran have regarded this treaty as a serious Soviet expansion in the region. While it is also meant for the capitalist world a serious step towards Soviet control of all development plans in Iraq, i.e. denying the West of any significant economic benefit in the potential Iraqi market. All these reasons have given rise to the possibility of intervention by foreign parties that tried with all their strength to drag Iraq into conflicts, problems and wars in order to drain its national resources and thwart its development projects. (This was also the case in Egypt under late President Jamal Abdel Nasser.) This does not mean that the leadership of Iraq (and before it that of Egypt, and later on Syria and Libya), has been removed from any criticism or responsibility for what happened to their countries due to the authoritarian nature of their governments, the absence of democracy and the establishment police states. The claims of these regimes that all these measures were necessary for three reasons, first, that post-independence era required strict centralized governments to put an end to the feudal system and the widespread poverty. Secondly, that the Arab people were not qualified for democracy because of their ill-education, and thirdly, the claim that the struggle with Israel necessitated certain patterns of rule, gradually lost its credibility. This could also be said about the argument of these regimes that their mistakes, suppression or interference should be forgiven because they were patriotic regimes working for the good of their countries and their citizens. These dictatorial measures ultimately weakened these regimes and caused their downfall. In other words, in the name of democracy, as it happened in Iraq, the actions of these patriotic regimes gave their enemies the arms with which they were able to put them down, often with foreign support. Unfortunately, the welfare of these countries or their population never really mattered. The invasion and occupation of Iraq is the clearest example of this.

Yet other observers maintained, with a reasonable amount of reason and accuracy, that if the Iraqi monarchy (1921–1958), had the chance to continue, it would have created another stable Iraq state that is more developed, flourished and prosperous. However, those who favour this opinion tend to forget the many mistakes committed by the monarchical regime which in the end led to its downfall.

Among these mistakes were: First, the insistence of the ruling political elites, mainly Premier Nouri al-Said and Regent Abdul Ilah, to adhere to power and refusing to allow young generations to take part in governing the country, something that neighbouring King Hussein of Jordan shrewdly implemented efficiently.

Second, not allowing the opposition, even if it were simple and ineffective, to play any role in Iraqi politics, through continuous attempts to rig the elections.

Third, the insistence on executing some peaceful opponents who did not practice armed resistance (such as the leaders of the Iraqi Communist Party in 1949) or the method of displaying the bodies of its executed opponents for days in public places (as it happened with the much loved Iraqi officers who led the May 1941 revolt, against the British domination of the country, despite the fact that their aim was not to overthrow the monarchy). Fourth, the complete alignment of the royal regime, or subordination to Britain, which was regarded by the Iraqis as instrumental in establishing a Jewish entity in Palestine.

Fifth, the decision to oppose the rising tide of Arab nationalism led by the late President Jamal Abdel Nasser, and especially the decision to abide with Britain during the 1956 British-French-Israeli aggression against Egypt following the nationalization of the Suez Canal.

Finally, the monarchical regime neglected the economic factor, which led to the failure of paying attention to the sufferings and poverty of the majority of the Iraqi people, while it continued to support and defend the feudal class.[1]

The plans to overthrow the Iraqi Baath regime and destroy the huge military power it possessed began to take shape immediately after the end of the Iraq–Iran war (1988). Against the wishes and expectations of all the international and regional opponents of Iraq, who wanted the war to drag on to weaken the two sides, or at best end with no victor and no vanquished, Iraq came victorious and obliged the Iranian leadership to accept ceasefire. These opponents, headed mainly by Israel, the USA, Britain and the Gulf countries, were more alarmed by the conduct of the Iraqi army during the final stages of the war, and the huge military arsenal and experience it acquired. Of course, the disastrous decision taken by Saddam Hussein to invade Kuwait (August 1990) was the straw that triggered the plan to destroy the Iraqi military power. From that day, the USA, Britain and Israel began to fabricate stories about Iraq's WMD to justify their actions.

The primary aim of this book is to verify the false and fabricated issues the US–British–Israeli coalition put forward to justify their military action against Iraq. Also, why this act was illegal and why the Security Council did not approve of it. It also aimed at explaining why a fair number of Iraqis felt indifferent to what was awaiting their country following the disastrous terrorist attacks of 11 September 2001. Second is to discuss the manifold problems that surfaced as a result of the invasion and the occupation that ensued. These issues cannot be understood without going back to study the many wars that the Iraqis have been subjected to since the arrival of the Ba'ath party to power in 1968, (the war in Iraqi Kurdistan 1974–1975, the prolonged, brutal and intensive Iraq–Iran war 1980–1988, the 1991 Gulf war to oust the Iraqi forces from Kuwait), and most importantly the inhumane thirteen years of harsh and unprecedented international sanctions (1990–2003) following the invasion of Kuwait. All these events have turned a fair segment of the Iraqi people into being indifferent to what was coming. A fair portion of the Iraqis even thought that removing the totalitarian Baath regime through external invasion was perhaps the only way to get rid of it, and that such a change could bring their democracy, prosperity and respect for human rights. Soon they discovered that they were very much disillusioned.

The book also aimed at discussing the outcome of the occupation; and more importantly, the policies of the two main occupying countries (the United States and Britain) which led to the sharp sectarian and ethnical division that overwhelmed the country. These divisive policies were culminated by the United States call to divide Iraq into three entities.

The book also concentrated on the major issues that caused the total disintegration of the Iraqi state, starting with the harmful decisions taken by the occupying administration, such as dissolving the Armed forces, the de-Baathification law, treating Iraq as an artificial state, denying the Arab identity of the majority of the Iraqis and ignoring the Iraqi identity of the people of the country.

There were other decisions that caused lasting harm such as:

First, was the fact that all these divisive actions were incarnated (embodied) in a permanent constitution that the Iraqis had a minor role, if any, in drafting it. In fact this constitution is still being regarded as the main cause of all the problems Iraq is facing, as well as the cause of the division inside the Iraqi society. Suffice it to say that it helped to create a weak central government and a strong Kurdish federal region. It was not surprising then that the major Kurdish parties resorted to its ambiguous clauses every now and then to claim separation from the Iraqi state, or behave as a de facto independent state. At the same time other oil-rich provinces are trying to depend on the same vague clauses to claim a status that enables them only to enjoy the biggest share of oil revenues.

Second, the sectarian, racial and quota policies initiated by the occupying forces, which created divisions among the components of the Iraqi society. Moreover, the quota system allowed the parties participating in the political process, (the vast majority of them came with the occupying forces), to dominate the key positions in the government. Of course this was done with the full support of the United States to some parties and that of Iran for others.

One can also add that the occupying administration regarded Iraq as an 'artificial country', and treated the Iraqi society as a society composed of Shiites, Sunnis, Christians, (not Arabs) Kurds and other smaller minorities, and not as one Iraqi people. On top of that, only the Shiites and Kurds were favoured by that administration, because, according to its allegation, they were the components that was largely encroached by the old regime, (of course not all Shiites or Kurds were favoured or treated in this positive way, only those who came or cooperated with the invading forces from these two components have received such a privilege). On the other hand, the Sunnis in general were looked at as Baathists, supporters of the old regime of Saddam Hussein and, in the view of the US administration and those who cooperated with it, were not worth treating equally or even protected as human beings.

The third damaging practice was that all those who cooperated with the invaders, regardless of their inefficiency, ill-education and tarnished reputation, were the ones who were entitled to rule Iraq. While all the Iraqis living in Iraq at the time of the invasion were regarded as followers of the old regime, regardless of their efficiencies, merits or high qualifications.

The two occupying forces were not the only elements to be blamed for causing the damage, indeed the policies of the successive Iraqi government after 2003 have also played a major role in this division.

Fourth, there are other assisting factors that contributed to the disintegration of Iraq. They included the role of regional powers, such as Iran, Israel, the Arab Gulf countries and Turkey, as well as the widespread corruption that engulfed the country following the occupation and because of it.

The damage and division caused by the national unity and integration of the country to these policies was, and still is, huge, and could only be fully apprehended by those who were living in Iraq. Thus, this book endeavours to give an Iraqi point of view, depending on Iraqi narratives, from someone familiar with all the events that took place in Iraq during the Iraq–Iran war, the sanctions and the occupation itself.

The book is divided into five chapters, to cover all the main issues mentioned above. The first chapter discussed the situation in Iraq prior to the invasion, in order to give a clear idea about how and what the majority of Iraqis were thinking regarding what was being planned for their country in Washington, London and Tel Aviv. It also tried to show how the leadership of Baath regime was thinking about what was planned against it.

The second chapter mainly discussed the invasion and its aftermath. How it was planned, what were the excuses put forward by the invaders, what were the mistakes committed during and after the invasion, what was the Iraqis' reaction to it, and importantly why the Iraqis failed to challenge the occupation and its disastrous outcomes.

As the new permanent constitution was, and still is, regarded as the major source of the division in Iraq, the third chapter tried to discuss the flaws of this document, who wrote it, how it was passed and what were its major loopholes.

The fourth chapter was fully allocated to discussing the chronic Kurdish dilemma in Iraq. The discussion however, was not meant to follow the development of this problem, which was covered in many writings, it was rather an attempt to find out why all the solutions to this dilemma have failed in Iraq.

Finally, the fifth chapter was devoted to discussing the damaged national unity and integration of the Iraq state and society. What were the causes, as well as ways to amend the split caused by the occupation and the new politicians that came with it. More importantly, what are the needed steps for successful national reconciliation?

Much has been written about the occupation of Iraq, or Iraq after 2003, particularly by Western writers. These writers had either supported the idea of the invasion, consequently the US–British colonization of Iraq, or had worked closely with the occupying forces, but due to the huge mistakes committed by the occupation they criticized the mistakes committed. In other words they were not against the idea of occupation; they were rather against the practice. Some of them still think that the United States could save Iraq by re-occupying it and amend the mistakes previously committed. Yet materials written by Iraqis who totally rejected the idea of invasion and occupation, and who lived through all the crises Iraq witnessed (the Iraq–Iran war, the invasion of Kuwait, the strict sanctions, the 1991 destructive war, witnessed the American invasion and lastly lived under the occupation and suffering from its after-maths), remained scarce. Therefore, the other objective behind writing this book is to record an Iraqi view about all these events. At the same time all these events are narrated by a person who not only lived inside Iraq but also chose to oppose the idea of one-party system, and at the same time strongly opposed the idea of relying on external powers to bring about change in Iraq, as well as adamantly refusing the occupation and its aftermath. All this in the hope that the arguments put forward would represent a national Iraqi vision in the midst of the many ones that represented foreign ones, and responding to the views that tried to justify the occupation or fully cooperate with it.

Two final notes for the reader: First: the author, against his beliefs and convictions of loathing and detesting sectarian language and terminolo-gies, was obliged to use such references as the events since 2003 forced itself to explain some of what happened. Second, the issues discussed in this book are so intertwined that it obliged the writer to discuss matters that were analysed in details in some chapters. For example it was neces-sary to discuss the role of the new constitution in the chapters dealing with the Kurdish dilemma and the one discussing national reconciliation, although there is a full chapter allocated for the constitution itself. Simi-larly, was the decisions taken by the occupation and the outcome of the occupation.

In the end I should take this opportunity to thank all those who helped in finishing this book starting with my wife Dr. Sawsan Ismail al-Assaf for her assistance in finding some of the sources for which this book was written and helping me to use the internet efficiently. I want to also thank our little daughter Mariam for her patience, and apologize to her for the times she felt, that she was not getting the attention she deserved. Thanks to the many friends and colleagues who helped in providing me with internal information from inside Iraq, especially after 2010 when I decided to leave the country permanently due to the threats I faced. Paramount among this category is the late Dr. Wathiq Salim al-Hashimi, my old student and close friend, who was enormously helpful, May his soul rest in peace. Thanks also to my friends Dr. Naji Sabri al-Hadithi, former Iraqi minister for foreign affairs, for his valuable comments and corrections, especially on the first chapter, to Professor Dhia al—Joburi and Mr. Leheb Abdul Wahab, for the English corrections they made to some drafts. I am grateful to all those who provided me with useful information, their names and contributions are cited in the book itself as sources.

Profound thanks and gratitude should also be extended to my friend and colleague professor Fawaz Gerges, LSE, for continuously urging and encouraging me to finish this book.

Finally, I am indebted to all the friends and followers of my writings who provided me, through their comments, with the incentive to continue to write.

NOTE

1. See the articles written by Dr. Kadhum Habib about that period: http://m.ahewar.org/s.aso?aid=647042&r=0.

CHAPTER 2

Iraq: Pre-Occupation Years

It is not easy to study the Iraqi situation before US–UK invasion without discussing a problematic dichotomy. Iraqis, on the one hand, suffered from cruel, inhumane and devastating UN sanctions. The embargo that lasted for almost 13 years (August 1990–April 2003), badly affected the life of the Iraqi people. More accurately, it made their life difficult. On the other hand, Iraqis showed a great deal of resilience and defiantly faced attempts by the USA, Britain, Israel and other allies to break their morale.[1]

Throughout those difficult years, Iraqis' position on who to blame for the situation that had befallen them split into two: First, some Iraqis blamed the government, while the others blamed the sanctions. Meanwhile, the vast majority felt helpless to do anything to improve their conditions.

Some scholars, including the writer, believed that the invasion and occupation would be inevitably coming regardless of the plight of Iraqis'. Subduing Iraq was simply a top American and Zionist objective for three reasons: First, the substantial military power Iraq possessed at the end of the Iraq–Iran war. Second and more importantly is Saddam Hussein's daring decision to fire 39 long-range Iraqi missiles at Israel during the 1991 Gulf war, and finally, the 9/11 events, which led the United States to accuse Iraq of being a culprit.

© The Author(s), under exclusive license to Springer Nature Switzerland AG 2021
S. N. Jawad, *Iraq after the Invasion*, Middle East Today, https://doi.org/10.1007/978-3-030-72106-0_2

This chapter will focus on three issues: first, the negative conditions in Iraq, which led to the April 2003 disaster of the invasion and full occupation of Iraq. Second, and more importantly, what made some Iraqis feel indifferent or silent about what was inevitably coming, i.e. the occupation. Finally, it will look at the factors that helped the invaders to fabricate and put forward certain pretexts to justify the brutal invasion of Iraq.

THE IRAQ–IRAN WAR AND ITS IMPACT

Discussing and analyzing the Iraqi situation that led to the invasion cannot be done without reflecting on the Iraq–Iran war (1980–1988), invasion of Kuwait, the ensuing international sanctions (1990) and the 1991 Gulf War. All these events led to the 2003 disaster. Only by understanding the consequences of these significant events can one know the exact picture.

Very briefly, and without going into details of the Iraq–Iran war, one can fairly describe it as needless and senseless. The war could have been avoided with some wisdom and self-reservation. More importantly, is the fact that the two countries concerned, Iraqi and Iranian, had no say or any interest in it.

It can also be said that both countries' leadership shared an equal blame and responsibility for insisting on going to war, and for escalating it. Each side believed that it could easily overthrow the other within a few months, if not weeks.

Immediately after the success of the Islamic Revolution in Iran, it was clear that the two regimes in Iraq and Iran were not comfortable with each other. The Iraqi leadership's manner in congratulating the Iranian Revolution leaders demonstrated mutual dissatisfaction and distrust. After that, the leadership of the Baath Party received a response from the Iranian Revolution leader, Ayatollah Khomeini that they justly regarded as an insult. Tension between the two sides began, ever since, only to escalate rapidly. The Iranian response did not start with the usual Islamic phrase (In The Name of God the Most Gracious the Most Merciful), instead it started with the phrase (Peace upon those who follow the guidance of Islam), a phrase that is usually addressed to the infidels.

The tension was especially clear after former Iraqi President Ahmed Hassan al-Bakir stepped down in July 1979, and delegated power to his deputy, the most powerful man in Iraq at the time, Saddam Hussein. The new Iraqi president had the ambition and desire to take advantage of the chaos that overwhelmed Iran. This desire was mainly because the man was obsessed or haunted by the bad memory of being obliged to cede half of the vital Iraqi river (Shatt al-Arab) to Iran during the Shah regime. It also seemed that he saw the fall of the mighty Shah regime and the ensuing chaos as a golden opportunity to abrogate the treaty of Algiers 1975, which he signed, to restore full Iraqi sovereignty over this pivotal waterway.

What supported this conclusion was the concern he voiced on more than one occasion about what will be said or written about him and his term in office, a hundred or five hundred years later. He did not want to be remembered or mentioned in the history books as someone who conceded Iraqi or Arab land or waters.

For his part, the leader of the new Iranian regime, Khomeini, felt so confident that his success in removing the most powerful government in the region would enable him to do the same with the second powerful one in neighbouring Iraq. If he succeeds, he would dominate the Gulf region. After living thirteen consecutive years in the holy Shiite city of Najaf-Iraq (1965–1978), he believed and repeated more than once that the 'Sunni Iraqi Baath party' was both unpopular and weak, and can be toppled easily. Of course this was not true as the Baath party was a secular one and included a fair number of Shiites in his rank and files.

It also seemed that the hearsay to which he used to listen, where he lived in Iraq was sufficient to make him confident that the process of overthrowing the Baath regime only needed an appeal to the 'spirit of defiance' among the people, like what happened to the Shah regime. Thus, he was unable to distinguish between the usual daily grumbling and clamour he used to hear from the amateur Iraqis and the earnest desire to overthrow the regime.

He also failed to understand that general chatters in closed and narrow circles do not represent the public opinion of all Iraqis, nor was it a clear indication of the desire to change the regime. Moreover, he ignored the fact that after a decade or more in power, the Baath Party was able to build a robust security system based on a fair number of loyal affiliates and supporters, as well as, robust security, intelligence and military agencies capable of defending the regime.

Khomeini's way of thinking and his ignorance were strange. During his extended stay in Iraq, he witnessed how the Baath regime prided itself on its toughness, especially when it encountered religious demonstrations in the 1970s. One can also add that what escaped Khomeini's mind was that the first Baath party cells and cadres were from the southern Shiite provinces, mainly Karbala, Najaf, and Nasiriya. This meant that the regime had strong popular affiliates in the circles where Khomeini wanted to start his opposition movement.

Finally, he did not consider, while in the euphoria of victory, that the international community was both shocked and scared by the extreme measures taken by the new Islamic Iranian regime. They were not ready to allow it to spread its influence and model over the whole region. In other words, they were not prepared to see another Gulf secular regime like Iraq surrendering to a conservative, theological and extreme power.

While the West and the United States were not keen to save the Shah regime because they thought that he began to show signs and ambitions to dominate the Gulf area, the same powers were not feeling the same about the Iraqi government. This US–Western attitude towards Iraq only changed following Kuwait's invasion in 1990, and the firing of Iraqi long-range missiles at Tel Aviv in 1991. In short, while rejoicing at his victory over the Shah most powerful regime, Khomeini believed it would not be difficult for him to overthrow the Baath party. After a short while, he discovered he was mistaken.

In 1980, all indications pointed out that both sides, Iraq and Iran, were competing for military confrontation, each side believing that it could defeat the other in a short period. Hence, Iraq began talking about the necessity of demarcating the mutual borders in the implementation of the Algiers 1975 agreement, which it did not insist on under the rule of the Shah.

The Iraqi Ministry of Foreign Affairs also published what they called a monitoring report. The report recited hundreds of Iranian attacks on Iraqi territories. The publication and circulation of this report were considered a prelude to, and justification for the looming war. Meanwhile, the new Iranian regime started talking about the principle of exporting the revolution and expressly declaring that Iraq is the first target and stage of this principle. The new Iranian regime also began to incite the people of the southern and central provinces of Iraq, particularly in Najaf and Karbala, to rise against what they described as 'the atheist Baathist regime'.[2]

This announcement was followed by Iranian military attacks on Iraqi border posts and towns, all because of the new Iranian regime's belief that overthrowing the Iraqi government only needs a spark for the masses to raise and topple it. Iran also helped form terrorist cells in Baghdad from

Iraqis of Iranian origin, which launched attacks against Baathist leaders and headquarters in the capital. Similar cells were also established in other Iraqi provinces bordering Iran.

The leaders of the Iranian Revolution did not consider two basic facts: first, is that Iraqis in general and the Shiite Arab tribes of the south whom Khomeini thought of instigating, may disagree with the regimes that ruled them, but they will not accept to be governed by a non-Arab Iran. This resilience was proven later during the war and, recently, by the popular Intifada that has been going on since October 2019 in the overwhelming Iraqi Shiite provinces.

The second fact is the ability and efficiency of the Iraqi Baathist security services to confront and suppress such amateur attempts. For its part, it was said that the Iraqi regime at that time took the advice of some Iranian exiles, ex-senior military and civilian figures loyal to the old Shah regime, who took refuge in Iraq. These figures, especially the ones that were ex-military encouraged the Iraqi government to take the initiative to attack Iran and topple what they described as a weak and shaky new regime that was overwhelmed by bloody turmoil.

It was also said that they provided the Iraqi leadership with information and logistics, about 17 Iranian military bases, camps, and airports. They affirmed that if Iraq could perform airstrikes and destroy them, Iran would lose any ability to respond, and the regime would collapse. Of course, this fact coincided with the strategy of the Iraq regime at that time which was built on the idea of taking advantage of the Iranian chaotic situation. What supported, and somehow confirmed this statement and strategy was the comprehensive airstrikes launched by the Iraqi air force in the first few days of the war, which targeted all Iranian airports, especially in the cities bordering Iraq.

This information was proven to be misleading as the Iranian air force launched significant counter-attacks on Baghdad, which meant that their air force remained operational. What slipped the mind of the Iraqi leadership was the principle that says: 'never wage war on a country embroiled in an internal division or civil war', as any external attack or invasion will unite such a torn and divided country, which happened in the Iranian case.

As a result, the protracted war lasted for eight years, against both countries rulers' expectations. It enormously affected the Iraqi society and the foundations upon which the Iraqi state and economy was built.

The most dangerous effect was that this war subjected the Iraqi society to an unprecedented Iranian sectarian propaganda, with the aim of creating a significant rift within Iraqi society. The regime indeed managed to control this wave, but it is also true that sectarian Shiite and Sunni talking became a common and subdued phenomena. This issue created a situation that the Iraqi society was never familiar with in the past. Of course, this issue and way of talking increased after 2003.

On the other hand, and as the war prolonged, Iraq became an indebted country. The amount of the debts reached 160 billion dollars, and some sources estimated the figure to be 200 billion dollars. This debt happened after a time when the Iraqi economy was in a state of unprecedented affluence. The Iraqi budget claimed cash reserves reaching more than $45 billion in the year when the war started.[3]

Moreover, the value of the Iraqi Dinar, which was one of the strongest currencies in the Middle East, decreased steadily. Before the war, the ID equaled 3.30 US dollars. When the war ended, the US dollar equaled 5 IDs. After the invasion of Kuwait and imposing UN sanctions, one US dollar equaled 3000 ID.

As a result of the continuous and intense war, the Iraqi society became heavily militarized. Freedoms were restricted on the pretext that any opposition or democratic measures could affect the morale of combatants. As the cost of the war increased, poverty and growing unsatisfied basic needs became the two significant features of life in Iraq, affecting families and individuals, especially the families of those called for military service. This situation was contrary to the flourishing Iraqi economy in the seventies, following the increase in oil revenues.

To better clarify these aspects accurately, show their impact on society and how much they indirectly contributed to the invasion of 2003, four issues will be addressed. These issues include the social, economic, military and political effects of the war on the Iraqi people. It is also worth mentioning that any difference between these issues, prioritizing or giving precedence to one of them over the other, is difficult, if not nearly impossible, due to the sizeable overlap between them.

THE SOCIAL, ECONOMIC, MILITARY
AND POLITICAL EFFECTS OF THE IRAQ–IRAN WAR

Although, the Iraqi society, since 1958, had experienced significant and violent turmoil,[4] the social, economic, military and political effects of the Iraq–Iran war were more substantial. The devastating shocks the society experienced during the 1980–1988 war were greater and more violent. It could be said that after eight years of a destructive war, no Iraqi family was spared from its adverse effects. Members of all the components of the Iraqi people like Arabs, Kurds Turkomans, Sabians, Christians, Shiites and Sunnis Muslims were either killed or wounded. The casualties of Iraq's war were 250,000 dead and about 750,000 disabled or injured.

If we add 100,000 casualties of the war in Iraqi Kurdistan between 1974 and 1975, double that figure of human losses as a result of the 1991 war and the chaos that followed,[5] one can imagine the magnitude of the impact of these human losses on each Iraqi family, and the Iraqi society as a whole. It is also important to remember that Iraq's population at the beginning of the Iraq–Iran war was 13 million. As a result of the wars, losses amounted to 10% of the total population.

The impact of the many wars, especially the 1980–1988 and 1991 wars, on the infrastructure of the Iraqi state, society and economy, was great and difficult to calculate. It was more difficult, perhaps, to take steps to fix the enormous damage in a short period. The other result of the strict, harsh and inhumane sanctions imposed on Iraq from 1990 to 2003 was the massive waves of emigration from Iraq. These immigrants were younger, skilled and educated, which led to very serious brain drainage.

It is also challenging to determine the number of those who left Iraq during that period. Some sources estimated the figure to be 4.5 million,[6] while others said it did not exceed 1.5 million. However, in both scenarios, the proportion remains significant and harmful for the society, family relations, and economic growth in a developing country like Iraq. Despite the detrimental effects of these sanctions, the United States and Britain continued to tighten them from time to time while encouraging and forcing other countries to abide by them.

Perhaps the worst part for Iraqis was the participation of Arab countries. The vast majority of Arab countries committed themselves to the sanctions only to comply with the orders of the United States. During the war with Iran, some Arab countries, especially Syria and Libya, sided with Iran and supplied Iran with armaments as well as long-range missiles to bomb Baghdad.[7] The casualties of the sanctions was higher. They claimed the lives of nearly 1.8 million people, over half a million of them were children under five. These estimates do not include those of the last few months of 2002 and the beginning of 2003.[8]

What was saddening and ridiculous is that some sources, especially the United States, insisted that these figures, which were adopted by UNICEF and the Harvard University team,[9] as well as by the former United Nations representative in Iraq, Sadruddin Aga Khan,[10] were exaggerated. They claimed that the right figure was just over half a million people, like half a million people is not worthy of guilt", a former US Secretary of State Madeleine Albright once stated.[11]

The percentage of fatal diseases, such as cancer, increased by a frightening rate compared to what they were before the sanctions and the 1991 war.[12] Diseases and epidemics that were eliminated reappeared in a dangerous capacity.

Hospitals lacked basic equipment and supplies necessary to treat patients with minor injuries, let alone difficult cases. The UN declared Iraq as the country with the best health services system in the Middle East in the seventies, but it became the worst under the sanctions. As a result of the wars and the unprecedented sanctions in human history, a psychiatrist in Iraq stated in a lecture that between 80 and 85% of the Iraqi people suffered psychological depression with varying degrees, apparent in some and muted by the vast majority. This phenomenon reflected on their daily behaviour, during work and in their families.[13] Expectedly, these issues also affected the country's economic situation, the individual citizens and a majority of Iraqi families.

Gradually, the economic burden on the society became more substantial, or even unbearable and overwhelming. Most of the goods and commodities which the Iraqis used to get were diminished as a result of the declining volume of import, the destruction of the State and private national industry, and the deterioration of the value of the Iraqi Dinar. While there is no official statistic on the size of inflation in the Iraqi economy, one can indirectly determine this by giving some examples such as; the country's highest salary was that of ministers, which was in the seventies and eighties around five 500 Iraqi Dinars, equivalent to about $1500. The second-largest salary was that of a university professor, judges and army officer reaching between 300 and 450 Dinars ($900–1350).

As for the majority of Iraqi employees, they used to receive between 30 and 100 Iraqi Dinars monthly. Workers were paid less. However, these salaries usually provided decent and adequate income for individuals and families. Most of the necessary goods and commodities, known as public or merit goods, as well as the supply of medications, free education and healthcare, were either subsidized or freely supplied by the government. The government also had a plan that included building housing units and distributing them at a meagre price with small monthly payments.[14]

As 40% of the society, mostly the middle class had an income that depended on government spending and salaries,[15] one can then figure out the extent of the negative impact on this large portion of society. Due to the devaluation of the Iraqi Dinar and the failure of government to support all social aspects such as health, construction, education, etc. the impact became devastating.[16]

As earlier mentioned, the exchange rate of the Iraqi Dinar began to reduce shortly after the initiation of the Iraq–Iran war, and the Dinar value steadily deteriorated as the war continued. Moreover, the deterioration sharply increased after Kuwait's invasion, the international sanctions, and the battle to liberate it. The value of the US dollar increased substantially until its price exceeded two thousand Dinars per dollar.[17] With the economic sanctions and embargo on oil exports, the state's financial capabilities were severely affected to the point where the government was unable to provide enough cash for salaries. To overcome this problem, the government chose to print banknotes locally, only to push up the inflation rate, which led to another devaluation of the Iraqi Dinar.[18]

In fairness, the Iraqi government at that time endeavoured to alleviate the sanctions' appalling conditions. Each family was allocated a ration card with limited items of essential foods and medications for chronic and detrimental illnesses such as cancer, heart disease, diabetes and blood pressure, as these drugs were also subjected to harsh sanctions.[19]

However, these measures harmed the moral and psychological attitude of the Iraqi people who were neither familiar with the rationing system nor with restricting their purchasing ability. To decrease inflation, the government increased salaries using locally printed banknotes without any gold reserve to back it up as oil export, the primary source of foreign currency, was stopped entirely. All these increment did not rescue the deteriorating economic situation of Iraq. The value of a university professor's salary, with all these increments became $25 at best. In contrast, the wages of the lower tiers and the majority of employees were equivalent to between $3 and 10 only per month.[20]

From the military aspect, the Iraqi society was militarized during the war in an unprecedented manner. Military units expanded, and the number of people enlisted multiplied exponentially, which meant that spending on such a large army also escalated, affecting spending on other areas.

It was officially said that the military budget, including the military industry sector, reached 68% of the general budget. Some experts accused the government of hiding the real figure, which reached 75% of the total government spending.[21] Spending large amounts on the military showed how small proportions were allocated to other areas, such as health, education, social affairs, social insurance, etc. This level of spending continued until 1991. When it was reduced after this date due to the sanctions imposed in 1990, military expenditures remained a priority. In other words, the financial and social burden caused by military spending and army expansion represented a massive burden on the state's budget and the society at large.

It is worth mentioning that military spending was not restricted to the official Iraqi army. The Baath regime was keen to form other military divisions, such as the Republican Guard and the Special Guard Units, to ensure its safety and protection. These military divisions and other local militias ran by the Baath party, such as the Popular Army and the al-Quds Army, required more spending.

In addition to the financial burden to sustain these units, they jeopardized the daily work of the other government agencies. Most units, especially those formed by the party, drew their members from employees in different government departments. This phenomenon led many official departments, sectors and public services to work morning and evening shifts, without any holidays apart from one day a week (Fridays) to cover staff shortage, only to add pressure on social life. Amid all the trouble and hardship, Baghdad and some other major cities in Iraq were subjected to air attacks and violent shelling, which reminded the people of the destruction of the capital in the 1991 war. Apart from the destruction of property, these attacks caused significant harm to civilians' morality and endurance.

Iraqi Kurdistan was also suffering from other violations, such as the intrusion of neighbouring foreign forces,[22] and the brutal fighting between the two main political parties there, the Kurdistan Democratic Party led by Mr. Massoud Barzani and the Patriotic Union of Kurdistan led by Mr. Jalal Talabani. The peak of this inter-factional fight was in

1994, which reached the stage of house-to-house street fighting. If one adds the many assassination attempts and counter the physical liquidation of opponents to the regime or members of the ruling Baath party, as well as between members of the opposing political Kurdish parties, one can perceive the plight and sufferings of the majority of the Iraqi people at that time.

How Did the Regime Deal with What Was Going on in Iraq?

The above-mentioned bleak picture made a significant number of Iraqis live in a state of despair, which consequently led them to be indifferent and careless of whatever happens to their country, even if it was an external intervention or invasion.

Others felt that it was impossible to improve things while the Baath Party remained in power. Thus, they thought that perhaps a foreign element could change things. Even when there were hints from the state that indicated an intention to carry out some reforms, most Iraqis doubted them due to the regime's dominating and totalitarian nature, the heavy-handedness of the security forces, and the fear infused in them as a result of previous experiences. Thus, it could be fair to say that this portion of people was also indirectly unwilling to oppose external interference.

Between these two views, there was a smaller group of observers who tried to analyze the events in a different, sensible, unbiased, objective and more rational way. Yet, members of this group felt that their position was very delicate, sensitive, and unenviable. Although, the group aspired for reforms carried out by the government and the Iraqis themselves, it was aware that the ruling party was not ready to accept their views. The regime was always unwilling to tolerate different points of view, but what made them venture on was their firm belief that dependence or counting on foreign assistance or elements was dangerous, futile, destructive and fraught with risks.

They also believed that the designs planned by the USA, Britain and Israel to invade Iraq were for reasons unrelated neither to the dictatorial nature of the Iraqi regime or the problems of poor human rights conditions in the country, nor the lack of democracy or the acquisition of WMD. These were instead, in the group's opinion, making excuses to occupy and destroy Iraq. Hence the group called for reformation from inside Iraq, and if possible, by the Iraqi regime itself.

This small group, or team of intellectuals, was brought together by Professor Wamidh Nadhmi.[23] The group was known as the Group of Eight, as eight individuals led it.

Members of the Group had both courage and foresight. Daring to convince the regime action tangible democratization measures, and vision to anticipate the catastrophes that has befallen Iraq should the regime fail to implement fundamental reforms. Knowing the regime's totalitarian and brutal nature, they had to adopt specific approaches:

1. To engage the regime constructively and not too blatantly challenging it.
2. Not to take any action that might lead the regime to think the group is conspiring against it.
3. To display the merits of implementing democratic changes, such as freedom of press, initiating national reconciliation, transparent elections, etc. in solidifying the internal front against foreign aggression.
4. To avoid publishing any material expressing the group's thoughts or ideas before notifying the regime in one way or another. To achieve these objectives, the group decided to directly and courteously address their approaches to the president, realizing he is the ultimate, if not the sole decision-maker.
5. Finally, and to avoid any possible unpleasant repercussions, the group wanted to make it clear to the president that they had no political ambitions. Their objectives were confined to advocating the implementation of needed reforms. They also wanted to publish a periodical journal and/or form a scholarly association to run public lectures and seminars. In other words, they tried to establish an independent platform allowed to openly discuss matters relating to the national interest to reflect alternative views to the discourse offered by the state-controlled media.

Perhaps it is useful to recall that what also encouraged this group to act, apart from fear of foreign intervention, was an incident that gave the impression that the government, or the president, thought of carrying out some reforms of a somehow democratic nature. This idea was presented by leaked information about discussions among the top Iraqi leadership, the regional command of the Baath Party and the Revolutionary Command Council, during mid-1988.

The main theme of these discussions was the future of democracy and multiplicity in Iraq. These deliberations were at the beginning, mere rumours that were subsequently published in a book titled 'Democracy and Multi-party System'. The book was strictly and exclusively for party members. The discussions revealed that few leading members of the party and the government thought that there should be some democratic reforms. Most importantly, it showed that the president of Iraq was leading those views.

Reading the discussions in the book showed that the President had a keen interest not to elaborate his opinion at first. He instead asked the rest of the leading members to express their views on the issue of democracy and Multi-party System. Two leading members at the time, Saadoun Hammadi and Tariq Aziz were the most knowledgeable regarding the President's way of thinking, or maybe the President had briefed them beforehand on some of his ideas, spoke in favour of such a scheme. After the military victory over Iran and forming a massive regional military power that guarantees the regime's survival and protection, they perceived that the President had the desire to make some reforms. Otherwise, they may have also thought that he would not consider raising an issue that he ignored throughout his rule and found it a serious challenge to his one-party system.

Based on this conclusion (or prior knowledge), the two men brought forth ideas about the necessity of holding a transparent general election for a House of Representatives preceded by legitimizing some 'national-patriotic parties' other than the Baath Party. Aziz also suggested that another council be appointed by the government that will consist of members of the regional and national command of the Baath Party. He argued that these people gained their positions in democratic elections within the party itself. This council, he added, shall have the right to veto decisions taken by the House of Representatives when necessary.

The rest of the party leadership, who lacked foresight, and were always keen to echo the President's ideas, thought that the President has never been interested in a democratic government that would challenge his authority and dominance. Accordingly, they stood against the idea.

The President rarely participated in the dialogues, but he concluded the discussions with critical remarks. He said that the Baath party is the only institution capable of establishing democracy and pluralism. If the party fails in that respect, other people or groups will begin to work under the pretext of implementing democracy to overthrow the regime and control the government. If they succeed and control the government, they will not carry out any democratic transformation.[24]

These words and discussions gave an impression to the Group of Eight that after the regime controls the external and internal dangers that threatened its existence following the end of the Iraq–Iran war; it will be more open and will ease some restrictions in the country.[25] The ideas obtained from the leaked book were not the only ideas that reinforced this impression. These ideas were more reliable when the two drafts were issued in 1990 about two projects, one for a permanent constitution and the other for the law of associations, political parties included.

Deputy Prime Minister, Tariq Aziz, was tasked with reviewing and amending the proposed draft of the constitution with the drafting Committee.[26] However, the disastrous decision to invade Kuwait and the destructive war led by an international coalition of 33 countries, kept the intention to issue a new constitution and make some reforms on the shelf. The Group of Eight continued to seek change from within, depending on the measures taken before the Kuwait's invasion.

Following the devastating, destructive and humiliating war of 1991, the group members considered the need for reforms a top priority like never before. In March 1992, they sent a direct letter to the President of Iraq. The letter stated that the sanctions, together with all the resolutions taken afterward, including the false claims of (WMD), were designed to completely destroy Iraq.

It concluded that the best response to all these external conspiracies were democratic measures, which could encounter and foil all United States' and Western intentions to find excuses for occupying Iraq. The letter also included a request for permission to issue an independent daily newspaper, in the name of 'National Fraternity', as evidence of the group's keenness to uphold and strengthen national unity. In its memo, the group considered that authorizing such a newspaper would be a platform for an independent, internal and domestic opposition that goes in line with the leader's desire to achieve democratic transformation, political pluralism, and encourage or contribute to democratic reforms and dialogues.

As members of the group held their breath in anticipation of the results or reaction to this boldness, they were surprised to find that their memo, meant to be a personal one to the President, was published two days later with an order from him. The publisher was the second most important official daily newspaper named al-Jumhouriya, which was regarded as the second regular media platform of the ruling Baath party.

Members of the group regarded this as a positive step that boded well for their action and decided to continue sending other letters to the President, urging him to carry out democratic reforms. The last letter was known to be the most convincing. It was sent following the escape of General Hussein Kamel, son-in-law of the President and third highly ranked man after him, and Qusai his son,[27] out of Iraq in 1995. The goal of this memo was to remind or bring the President's attention to some facts:

1. Whoever relies on such people should expect and accept their shameful actions and behaviour.
2. There is no alternative to democracy and multiplicity measures.
3. The selection for top positions should be made according to competence and merit.

The President's response that time was even more positive. In addition to publishing the memo in the daily newspapers, all the group members were called to have a private and closed meeting with the Deputy Prime Minister, Tariq Aziz, who was also known to be the President's representative to meet intellectuals at home and abroad.

When we, the Group members, attended the meeting, we were greeted warmly and friendly by Mr. Aziz. He started by saying that he was meeting us by an order from the President. He added that the President thanks us for our patriotic position and frank views and told us that he ordered that we prepare ourselves to be part of the next government.

Then he asked to hear our opinions.[28] Everyone spoke, expressing their observations and criticisms about the situation in Iraq. Lawyers Hassan Shaaban and Judge Salim Al-Mandalawi discussed the necessity for an open-door policy, openness, easing restrictions and adherence to the rule of law. They also spoke about the release of political prisoners, and not arresting anyone without a warrant, something that Dr. Husain al-Jumaili elaborated on. Economist Duraid Saeed Thabit spoke about the sanctions, government's role in easing them, and ways to stop the deterioration of the Iraqi currency. Other political, social, educational and economic issues regarded as a taboo at that time, were also raised in that meeting. Mr. Aziz responded calmly and courteously.

I remembered that in answering our complaints, he mentioned two critical issues that remained in my mind: First, he said that we should be aware that inside the Baath Party leadership there exist two different attitudes: one is a (leftist) minority that included President Saddam Husain, Saadoun Hammadi and the speaker, Tariq Aziz. The other is the (right-wing) that included the rest of the leadership. This answer was to give us the impression that carrying drastic changes was not an easy job, and to draw our attention that the resistance to reformations was in the majority.

The second important issue he mentioned when answering our request for reconciliation was when he said: 'You are asking us to open up, have a dialogue with the so-called external opposition groups or parties. These are not parties; these are gangs and groups of thieves. Religious and sectarian groups attempted to seize any opportunity to control the power by calling for democratic measures and free elections. Once they achieve this goal, they will not leave power, and will abolish democracy. More-over, they will be ready to burn the whole country if they felt that they were about to be forced out of power'. Not all of us agreed with him, but the post-2003 events proved that his judgement and analysis were correct. I was the last speaker. I was keen to convey that our ambitions are not political, and we were not interested in joining a future government. I said: 'Mr. Aziz when we wrote what we wrote, we did not do that in order to obtain a position. We were seeking democratic reforms and permission to publish an independent newspaper. If you honour us by granting us a license, we will be grateful, and if you refuse, we will be thankful too. Then, let me tell you frankly, Mr. Aziz, and I hope you will not be offended by what I will say. Neither your experience nor your actions indicate that you are willing to accept different views or people like us. In order not to lose each other, please leave the relationship between us in this form. Mr. Aziz, believe me, being part of the government is not one of our aims or objectives'.

His answer to me was: 'Soon you will find that you were wrong. Within two months at most, there will be a shuffle and you will be part of a new government'. He concluded by repeating the sentence 'be prepared to participate in the government soon'. Of course, this promise never materialized. All that happened following that meeting was that we were asked to form a political party, an idea we rejected right away. We were sure that creating a political party would allow the security agencies to infiltrate and dominate it.

Long after that meeting, and following the occupation of Iraq, I met with a friend of mine, lawyer Sabah Al-Mukhtar in London. He told me that he was invited, with some other expatriates, to visit Iraq during the same period. He said that he met with Tariq Aziz during that visit who asked him how to improve Iraq's image externally. In response, Al-Mukhtar advised that one of the ways could be to allow our group to operate freely and publish an independent daily newspaper. This would be a good indication that the regime was intending to make some reforms.

Aziz's response to him was that he had doubts about the intentions of our group. He added that the state of Iraq, due to the sanctions, oil embargo and the scarcity of printing papers, had to reduce the size of its newspapers and reduce the number of pages. 'If the state itself is finding it difficult to publish its newspapers, how could a small group publish a daily newspaper?' Aziz asked al-Mukhtar. Then he added, 'This only means that this group has external connections and financing'.

It was an explicit accusation that our group was having external links, or being manipulated from abroad. Aziz's opinion on this matter was not surprising, giving the conspiracy theory that the Baath leadership lived with throughout their governing period. What Mr. Aziz did not say was that the state at the time, due to the sanctions, provided printing paper for all newspapers. Following the publication of our first memorandum, we were asked to meet the Minister of Culture, Mr. Hamid Hummadi, who wanted to discuss our latest memorandum to the president before publishing it. When we arrived at the ministry, we were asked to wait in the office of Mr. Amir al-Hilu, the Vice Minister, who confided to us that our proposed newspaper was also included in the programme of the ministry, together with other publications. He also said that it would be issued with printing paper at a reduced price, a privilege similar to that bestowed on the government's newspapers and magazines. But following our meeting with Mr. Aziz, we were almost sidelined, and nobody approached us. Finally, in our group's opinion, all our efforts to convince the government to carry out some reforms were over. The reason we came to this conclusion was the impression that Tariq Aziz got after meeting with us, and the bold and frank way we spoke to him.

The funny thing is that some malicious people inside and outside Iraq, who did not dare to say what we were saying, accused us, our memoranda and activities of working at the behest of the government in order to improve its image both internally and internationally.

The important conclusion from all that was said above is that the constant feeling of an 'external conspiracy' was deeply embedded in the leadership of the former regime. The regime, especially the president and his entourage, as well as the security agencies, were obsessed with the conspiracy theory. Following the occupation, it appeared that most of those, whom the regime was suspicious and doubtful of, were patriotic and proved to be loyal to Iraq. On the other hand, it turned out that a fair number of the regime's closest associates had links with the intelligence services of the powers that occupied Iraq, or were willing to cooperate with the invaders.

As the sanctions intensified, all talks about possible reforms faded away. They were replaced by a feeling of suspicion and an increasing belief that there were plots to topple the regime through calls for democratic reforms. In the regime's opinion, fears of conspiracies, real or alleged, could only be foiled by increased security and intelligence measures, which added to the sufferings of the people due to the unprecedented sanctions.

The United States, in particular, and the West in general, contributed to the perpetuation of this situation by tightening the sanctions, and rejecting any compromises or initiatives by the Iraqi government to settle their differences. Despite the confirmation of all specialized agencies of WMD disappearance or nonexistence in Iraq, the USA, UK and Israel continued to spread lies about the alleged existence of these weapons.[29]

Throughout the time of the Iran–Iraq war, the 1991 war, and the sanctions, the regime used argument to defend its policies and its refusal to undergo any reforms. This argument was that the time was not suitable for democratic reforms due to the many (conspiracies) the country was facing. The regime considered any criticism to its performance, no matter how mild it was, as part of these conspiracies, or as an alliance with the regime's enemies. At best, it considered that criticism indirectly supports these conspiracies, only to justify the refusal to share power.

They kept repeating that a complete centralization was the only way to confront the many crises and foreign designs that the country was facing. The calls for reforms became a pretext to imprison or liquidate everyone who asked for them. The excuse was that these calls were in harmony with the USA, Western and Israel agendas towards Iraq. As for the generally deprived and besieged population, they were mainly troubled with solving their daily problems and seeking essential commodities for their families. Talking about democracy, multiplicity and pluralism was meaningless for them. We cannot blame a population that was subject to unprecedented sanctions, poverty and family burdens, accompanied from time to time by violent airstrikes on Baghdad and other regions, for thinking this way.

To understand the Iraqi situation, it is necessary to address the Iraqi opposition's attitude abroad. This opposition was divided into two parts: A small section comprising minor parties and some national figures. It had some followers inside Iraq who generally alienated themselves from the preparations for the war against Iraq. The substantial part was made of parties and people associated with the plan to invade Iraq, and provide full support for the preparations and implementation of this plan. These groups went as far as making false allegations and stories about WMD to justify American and British plans to invade Iraq. As a result of putting forward misleading information and adopting these allegations, both the American and British governments formed commissions and directed accusations to the politicians who took the decision to invade Iraq. So did some of the leading newspapers in Europe.

These groups called themselves the Iraqi opposition abroad. They took advantage of the large and capable media agencies in the West to wage a media campaign to smear the reputation of the Iraqi regime and its leaders. These groups and individuals were generously funded by many countries like the USA, Britain, Gulf countries and Israel. Moreover, it later appeared that they worked under the direction and orders of these countries' intelligence services.

The tragedy was that all these efforts were made to overthrow the regime. No plan was put in place to seriously study how Iraq would be governed after the invasion. In other words, overthrowing the government by any means was the only thing on their mind, even if it was through deception that meant the occupation and destruction of their homeland. Some of them also tried to convince Iraqis that the occupation is better than indigenous or national systems, and that colonization was the only way to provide democracy and prosperity to the country and the region.

The Iraqi government tried to offset their failures to bring the majority of the population behind it to counter the allegations of the external opposition and foreign supporters. It failed to convince the majority of the people that the claims made against Iraq by these hostile parties like the USA, Britain and Israel were false and misleading.

Instead, the Iraqi Baath government resorted to the idea of using religious beliefs and organizations, a natural enemy to the west in general and the United States and Israel in particular, to confront the campaign that aimed to overthrow the government. Thus, the state encouraged the plan of returning to religion, and it supported religious groups, which wanted to act somehow freely.

Ironically, when the effectiveness of these religious groups became apparent in the society, the government turned against them and initiated a campaign to curtail their influence, at a time when the government was facing significant challenges. In the absence of capable political parties and convincing political and social organizations, mosques, religious circles, Husaini centres (Shiite mosques) and shrines remained the only places that could accommodate people.

This situation may explain the emergence of religious groups and resistance following the occupation. On the other hand, the Iraqi government was living in another contradiction as a result of the promotion of the religious factor. This contradiction was represented by glorification, praise and commendation for everything that the religious movements in the Arab and the Islamic world do, such as the Lebanese Hezbollah, the Palestinian Hamas and Bin Laden group in Afghanistan. They, of course, did not mention the exact names of these movements. They replaced them with words like the national movement in Lebanon, Palestine or Afghanistan, while the government would not tolerate anyone who acclaimed these movements in Iraq.[30]

The second method adopted by the regime to defend itself, was by mobilizing support through material temptations. Of course, these temptations were not available to everyone. It was restricted to members of the Baath party, its loyal organizations, the security and intelligence services, and the private republican guards. Through these methods, the regime did not realize that it created greedy groups that began to care more about protecting their material interests rather than their homeland. On the other hand, while these security institutions succeeded in strengthening the regime's grip at home and could crush and liquidate any internal resistance, this method has certainly not been able to mobilize great public support for the party or prevent the aggression that led to the country's occupation.

The opposite party, the United States and the other rich countries allied with it, began to use the same method. They had another advantage in this field by mixing financial donations with promises of a high position after the change of the regime. By comparing the financial abilities of the two opposing parties, the Baath government and the US coalition, one could easily prejudge which party will prevail. The US administration was able to attract a fair number of Iraqi officials, party members, and military and security commanders to work for its side. It was discovered later that the United States managed to recruit people close to the regime's top officials.[31] However, the Iraqi government's method of securing support through financial donations had an adverse reaction, especially among the majority of the deprived Iraqis. This majority was finding it difficult to secure their daily needs; while in contrast, others were blessed with different privileges.

Most observers were puzzled by Iraqis' reaction before and after the invasion. The situation in Iraq was unique, and it represented some rare and contradicting phenomena that may not have been found in other countries and among other people.

On the one hand, the state of deprivation felt by the majority of the people resulted in the sense of indifference about what was coming even if it was foreign occupation. On the other hand, the sanctions generated a desire for persistence, challenge, and steadfastness, which was translated into hard work. Universities, factories, schools, and all other state administrations were working efficiently and impressively. This work was accompanied by the state's enthusiasm to provide a regular monthly food basket for each Iraqi family using a rationing system designed by the Iraqi Ministry of Trade and commended by the United Nations.

What was more impressive about this programme was that international inspectors did not register a single case of corruption in that system. Likewise, the Ministry of Health was working hard to provide medication, especially for chronic illnesses. The Ministries of Higher Education and Education provided all the necessary supplies and materials to keep universities and schools running, while state and private factories kept working.

Iraqis also showed rare persistence to reconstruct what the war (1991) and the repeated airstrikes destroyed. New projects like building of bridges, opening new universities, carrying out significant water maintenance, building sewage and providing electricity were executed. No wonder these projects surprised and confused external observers. They could not comprehend or explain this sense of dedication by a population that was supposedly unsatisfied with its regime, a regime that did not provide them with a reasonable margin of freedom and democracy. This confusion and surprise increased during and after the invasion due to the strong resilience the Iraqis showed until the fall of Baghdad. The strong resistance which occurred after the occupation was due to the standard, patriotic and overwhelming anti-occupation feeling and not an attempt to defend the regime as some observers noted.

Although, the neighbouring countries' position fell outside the scope of this research, it is useful to recall that these countries had either aligned with or tacitly approved the plans to occupy Iraq. Because of Iraq's foreign policy, which managed to alienate it from most neighbouring states, or the success of the USA, Britain and Israel in attracting support for anti-Iraq plans, Iraq was surrounded by a 'sea' of enemies. Some of these states were even against its existence as a unified state. The regime's failure to find solutions to neighbouring and internal problems, like the problems of democracy, reconciliation, and the Kurdish conflict, provided the international coalition with a reason to invade Iraq using extra tools to implement this strategy. Some analysts believed that this was almost an impossible job for the Iraqi regime, especially with the Kurdish conflict, due to external factors and encouragement. This claim was not valid. At that time, the government could have reached a peaceful solution if it was ready to give the Kurdish parties some additional concessions, such as federalism. After the occupation, these Kurdish parties did not only get more than what they were asking for, they also 'took the whole Iraqi state hostage', as the previous Prime Minister Nouri al-Maliki said in one of his declarations.

The Baath regime strategy concerning the Kurdish problem was built on keeping secret relations with the various Kurdish parties by providing them with financial gains. On their side, the Kurdish parties were also comfortable with this situation, which enabled them to also establish secret relations with other states, especially with the coalition formed to invade Iraq.[32] In conclusion, the regime continued to believe that it still had the chance to subjugate everyone inside Iraq, and that all it needed was to try and stay in power and wait for the right opportunity.

However, there remains a collection of important questions that might be useful to address, despite the difficulty of answering them accurately and in a transparent and documented manner. Answering these questions can, or may be done by relying on the information, living experience and evidence that emerged after the occupation. These questions are:

1. What was the head of the regime, Saddam Hussein, thinking about the things going on around him or Iraq?

2. Did he see what the situation in Iraq will lead to in light of the explicit United States threats?
3. Did he have a clear idea about the scale of the military power that the United States and its allies were preparing for the invasion?
4. Did he carefully consider the results of the forthcoming war?
5. Was he convinced that the primary goal of the war was to remove him from power and Iraq's occupation at any cost? Or did he merely believe that it would be a war to destroy what remained of the Iraqi military power and the infrastructures?

As was mentioned earlier, it is not easy to answer these questions accurately and conclusively. However, the researcher tried to find answers to these questions, despite the difficulty of documenting them academically. Perhaps it is useful to include these observations to complete the whole picture of Iraq's situation at the beginning of war and invasion.

Initially and repeatedly, the regime believed that there was no need to make any reforms or change in its policy. Any demand to do so was classified as a conspiracy against it. Even after neo-conservatives came to power in the United States and announced their plans to change the government in Iraq by force, the regime continued to have this belief. The Iraqi regime continued making fun of these announcements and ideas, considering them merely as a whirlwind in a teacup, or at best desperate attempts that will end after a while that may be long or short, depending on the duration of the presidency of George W. Bush (The then president of the United States of America).

Then the regime felt that it could hinder these plans by demonstrating its ability to resist and challenge them. For example, even though the international inspectors relayed to the US administration, they were convinced that Iraq no longer possessed WMD or the ability to manufacture them,[33] Saddam Hussein persisted in pretending that Iraq can revive this programme, or maintain the ability to build other unconventional weapons capable of countering any possible attack. For example, the head of the regime insisted on meeting regularly with the military industry and the atomic energy leaders, and ordered that these meetings be on TV.

In reality these meetings were to discuss matters such as restoring electricity, re-operating state factories and had nothing to do with manufacturing weapons of mass destruction. The former president was informed by some people who attended these meetings that the meetings began to raise concerns inside the US administration. The administration was under the impression that Iraq was still seeking to revive its WMD and other programmes. A suggestion was put before the president that it was better to reduce these meetings or make them off-camera. His answer was: let them say what they want.[34] Instead, he made these meetings almost a daily event with the Iraqi TV showing them every evening.

At a later stage, the former president believed that deterrence could be achieved by increasing the number of Iraqi militias and giving them indicative Islamic titles, such as al-Quds Army. Those responsible for the armed militia said that it consisted of seven million fighters, and was made to face any external threat. Yet most military experts, talked about its poor organization and training, let alone its ability to fight a severe battle.

Another example of the former president's understanding of the seriousness of the international and regional situation and how to confront it was his speeches. During the few months leading up to the occupation, he was eager to appear almost every day on TV, sitting among a group of Iraqi army officers. They used to brag and swear to him, falsely, that they were ready to face any aggression and defeat it. In one of these meetings, one of the president's cousins, a junior officer, interrupted the bragging of the officers, and expressed his doubts. He was ordered by the president to leave the hall immediately and his remarks were deleted from the recording that was to be broadcast to people in the evening of the same day.[35]

The fourth and most indicative example of the president's failure to grasp what was coming was his insistence to accumulate and hide millions of US dollars in remote or unexpected areas, such as the back garden of the Republican Palace on the bank of the River Tigris. For this purpose, he supervised the building of sealed rooms in which he deposited this cash. After knowing that they will be filled with millions of dollars, one of the men building these rooms said: 'It is better to make these rooms more fortified'. The president replied: 'there is no need for that, no one will reach any of these rooms, the cash will be safe and ready for us to use to reconstruct what the evil bombings will destroy[36]'. He also added that American and British forces only aim was to destroy the governmental palaces, the infrastructure and military sites, and retreat after accomplishing this mission. He repeated this statement more than once in his previously mentioned secret and often televised meetings. He said that the Americans can only destroy from a distance, and that they will not risk a direct military confrontation.

If we follow the other top members of the Baath leadership and the ministers' statements, we will find a reflection of the president's ideas and speeches. There was no way to judge how much they believed in the inability of American and British power to occupy the country and remove the regime, as they were afraid to speak out their minds. However, it was clear that this idea, and similar ideas, were very much spread across the party. Few party and military leaders thought that there was a possibility that the invading forces will succeed in occupying some Iraqi territories for a short period.[37] But they used to assure their audiences that the Iraqi troops will expel them in due time. As it was mentioned, all that was relayed above cannot constitute a reliable scientific material for academic research. However, these narratives were drawn directly from people who were involved in the events. They may answer some questions for those interested in knowing the thoughts of the Iraqi leadership before the invasion.

Last but not least, it is fair to say that the desperate internal situation in Iraq due to the sanctions and the regime's continued oppression facilitated the process of penetrating and then occupying Iraq. It made a fair number of people feel indifferent to the outcome of the United States' plans to occupy their country. One should not overlook the fact that the United States was planning to occupy Iraq whether the regime was popular or not, or whether Iraqis were satisfied with it or not. The other saddening fact was that some people who appeared indifferent about the occupation went as far as naively thinking that occupying forces will provide a better life and a more prosperous future for their country.

When these people realized that the outcome of the invasion was destruction, torture and disrespect for human beings, the country was already occupied and fragmented. The country's sovereignty was shattered, its wealth was in foreign hands, and its dignity was lost. The result, as the anti-occupation groups envisioned, moved from bad to worse. Nothing was accomplished in the field of human rights, and people were appointed in positions according to the degree of loyalty they had towards the invaders. The country's wealth was left to the occupying administration and was stolen or dispersed irrationally. Sectarianism and racial differences were accentuated, and the killings of scientists and top army generals increased. Government banks, buildings and ministries were robbed, and many other chaotic events occurred daily.

NOTES

1. Saad N. Jawad, Dirasah wa Istiqraa fi Taamul al-Iraq Maa al-Hisar al-Dawly, qadhaiya Sharq Awsadia Journal, Amman, December 1999.
2. Abdul Sattar al-Rawi's review of Ali Sabti al-Hadithi's book, the Iran–Iraq war 1980–1988, http://wijhatnadhar.org/article.php?id=11947.
3. See the declaration of the director of the Iraqi Central Bank in al-Thawra newspaper (Baghdad) 25/12/1980. One of the saddening issues was that some Arab Gulf countries supported Iraq to continue its war against Iran based on their perception that this war will drain the power of the two central regional countries they feared. When the war was extended to reach the oil industry and tankers, the Syrian government decided to close the oil pipeline that goes through its territories, making it more difficult for Iraq to export enough oil to finance the war. As a result, Iraq signed an agreement with Arab Gulf countries who agreed to export certain shipments of their oil on behalf of Iraq. In return, Iraq agreed to export the same quantities on behalf of these countries after the war. Following the catastrophe of invading Kuwait and the implementation of international sanctions, these countries considered these shipments as debts that should be settled with their interests. Interview with Dr. Ramzi Salman, who signed these agreements with the Gulf countries on behalf of Iraq through the Ministry of Oil, Beirut, April 2004. An email from Dr. Salman 16/06/2019.
4. Since 1958, Iraq witnessed four successful coups: July 1958, February 1963, November 1963 and July 1968. Eight foiled attempts and an unspecified number of failed attempts that got caught before they erupted. Sometimes, these attempts were imaginary and were created by the different regimes to liquidate the opposition. Let alone the intermittent fighting that was taking place in Iraqi Kurdistan.
5. Jeoff Simons, al-Tankeel bil Iraq (The Scourging of Iraq) al-Uqobat wa al-Qanoon wa al-Adalah, Centre of Arab Unity Studies, Beirut, 1998, p. 44.
6. According to a report issued by the British Foreign Ministry and shared with Reuters, the ministry claimed that this number constituted 15% of the Iraqi population. It was discovered later that these figures were exaggerated to justify the invasion and occupation.
7. https://www.syria.tv/content/-كيف-ساعد-حافظ-الأسد-إيران-بصواريخ-السكود-في-
وزير-الحرس-مع-العراق؟   https://ar.mehrnews.com/news/1888108/-الحرس-
https://www.syria.tv/content/الثورى-سابقا-القذافى-أعطى-ايران-صواريخا-وطلب-منها
https://ar.meh   .كيف-ساعد-حافظ-الأسد-إيران-بصواريخ-السكود-في-حربها-مع-العراق
rnews.com/news/1888108/-وزير-الحرس-الثورى-سابقا-القذافى-أعطى-ايران-صواريخا-حربها-مع-العراق
وطلب-منها.

8. Jeoff Simons, op. cit., pp. 197–199. See also Tim Niblock, al-Uqobat wa al- Manbothoon fi al-Sharq al-Awsat, Iraq Libya and Sudan, Centre of Arab Unity Studies, Beirut, 2001 (Translation of the book Pariah States and Sanctions in the Middle East). See also, https://www.psr.org/wp-content/uploads/2018/05/body-count.pdf.

9. Summary of the report in Saad N. Jawad, op. cit., pp. 43–44.

10. See Sadruldin Agha Khan's report, in *Journal of Arab Association of Political Science*, Baghdad, nos. 5–6, 1993, pp. 186–188.

11. As an example of these harmful attempts see: Amatzia Baram, The Effect of Iraq Sanctions: Statistical pitfalls and Responsibilities, *Middle East Journal*, Vol. 54, no. 2, Spring 2000.

12. See Geoff Simons, op. cit., pp. 190–193. Letter from the Iraqi Foreign Ministry to the UN Secretary-General 27 June 1998 (S/1998/661 and A/53/165). See Tim Niblock, op. cit., pp. 146–147; and Jeoff Simons, *Targeting Iraq: Sanctions and Bombing in US Polices*, Saqi Books, 2002, pp. 80–82.

13. Lecture by the late Iraqi psychiatrist Professor Mohammed Taj al-Din. While Dr. Niblock affirmed that the number of those affected by these illnesses rose to 200,000 in 1990 to 510,000 in 1998. Niblock, op. cit., p. 146. It should be noted that these figures include only the severe cases that got referred to hospitals. See Hussein Ali al-Saadi, Tathirat al-Harb al-Idwania ala al-Bia' wa al-Siha al-Ama' fi al-Iraq, Um al-Marik Journal, issue no. 4, Autumn 1995.

14. These residential compounds and lands were distributed almost for free to all government employees and pensioners, giving loans with zero interest. They provided those employees and their families with stability and social security. For example, in the eighties, all university lecturers who did not own a residence were supplied with modern luxury flats in Baghdad's centre, with small monthly payments divided in ten years. The price of these flats was estimated according to the cost. As for those working in other cities, they were provided with a piece of land in their place of birth and a loan to build a house with zero interest.

15. Abdul Munim al-Saed Ali, 'al-Iqtisat al-Iraqi: Ila Ain? Tamulat wa Tadaluat', al-Mustaqbal al-Arabi, year 20. Issue no. 228, February 1998, p. 75. See also Jamal Aziza Mishaf, Athar al-Idwan al-Thalathini fi Mua'shirat al-Iqtisad al-Iraqi, Um al-Marik Journal, no. 7, 1996.

16. Saad N. Jawad, op. cit., pp. 41–49.

17. Niblock, op. cit., p. 175.

18. Al-Saed Ali, op. cit.

19. For more details, see Saad N. Jawad, op. cit. An example of the haphazard way the UN Committee observed the sanction, dealt with one of Iraq's most essential and vital medicine to people with heart disease. Isordil was sanctioned on the pretext that it contained a component that could be

used to manufacture WMD. The same excuse was used to prevent Iraq from importing writing pencils for primary schools. The United States and British members of the Committee were the ones who suggested such weird ideas.

20. Niblock, op. cit., pp. 174–176.
21. There are no official statistics that could confirm this figure, as official statistics and the country's budget did not contain such statistics. They were regarded if deemed harmful to national security. General Hussein Kamil, Minister of Defense and the man managing the military industries, mentioned this percentage to some staff members in the College of Political Science. In May 1992, he was a student in that college, while he was a minister.
22. See a statistic of these breaches in Jeoff Simons, al-Tankil bil al-Iraq, op. cit., pp. 287–288.
23. This group included Professor Saad N. Jawad (academic), Hassan Shaban (lawyer), Salim al-Mandalawi (Lawyer and Judge), Duraid Saeed Thabit (economist), Professor Khalil al-Jazairi (academic), Professor Hussein al-Jumaily (academic) and Basim Said al-Hajj Unnis (lawyer). After a short while, Basim al-Hajj Younis left the group and Dr. Majid Abdul Ridha joined. Then Abdul Ridha also left the group after his request to be the editor in chief of the forthcoming journal was refused by the other members of the group. Khalid al-Salam and Hussein Sultan also signed the second memorandum. The Baath leadership named this group 'the internal national opposition' as opposed to the external opposition controlled by some foreign intelligence agencies.
24. Saddam Hussein, al-Dimocratia wa al-Ta'adodia al-Hizbia, al-Huriya publication House, Baghdad, July 1989. Exclusively for party members. It contained all the referred discussions.
25. An incident that showed the Baath Party leaders' way of thinking about what was happening around Iraq after it came out victorious in the war with Iran. It also reflected how they dealt with external parties who were not satisfied with the great military force Iraq possessed after the war. The famous speech of President Saddam Hussein on 2 April 1990 said: 'We will make the fire swoop half of Israel if it dared to attack Iraq again', referring to the Israeli attack on the Iraqi nuclear reactor near Baghdad in 1981.

This speech was preceded by the execution of a journalist of an Iranian origin named Farzad Bazoft. The journalist, who was working for a British newspaper, was accused of carrying an espionage mission inside Iraq. A major attack on Iraq followed the two incidents. Western media deliberately deleted the phrase 'if Israel attacked Iraq' from the President's speech, and insisted that Bazoft was innocent. General Hussein Kamil, the President's right-hand man, the Minister of Defense, and the president son-in-law, was at that time my student at the college of Political Science at the same time he held his official position.

Kamil asked me what I expect to happen after the execution of the British journalist and the President's statement about burning Israel. I replied: 'The situation is critical and can explode at any moment for several reasons: First, Israel is not satisfied with the tremendous power that Iraq has after the war with Iran. Secondly, I believe that the United States, with enormous pressure and incitement from Israel, is also not satisfied with the power that Iraq possessed. The two sides are cooperating in preparing an action against Iraq to destroy it. Lastly, Britain and Israel wanted the Iraqi regime to execute an Iranian journalist who had not yet obtained the British nationality and had previously been imprisoned in Britain for petty crimes he committed, to provoke a new action against Iraq and the Baath regime. Therefore, in my view, the government should be wary of what is to come'. Hussein Kamil's answer to me was: 'do not worry doctor; there is nothing more significant and dangerous than the plot of the Iran-Iraq war that was orchestrated against Iraq. Since we won against this plot, there is no fear for Iraq'.

26. Raad al-Jida, al-Karitha al-Disturiya: Dirasah fi al-Shuoun al-Disturiya al-Iraqia, Dar al-Manahij lilnashir, Amman, 2018, pp. 23–27.

27. General Hussein Kamil, who climbed the ladder of power very quickly, started as a junior bodyguard of the president. Then he became the man in charge of the Special Republican Guard forces. After a short while, he was appointed head of the Military Industry Corporation, Minister of Industry, then Minister of Defense and inspector of the Ministry of Oil. He married the eldest daughter of the president, and married his younger brother to the president's second daughter. The two brothers were almost the only men in charge of the security and safety plans concerning the life of the president. That is why their split and defection greatly shocked Saddam Hussein and caused a sharp deterioration in his morale.

28. Dr. Wamidh Nadmi did not attend because he was on a trip outside Iraq.

29. Scott Ritter, *Endgame: Solving the Iraqi problem Once and for All*, Simon and Schuster, New York, 1999. Ritter was a leading member of the UNISCOM team, and he affirmed in his book that Iraq was clear of the WMD since 1993.

30. Al-Thawra newspaper, Baghdad, 4/12/2002, and al-Jumhoriya Baghdad 17/12/2002.

31. After the invasion, there was a rumour that a member of Qusai, Saddam Hussein's office was one of the collaborators with the US–British invaders, and that there were others who had links with the Iraqi opposition abroad. The writer himself saw with his own eyes a number of middle-rank

Baathist officials streaming towards Ahmad Chalabi's temporary headquarters at the Hunting Club in Baghdad to congratulate him on his
'triumphant return'. Other did the same with Ayad Allawi and Mishaan
Jubouri, on the pretext that they were 'old comrades'. Also, as soon as
the invasion started, the Iraqi security forces waged a fierce campaign
to collect the satellite phones (Thuriya), which were the only cellular
phones used at that time, after they discovered that the invading forces
had distributed a big number of them to their stooges in Iraq to give
direction to the invading forces.

32. Two weeks before the invasion, there was a round of talks between
    the Iraqi government and the Kurdish parties. The last director of the
    Iraqi Intelligence Service, al-Mukhabarat, Major General Tahir Habboush,
    published some materials confirming these facts. https://www.knoozm
    edia.com/92385/طاهر-جليل-حبوش-ماذا-قال-عن-مسعود-برزان/amp/. See also
    Chapter 5.
33. See some of the declarations of the inspection team, Ritter, op. cit.
34. Interview with Dr. Fadhil al-Janabi, the last head of the Iraqi Atomic
    Energy Commission before the invasion, April 2003.
35. The officer was Captain Maan Khairullah Talfah, a maternal cousin of
    Saddam Hussein. He was the one who made the comment. The president
    was outraged, and he ordered him to leave the meeting. He instructed
    the team that recorded the event to delete the comment—interview with
    Captain Maan Khairallah Talfah, April 2003.
36. This was relayed to the author by one of the builders who preferred to
    remain anonymous. The man, who took part in this mission, was so keen
    in April 2003 to find someone to help him reach these sealed rooms.
37. Conversation with Zuhair Abdul Ghaffour al-Younis, the last head of the
    Iraqi Chamber of Commerce before the occupation. Immediately after the
    invasion, he spoke to me about how he headed a team to meet with the
    Minister of Trade, asking his permission to move some essential docu-
    ments and belongings of the Chamber to a secure place. The Minister
    reproached them and mocked their concerns telling them: 'Iraq would
    never be occupied. The military campaign will only result in destroying
    some of the presidential places and headquarters and will end in a very
    short time'.

CHAPTER 3

Occupation and Its Aftermath

Iraq and the United States, Historical Background

The US designs to replace the British influence in the Middle East goes far back as 1945, the year World War II came to an end. At that time, the US policy makers began to look at their country as the main international power that saved not only Europe, but the world at large from Nazi Germany. Thus, they felt that most of the privileges acquired by the old European Empires, especially in the Middle East, had to be revised. For the US ruling elite, it was not acceptable to keep the United States sidelined and deprived from having a share in the natural wealth of, and presence in the colonies dominated by the European powers following World War I. Thus, the 1950s witnessed United States attempts to take advantage of the decline of British and French power in the Middle East. It started in Saudi Arabia when the US secured almost all the oil concessions in that country. The next was Iran when the United States overthrew the Cabinet of PM Mosaddegh (1951–1953), who nationalized the oil industry, and re-installed the Shah once again, getting in return a share for US oil companies in the Iranian oil concessions. Two years before that, it propitiated the influential man of Iraqi politics under the monarchy Nouri al-Said, and encouraged him to strengthen Iraq's ties with Washington. Al-Said, who was impressed by the power of the United States and their advanced technology, arranged a visit in 1951 to United States

© The Author(s), under exclusive license to Springer Nature Switzerland AG 2021
S. N. Jawad, *Iraq after the Invasion*, Middle East Today,
https://doi.org/10.1007/978-3-030-72106-0_3

for the then young King of Iraq (Faisal II, a year before his inauguration) and his uncle the Regent. This visit resulted in many military, trade and oil agreements between the two countries. By 1957 US military supplies were flowing into Baghdad and Iraqi officers, especially from the police department, were attending training courses in the United States. This cooperation continued until 1966 when an Iraq military pilot was killed by Mossad agents because he refused to cooperate in a famous operation, later carried out by another pilot, to smuggle an Iraqi Soviet made fighter Mig 21 to Israel.[1]

The United States attempt to replace, or at least share, British influence in the area was culminated in the indirect role it played in foiling the Tripartite war against Egypt (waged by Britain, France and Israel) to foil the nationalization of the Suez Canal, which ended the British military presence in Egypt (1956). Some supporters of Iraqi monarchy went as far as claiming that Britain was behind the coup that toppled the royal regime (July revolution 1958) which put paid to the attempts of Nouri al-Said to establish stronger ties with the United States to replace the British ones. In the end, and with the declining British influence in the Middle East after the Suez adventure, the United States influence increased in the area. Its main bases were Israel, Iran and Saudi Arabia, with some overtures towards Iraq and Egypt. But the rise of President Jamal Abdul Nasser in Egypt (1952) and the Iraqi revolution (1958) dealt a heavy blow to US–Western influence in the area. The United States and Britain in particular were more alarmed by the increasing influence of the old Soviet Union in the area. This was manifested by spreading many communist parties in the region, especially in Iraq, following the coups that replaced the monarchies in Egypt and Iraq, and also with the strong ties of the two countries and the defunct Soviet Union. As the two major international powers found it difficult to overthrow the nascent republican regimes in the Middle East, they reverted to the policy of subverting them. In Iraq, Britain and the USA, following the decision of the first republican prime minister General Abdul Karim Qasim to end the domination of the international oil companies (mainly British) (Law no. 80 1961), reverted to the policy of creating internal troubles to the regime by instigating the Kurdish tribes in the north of the country. Meanwhile, assistance and encouragement were extended to the officers and parties that opposed Qasim.

Britain, Israel and USA were consecutively accused of playing a major role in financing and arming the Kurdish armed revolt (erupted in 1961) through Iran. In fact Iran, Israel and the USA went further in their support for the Kurdish armed revolt financially and militarily, to destabilize the Iraqi Baath regime in the war between the Kurdish armed fighters (the Peshmarga) and the Iraqi army that resumed between 1974 and 1975. The United States surge in opposing the Iraqi regime of the Baath Party (that succeeded to come to power in 1968) was based on the many decisions taken by that regime, which were regarded by Washington as hostile to its national interests and to the existence of its protégé entity in Israel. High among these decisions was the nationalization of the Iraqi oil industry in 1972 and the signature of the treaty of friendship between Iraq and the Soviet Union in the same year.

The brief 'honey moon' in the Iraqi–US relations following the crisis of the hostages of the US embassy in Tehran, the fall of the Shah's regime (1979), and during the war between Iraq and Iran (1980–1988) did not progress and was related with many periods of tension.

However, there were times when there were indications that there was a sort of rapprochement between the two countries. In fact when the coup that brought the Baath party back to power succeeded some analysts argue that this change was influenced, sponsored and backed by the United States and to a lesser extent Britain. This was because of the good relations and affiliation of some prominent figures of this change that linked them to 'intelligence circles' in both countries. This belief changed, however, 13 days later when the Baath Party leaders managed to remove all the non-Baathists from the government. Immediately, a new era characterized by hostility to US–Western policies began. The new regime also looked like it was strengthening itself by taking new and daring internal measures. A new front comprising the Iraqi Communist Party was established, a peaceful solution to the Kurdish problem was introduced, very ambitious development plans were initiated and a treaty of friendship with the former Soviet Union was signed. Nonetheless, this period also witnessed brutal measures used against anti-Baath elements, and sometimes some Baathist dissidents. All these measures ended with the total domination of one person—Saddam Hussein—over power and the party.

A new era in the US–Iraq relations loomed in 1980. Weeks prior to the US presidential elections of November that year, a team from Ronald Reagan's election campaign approached King Hussein of Jordan asking him to help amass support for the republican candidate. King Hussein

suggested that the team met with members of the Iraqi intelligence directorate ('al-Mukhabarat) who he knew had good influence inside Iraqi,
Arab and Muslim communities in the United States. The King convinced
the two sides to meet in Aqaba in the middle of October in his presence.
During that meeting, the Reagan team promised the Iraqi delegation that
if Reagan wins he will endeavour to make Israel withdraw from the lands
occupied in the 1967 war and implement the two states solution (Palestinian and Israeli), as well as helping Iraq in its war against Iran. According
to the head of the counter-intelligence service in the Iraqi Mukhabarat,
who was the second man to attend this meeting with the director of the
Iraqi intelligence, his office was managed in a very short time to manipulate the support of Reagan among all the communities mentioned above,
which was helpful to him becoming the 40th US President.[2] According
to the same source, President Reagan did not keep his promises, and the
relations between the two sides, Iraq and the United States became luke-
warm once again. However, in 1982 when the Iraqi armed forces had
some debacles in the war with Iran, the late King Hussein relayed to
the Iraqi president Saddam Hussein, the desire of United States to send
a team from the CIA to help with information, the Iraqi armed forces.
As a result, a three-man team arrived in Baghdad in February 1982, and
secretly met with delegates from the Iraqi Mukhabarat, and stayed for two
weeks only. The meetings were merely to exchange views about future
cooperation.[3] The Iraqi president, after being informed about the details
of the talks, ordered the immediate departure of the CIA team out of
Iraq. According to the man who headed the Iraqi side, the president,
because of his distrust in US politics, discerned that the United States
was not sincere in their intentions. He was also angered by some reports
filtered from the United States which spoke about the latter's desire to
see the war ending with 'no victor no vanquished', and about the United
States hope that the war would weaken and drain the resources of the two
countries.

A more serious and longer cooperation started between the two sides
in July 1982 following the defeat of the Iraqi armed forces in Khuzistan
(al-Muhamara) area in May of the same year. As a result, the late King
Hussein of Jordan asked for a top secret meeting between the Iraqi
Mukhabarat and himself. In this meeting the King showed the Iraqi dele-
gates satellite pictures about the last battle which the Iraqi Army lost.
He advised the Iraqi side to benefit from the CIA assistance. President
Saddam Hussein, on the many advices and instance of the Mukhabarat,

reluctantly accepted the idea. Another five-man CIA team, headed by the chief of Middle East operations arrived secretly in Baghdad, this team stayed till 1986.[4] According to the same source, this operation was again a top secret one, only the President, the head of Mukhabarat directorate, the head of the counter-intelligence service and a translator from the same directorate were aware of this team and operation. Members of the team were furnished with a house in a safe area and its members were given Greek names to camouflage their identity before the Iraqis who were serving them, (the head of the team was B. Johnson, whom we nicknamed Abu Erick, father of Erick).[5] As the liaison officer dealing directly with them, the head of the counter-intelligence service, said that he sensed and noticed on many occasions that while that team was willing to fully coop-erate with the Iraqi side and provide it with all the information needed, their superiors in Washington were not. That is why (the Baghdad team in many instances was bewildered and refrained from giving us all the information they have about the battle fronts with Iran).[6] The mission of this team was also terminated upon the orders of the Iraqi president for four reasons: First, he was informed by his military advisers that the CIA team used the tactics of holding the information concerning any major intended attack by the Iranian side, while they handed all the details of the battle to the Iraqi side after it ended, Second, he was informed by his security advisers that the CIA team was conducting some activities that could be considered harmful to the Iraqi national security, such as estab-lishing contacts with Kurdish separatist parties, and collecting information about the internal situation in Iraq.[7] Third, was leaked information about the Iran–Contra scandal, which unveiled the operation that was going on between the US–Israel and Iran to supply the latter with advanced military equipment since 1985.[8] This deal-affair took place despite the fact that the Iraq–US diplomatic relations was improving, and would finally resume in 1984. The fourth reason was the almost certain information that reached the Iraqi intelligence that the CIA had a similar team in Tehran providing Iran with similar information about Iraq. However, in 1983 there was another round of cooperation between the Iraqi intelligence service and its United States counterpart, when the latter approached Iraq, through the (West) Germany side to help in collecting informa-tion about the huge blast the hit the Marines headquarters in Beirut that year. The Iraqi side agreed, but refused to do that directly and insisted on doing that through the German side. But the source admitted that during that time the United States turned a blind eye on the Iraqi's croaked ways to obtain armament from all over the world, and sometimes from the United States itself.[9] One should also add the two famous visits in 1983 and 1984 made by then US defence minister Donald Rumsfeld to Baghdad and his meeting with Saddam Hussein.

The end of the Iraq–Iran war caused major concerns for Israel, and consequently the United States. These concerns were represented by the enormous military power Iraq possessed at the end of the war. In other words, all the United States and Israeli attempts to weaken Iraq, or the plan to divide it into three separate entities according to a notorious plan put in place in 1982 was in vain. At that time, Israel was the first to speak about the necessity to divide Iraq during the intensity of the Iraq–Iran war. This came in an article written by the Israeli journalist and former diplomat Oded Yinon, first published in Kivunim in February 1982,[10] His paper spoke about the need to split Iraq into Kurdish, Shiite and Sunni entities as a way to protect Israel's security.[11] He also thought that this objective would be achieved indirectly through the continuation of the Iraq–Iran war. Yinon's hope was dashed, as the war ended with a clear Iraqi military victory. Nevertheless, his 'plan' remained useful for all those who opposed a strong Iraq. It was not surprising, therefore, that the neo-conservatives were quick to revive this idea following the occupation of Iraq in 2003. Thus, it could be concluded that the plan to divide and fragment Iraq was older than the occupation by at least two decades.

The tension between Iraq and the United States began to grow at the same time and for the same reason. But the US government of George H. Bush (the father) preferred to keep links with Iraq. Even when the Iraqi president declared in April 1990 that if Israel attacked Iraq he will let fire engulf half of Israel, (following the leakage of information that Israel was preparing an attack to cripple the Iraqi military power), the US government tried to put the growing tension on ice. A high-level delegation, headed by Senator Robert (Bob) Dole, apparently upon President George Bush request, arrived in Baghdad in April 1990 and met with President Saddam Hussein. The Iraqi president was told that the United States wanted to improve relations with Iraq, but at the same time wanted assurances that Iraq will not attack Israel. Later on Dole declared that the meeting and the frank conversions were successful.[12]

But the threats to Israel and the defiant attitude of the Iraqi president, at a time when the United States was left as the only power in the world, following the collapse and dismantling of the Soviet Union, made the

US administration seriously feel that undisciplined Iraq, with all its military might and economic capability, would present a threat to America's influence and interests in the region, as well as threatening the security of its protégé Israel. Thus, immediately following the end of the Iraq–Iran war, think-tank centres inside the US administration began to put plans to contain the growing power of Iraq.

THE INVASION AND OCCUPATION

The occupation of Iraq in 2003 was neither an impulsive decision nor the result of the 9/11 attacks, as propagated at the time; rather, it was the culmination of United States plans aimed at including oil-rich Iraq into America's sphere of influence, as well as ending a regime which was an obstacle to the US vision of a new middle East in which Israel will be a player.

The main factor that assisted and encouraged United States plans was, in addition to the downfall of the Soviet Union, the arrival of the neo-cons to power. The neo-cons also thought that they could dominate the world through different methods: the use of strict economic and military sanctions claims of spreading democracy, using creative chaos and deposing unfriendly regimes on the pretext that they possessed 'weapons of mass destruction' (WMDs) and supporting terrorism. According to Fukuyama, these deceptive illusions were what encouraged the neo-con leaders, the majority of whom were Zionist Jews, to do anything in order to serve the interests of Israel, which was not in the interest of the United States.[13]

The invasion of Kuwait in August 1990 by the Iraqi Republican Guards, and the refusal to withdraw from it, was the final straw that gave the United States and Britain the excuse they needed to wage a destructive war against Iraq (1991). Although, the war did succeed in driving the Iraqi forces out of Kuwait, but it also had two important by-products: the first was, the daring decision of Saddam Hussein to fire 39 long-range missiles on Israel, an action that not only exceeded all limits but also initiated a new strategy in the Arab–Israeli conflict which put a definitive end to the idea of (impregnable Israel). It also proved that the then Iraqi president was not ready to succumb to American and Israeli ambitions. The second by-product was that, the ability of the Iraqi competencies and know-how was capable of rebuilding what the war to liberate Kuwait had destroyed in an efficient and speedy manner, something that had never been envisaged by the West and the United States. This was clear in the prompt reply of former US Secretary of State Madeleine Albright when asked about the feasibility of continued inhumane sanctions on Iraq following the destruction of all its capabilities, she said: 'Yes, but the brains are still there'. But neither the unprecedented sanctions, which lasted for almost 13 years and claimed the lives of 1.8 million Iraqis, mainly children, women and elderly people, nor the intermittent aerial bombardments of Baghdad succeeded in changing the defiant attitude of the late Iraqi president. On the contrary, he increased his assistance and support to the Palestinian Intifada by generously compensating the wounded and the families of those killed. He also refused to comply with America's plan to create a new Middle East. The decision to change the regime by force was officially taken by the United States in 1998 when the Bill Clinton administration issued the Iraq Liberation Act.

At the same time the United States and Britain continued to fabricate pretexts in order to tighten the sanctions on Iraq as a prelude to occupying it. In spite of the fact that the United Nations (UN) teams, which included many Zionists—whose mission was to observe Iraqi compliance with the resolutions to rid Iraq of its WMDs, affirmed offstage that Iraq did not possess such weapons, the United States and Britain continued to claim that Iraq was still concealing WMDs. It was also revealed that the United States interfered on many occasions to force the heads of the UN teams to declare Iraq is in possession of WMDs and the ability to manufacture them.[14]

To justify the plan to occupy Iraq, the United States and Britain initiated many inventive reasons which included possessing a secret programme to manufacture WMDs, and having links with al-Qaeda.[15] Other reasons were also added such as the miserable state of human and women's rights,[16] which could only be described as 'right' reasons to justify 'wrong' objectives. To all reasonable and impartial researchers, there were two main reasons for the occupation: Iraq's oil wealth and the security of Israel.[17]

In preparation for the war, American, British and Israeli intelligence services recruited a number of Iraqi stooges, presented as Iraqi nuclear scientists, who alleged that Iraq still possessed WMDs and programmes to manufacture them. Despite the fact that all these intelligence services were certain that these collaborators were lying and that their main objective was to obtain the nationality of the countries to which they sought to flee, the governments of these services regarded their fabricated information as crucial facts to justify the war on Iraq. What is more harmful, was that all the Western media, even the respected ones, accepted these lies and had them published. Up to the present-day, we still have not heard or seen any of those who put forth these lies taken to account, whether they be officials, media representatives or journalists alike. The Chilcott Committee in Britain, investigating the war on Iraq, after years of works and interrogations, failed to direct accusations to those who lied to the people to justify their participation in the war the United States was planning.

From the outset, all the efforts of the American, British and Israeli intelligence services were concentrated on the Iraqi elements living in the West who introduced themselves as the opposition to the Baath regime. These elements were supported materially and morally to act as a facade to the moves against the Baath regime. The differences between these elements were muted by United States and British pressure. The so-called Iraqi opposition in the West consisted of three elements:

- Religious Sectarian Parties and Personalities.
- Some secular ones, such as the Iraqi Communist Party, that was in the minority and who succumbed to the religious parties and American influence.
- Some personalities that was notorious for their tarnished reputation and long-established connection with American, British and even Israeli intelligence services.

Thus, sectarianism, chauvinism, selfish personal interests and submission to foreign intelligence services, as mentioned above, constituted the majority of this opposition. Furthermore, it was clear that the majority of this opposition had no support or influence inside Iraq. More harmful than the role these elements played was the one played by some Iraqis inside Iraq; some were members of the Baath Party. They were successfully recruited by Western and Israeli intelligence services between 1998 and 2003 and played a crucial role in providing the invading forces with valuable information before, during and after the invasion.

THE OCCUPATION OF IRAQ, THE POLICY
OF THE OCCUPYING FORCES AND THEIR COLLABORATORS

In March 2003 the operation to occupy Iraq by an international coalition forces, mainly comprised of US and British forces stationed in Kuwait, got under way. This operation had no international legal cover, especially from the UN. It was also ineffectively opposed by some members of the UN Security Council. The administrations concerned, adopted a disparaging attitude to the opinion of the millions who took to the streets, especially in the United States and Britain. After two weeks of heavy fighting, Baghdad was occupied on that fateful day of Wednesday, 9 April.

Right from the early days of the occupation it was clear that America's and Britain's sole aim was to remove the regime of Saddam Hussein and to destroy Iraq to the extent that would prevent it from becoming a regional power. What facilitated the application of this policy were the people who governed Iraq after the occupation. For example, the first US civil governor of Iraq, Jay Garner, knew nothing whatsoever about Iraq, so was the team that came with him. I had the opportunity to meet with him and his team in April 2003, when they were invited by a neighbour of mine in Baghdad. This neighbour asked me to come and tell Garner what I thought.[18] I was amazed about how ill informed and ignorant he and his team were about Iraq.[19] His questions showed that he knew nothing, while his team seemed angered by my frankness. Instead of listening to me they felt restless and thought that I was ruining their evening and the big banquet my neighbour had prepared for them. When I finished my talking Garner offered me a job to be his right-hand man by the next day. I immediately declined his offer by telling him that he had chosen the wrong person. I added that I attended this meeting mainly because I wanted to relay to him the voice of a big portion of the Iraqi people, and that I was not ready to cooperate with the occupiers. When Garner told me that things will be better in the coming days I told him: 'remember me when you find out or hear that your causalities under the occupation will be more than your loses during the invasion'. Few months later, when the number of US soldiers killed in Iraq had risen, my neighbour told me that Mr. Garner says hello to you and that he still remembered what you told him in that meeting.

Perhaps another incident happened with me could give a better example about the ignorance of Garner's team, and in fact all those who came to govern Iraq following the occupation, about Iraq. The day after my meeting with Garner, one of the advisors of his team called at my house and asked if I could spare few minutes to talk to him. I showed him in. Immediately after he sat down he said: 'could you please tell me what the Maria'iya al-Diniya in Najaf is?' I was really shocked; I said 'I beg your pardon?' Do you mean to tell me that you know nothing about the most important religious institution in Iraq? 'All your plans and preparations to occupy Iraq did not include a single study about al-Marja'iya in Najaf?' He simply replied 'we know nothing about it'.

As a result of Garner's flops, chaos prevailed as there was no plan to administer the occupied country. Even the traffic police and Public service men were not allowed to carry out their job. Moreover, the occupying forces did not declare the necessary curfew, something very normal in such cases. Banks, museums and public places were looted and burned before the eyes of the occupying forces which did nothing to stop these activities. In addition to this, armed contingents of the so-called opposition converged in Baghdad and other cities and began to take the law into their own hands. People were terrorized and a systematic wave of assassinations ensued. This wave was directed mainly against scientists, academics and members of the Iraqi armed forces.[20] Iraq's borders were left open allowing different militias to infiltrate Iraq from neighbouring countries. Al-Qaeda was the first organization to take advantage of this situation. The new incoming militias from Iran strongly supported the religious and sectarian parties, something that gave them the upper hand in Iraq. The Iranian influence became excessive, giving the impression to many analysts that Iraq was being presented to Iran (on a platter of gold) by the United States. It was clear that the policy of the new US administration in Iraq and its supporters were operating on five basic principles:

- It regarded whoever was living in Iraq as a stooge of Saddam Hussein and the Baath Party, even if they were efficient people, known for their integrity; and whoever accompanied the occupying forces, no matter how ignorant they were and how tarnished their histories, had the right to govern Iraq.
- The old regime was regarded as Sunni, discriminating against the Shiites and the Kurds, and only these latter two elements now had the right to dominate Iraq at the expense of the Sunnis.
- All Sunnis were seen as Baathists or 'terrorists', and there was no objection to them being annihilated.

- The newcomers had the right to confiscate public places without any accountability or legal consequences.
- All public places could be ransacked, except the Ministry of Oil and the intelligence headquarters (Mukhabarat); the latter was protected until certain elements confiscated all its records, especially the ones relating to Israel, and was later burned down.
- As a result of the chaos, US administration removed Garner and appointed Paul Bremer as the undisputed civil governor of Iraq. It could be said that Bremer, who could be regarded as the one who institutionalized the sectarian and quota policy, was very much aware of what to do in Iraq in order to implement the US–Israeli plans for the country.

Bremer also had no knowledge about Iraq and its affairs. He admitted later in a book he published in 2006,[21] that the most important and critical decisions he took, which were devastating to the Iraqi state, were actually prepared for him in advance by the Pentagon or the State Department. In addition to the five basic principles of rule mentioned above, he also added his own ignorant opinion in describing the Iraqi state. He regarded Iraq as a fake and artificial state created by the British after World War I emphasizing that it was a diverse ethnic blend founded on a sectarian basis. Equally harmful was his belief that there was no such thing as an 'Iraqi people'; instead, there were Shiites, Sunni, Kurds, Turkomans, Assyrians, Christians and Yazidis. Thus, he erased the presence of Arabs or the Arab national character in Iraq, despite the fact that this identity constituted 80% of the population.[22] Another harmful idea was that the Arab Shiite population of the southern provinces was more attached to Iran than to Iraq, intentionally neglecting the fact that the population of these provinces were, and still are, proud of their Arab origin and heritage. Bremer also kept repeating that the Sunnis had ruled Iraq for over 400 years, and that the time had come to relinquish their political domination.[23] Of course, this idea of his contradicts what he said earlier when he claimed that Iraq was an artificial state; he did not ask himself how an artificial state, which did not exist before WWI, was dominated by the Sunnis' rule for four centuries? Needless to say, these ideas were very much welcomed by the Kurdish and the Shiite parties who collaborated with him, as they viewed them as victories over their opponents.

Bremer immediately put his ideas and thoughts into practice. He established the Governing Council (GC) and selected 25 members for it. His choice was made on a sectarian ethnic and quota basis. Its members comprised 13 Shiites, five Sunnis, five Kurds, one Turkoman, and one Assyrian Christian. To confirm his policy, he named the sect of each member after his name, instead of citing his or her qualifications. It was really ironic, for example, to see the word 'Shiite' written after the name of the Secretary-General of the Iraqi Communist Party; the same was applied to members who had always been known to be secularist. Yet, this was not applied to the Kurdish members of the council, instead they were kept as one nationality. This arbitrary policy was also followed when he formed the first transitional cabinet and the national assembly, which he wanted to ratify the laws he issued. During his term in office Bremer issued 100 compulsory laws, two of which were specifically harmful. The first was a law that disbanded the Iraqi army. This resulted in evicting 1.5 million well-trained and experienced servicemen from the army, security and intelligence services into the street, and without any compensation. This decision explained the effectiveness of the Iraqi armed resistance that erupted during the first two years of the occupation, and later on, the successes of the Islamic State of Iraq and the Levant (ISIL), better known as (Daesh) in Iraq, which included a fair number of Iraqi officers from the old army. The second law he enacted was to dissolve the Baath Party—the 'De-Baathification law'—which resulted in firing thousands of efficient people from their jobs. In the meantime the De-Baathification law, which had a very terrifying synonym in Arabic—'uprooting the Baath', was used haphazardly to annihilate those who opposed the occupation. Bremer declared in many occasions that the Shiite and Kurdish parties that cooperated with him strongly supported his decisions and, on some occasions, even proposed similar ones to him.

Shortly after dissolving the armed forces, Bremer issued a law to form the 'National Guards' to replace the old army. In fact, his choice of the word 'guard' was very indicative of his intentions, as he wanted the new force to simply be guards and not a real army. Moreover, he did not build the new force on professional considerations but on an ethnical, sectarian and quota basis, and by mainly amalgamating the militia forces that was established abroad before 2003 and who came to Iraq later on. These militias were given the right to give military ranks and positions to their members who were, in general, without any professional military training or experience, or even any education for a large number of them, some were virtually illiterate. It should also be stated that there was no real military discipline or law to organize these militia contingents, and all remained loyal to the parties to which they belonged. The new alleged Iraqi army, therefore, consisted of the Badir Brigade which was initially formed in Iran and fought with the Iranian army during the Iraq–Iran war; the Free Iraqi Forces which were composed of Iraqis trained by Americans in Bulgaria and airlifted to Iraq after the occupation; the Peshmarga Kurdish forces stationed in Iraqi Kurdistan which were almost independent and never followed orders from Baghdad; and the al-Sadir militia which later fought against the American and British armies, as well as other militias belonging to other parties taking part in the political process.

As was expected, corruption and sectarian affiliations were the main characteristics of the new National Guards which was now called the 'Iraqi Army' by the government, after the American withdrawal. The occupation of Mosul by the ISIL fighters (Daesh), revealed all the defects that this force had, as it fled the battles in Mosul, Tikrit and Anbar. Prime Minister, Haidar al-Ibadi (2014–2018) declared, after he took office, that the new force had as much as 60–70% of personnel who were not actually in service but were receiving salaries. He said that one calculation he made of some forces serving in Mosul revealed that there were 50,000 imaginary or non-existing members of these forces whom he called 'ghost recruits'.[24] His Minister of Interior made a similar declaration about the police force. Not only was this force dispersed following the Mosul incident, but also before that many contingents of it had left the service and joined their own rebelling militias in Baghdad and other southern cities.

As soon as the US–British occupation of Iraq was completed, both countries obtained a resolution from the UN (1483/May 2003) that deemed Iraq as an occupied country; a resolution that made Bremer even more authoritarian. As an example, he told a reluctant UN official responsible for Iraq's frozen assets to hand the money over to him. When the official refused to release the assets belonging to the Iraqi government, Bremer replied: 'I am the Iraqi government, and I am asking you to free the money immediately'.[25] Bremer was also accused of corruption and mishandling of large amounts of Iraqi money put at his disposal. About US$8.8 billion were never accounted for after he left his post 'So, Mr Bremer, where did all the money go?' The Guardian wrote in 2005.[26] The Iraqi politicians who came after him followed his example. One could also say that the US and British administrations in Iraq laid the foundations for a corrupt system by distributing large amounts of money to their collaborators for fake projects, or by paying huge salaries to people who never earned them. Both administrations also turned a blind eye to those who were stealing public money and transferring it to European countries of which they were nationals, regardless of the fact that up to 2003 these people were living in these countries on social benefits. On one occasion a private security company working with the US Army abducted from prison a former Iraqi minister who was serving a prison sentence for corruption and smuggled him out of jail in broad daylight through Baghdad's international airport.[27]

Although, Bremer was directly responsible for what happened in Iraq after 2003, this does not exonerate the Iraqis who took over the responsibility after him for maintaining the sectarian, ethnic policies and encouraging corruption, nepotism and foreign interference. Due to the fact that the majority of the Shiite, Sunni and Kurdish newcomers had little or no support inside Iraq, they used sectarian and ethnic discourses to lure the people. For example, Ahmad al-Jalabi, who was known as secularist and a person who never practised religious rites, established the 'Shiite House' in Baghdad to secure the backing of the Shiite parties and population. While one of his partners, Mudhar Shawkat, who has never been known for his adherence to religion, and who, since returning to Iraq after the invasion, mainly focussed his efforts on greedily collecting a huge fortune, courted the Sunni component, in a distasteful sectarian manner, by holding a big meeting for the displaced Sunnis in Erbil to promote the idea of a Sunni region.[28] On the other side of the spectrum, the Shiite politicians encouraged Shiite sectarian discourse to gain the trust of Iran, while their Sunni counterparts presented themselves as the guardians of the Sunni sect to court the Arab Gulf rulers as a source to generate huge amounts of money. The Kurdish parties, on their part, were more than happy with this fragmentation that served their objective of establishing a de facto independence. All they were concerned about was how much the Kurdish region could get from the centre. Moreover, the Kurdish region strengthened its relations with Israel, the only entity that openly supported the separation of Iraqi Kurdistan. The existence of Israeli companies, military trainers and advisers was no longer a secret.[29]

THE DIVISIVE NATURE OF THE NEW CONSTITUTION

The damage that Bremer's policies and decisions caused to national unity and to the fabric of society became more harmful as these divisive issues were enshrined in the Transitional Administrative Law (TAL), issued in 2004 by Bremer, and later in the permanent constitution of 2005. It was clear in these two documents, especially the constitution, that the American desire to establish a weak central government alongside strong regional entities, as well as asserting other controversial issues, would cause blood-letting and would take ages to resolve. Perhaps the most dangerous thing asserted in the TAL (became effective 28 June 2004) was the limited time it fixed to complete writing the draft of the permanent constitution (by August 15) and to carry out the first legislative elections in December of the same year.

It is worth noting that the insistence on such a short time to draft the constitution was not because the interest of the Iraqis was a primary concern, or because the United States wanted to establish democracy in Iraq. Rather, it was because of the escalating Iraqi resistance which claimed the lives of 4487 American soldiers according to US statistics, and more than 10,000 according to other statistics, let alone the number of people who were disabled.[30] This fact drove the American government to seriously think about an early exit strategy. They wanted the permanent constitution to be approved quickly, followed by general elections, so they can claim that it withdrew after it had established democracy in Iraq.

There was much controversy about who wrote the permanent constitution of Iraq. Although, the leaders of the Iraqi parties involved in the political process insisted that they were the ones who drafted it, two facts subsequently emerged proving the contrary. Firstly, it was said that the 32-year-old orthodox Jew and junior US academic Noah Feldman drafted it. He himself confirmed this fact indirectly when he admitted that he had been an adviser in writing the draft.[31] The late Edward Said, relying on what was published in US media, also confirmed the fact that it was Feldman who wrote it.[32] The second fact was that the permanent constitution was almost identical to the TAL, in which the Iraqis had no real say and which was approved by the GC on Bremer's order.

Full enumerations of the shortcomings of the constitution will be discussed in Chapter Four of this book, suffice it to say that the hidden and malicious intentions behind drafting the constitution in such a divisive way, could explain the reasons for the endless and continued crises the country has been undergoing ever since.

Following the approval of the constitution, Iraq witnessed its first general elections since the occupation in December 2005, to elect 275 members for a new parliament according to the new constitution. It was clear before the announcement of the results that the Shiites and Kurdish parties will have the majority of the seats. After a short lull due to some objections, or accusations, from the Sunni list claiming that the results were tempered with, the final results were announced as follows: the Shiite coalition won 128 seats, the Kurdish coalition 53 seats and the Sunni coalition 44 seats. Under the terms of the constitution the list (coalition) that gained the majority of votes/seats would have the right to form the cabinet. Accordingly the Shiite coalition, in an internal election, chose Ibrahim al-Jaafari, (holder of British citizenship) from al-Dawa religious party, to be the new premier. But this choice was strongly opposed by the US administration. The impasse was increased when the Kurdish parties joined in objecting to this nomination. In the end, and upon the insistence of the US administration, Jaafari was (advised) to relinquish his nomination. Four months later (May 2006), Jaafari agreed to step aside in favour of his fellow party member Nouri al-Malki.[33] In other words, all the United States claims about initiating and respecting democratic procedures in Iraq were ignored or disregarded as Jaafari was forced to drop out.

Maliki's two terms in office (2006–2010 and 2010–2014), augured ill for Iraq and Iraqis. Under his rule sectarian violence increased, corruption was widespread and the biggest disaster was the success of the terrorist Daesh forces in occupying third of the Iraqi territories (Mosul, Anbar and Salah al-Din provinces), in June 2014. All his boasting about the army and the military forces he organized, on which he spent billions of dollars, vanished in thin air, as all these troops ran away in front of few hundreds of Daesh fighters.

Interesting to note that following the second elections (March 2010), the coalition of the Prime Minister Maliki, (which he named The State of Law), came second with 89 seats. The first winning coalition (al-Iraqia list), of the former interim premier (2004), Ayad Allawi (another holder of British citizenship), won 91 seats. Maliki claimed that constitutionally he still had the right to form the new government because he managed to form a majority inside the parliament, i.e. after the elections, by coalescing with other groups. He also managed, with the backing and pressure of Iran to: first, convince the president of the republic Jalal Talabani, (holder of British citizenship) not to ask Allawi to form a new government, second, to make the High Court support his claim by giving a verdict in his favour concerning the clause in the constitution that spoke about the winning list. (The court's verdict was that the majority does not mean the party that wins the biggest number of seats, rather it means the side that could manage to form the biggest block [majority] inside the parliament).[34] These contradictions and controversies lasted until November 2010, almost eight months following the announcement of the results. One month later, in December, Maliki was able to form an incomplete government that was passed by the parliament, (mainly without ministers for defence and interior).

Following the third elections (2014), Maliki tried to gain a third term, claiming that the results of the elections allowed him such a right. This time the US administration objected, despite the fact he had the backing of the Shiite coalition inside the parliament. In the end the United States pressure prevailed, making the president of the republic, Fuad Masoum, (holder of British citizenship) assign Haidar al-Ibadi (also a British citizen) to form the new government, four months after the announcement of the results of the elections and two days before the end of the extended constitutional period. This was done amid sharp objections and threat by Maliki to sue the president. In the end Maliki's objections were silenced by his coalition and the Najaf religious Shiite Marja'iya al-Diniya of Sistani.

Although, Ibadi (also from al-Dawa religious Party) enjoyed an unprecedented internal and international backing, most importantly from Ayatoullah Sistani Marja'iya, he failed to exploit this support to fight corruption, nominate efficient ministers or complete his cabinet in the first attempt. Nevertheless Ibadi's term in office (2014–2018) was marked by two positive issues: first, the significant decrease in the official sectarian language-attitude, and second, his success in leading a military campaign to liberate all occupied Iraqi territories controlled by Daesh since 2014, especially Mosul. Indeed this campaign, which lasted for almost two years (2016–2018), resulted in almost total destruction of the liberated areas.

The fourth elections of 2018 were also inconclusive, in the sense that no party had the majority inside the parliament. However, Ibadi's bid to gain a second term was blocked this time by Iran and its Iraqi allies. This was simply because of Ibadi's statement in which he said that his government will comply with the sanctions imposed by president Trump on Iran. The other reason was his dissatisfaction with the growing influence and presence of the pro-Iran militias, al-Hashid al-Shaabi, the Popular Mobilization Forces (PMF). In the end, and after the usual delay, which became characteristic of the Iraqi elections, it was agreed in October 2018 (more than six months delay) to select Adil Abdul Mahdi (holder of French citizenship) as a new (conciliatory) prime minister.

Abdul Mahdi's term in office was disastrous and a failure by all standards. To start with, and despite his claims that he will fight corruption, his cabinet included ministers who were indicted by Iraqi courts for corruption, and were released due to a controversial pardon issued by the parliament. Then he gave the PMF units the upper hand inside the military institution. In fact, the PMF had enormously strengthened their position by enlarging their forces and participating in the elections, managing to send a big number of their representatives to the parliament, (around 47 seats of 328). It could be fairly said that Abdul Mahdi's major failures were: his total subordination to Iran and its allies in Iraq, (especially the PMF), failure to provide the minimal services to the majority of the Iraqi people and finally the huge size of corruption inside his government. All these facts were accentuated by the sharp drop in oil prices, which caused a huge economic problem for Iraq in general. In the end Abdul Mahdi's lethargy, incompetence and his inability to take decision to alleviate the sufferings of the people caused huge protests and demonstrations in Baghdad. These demonstrations which started in October 2019 spread to all the southern provinces, especially Basra and Nasiriya. To add to his government's bad conduct, he took the unwise decision to deal with these demonstrations in an excessive way, ordering the use of force against the demonstrators. The brutal way with which he dealt with these demonstrations, resulted in about 700 people killed and more than thirty thousand injured, as well as an unspecified number of demonstrators imprisoned or abducted. In the end, these overwhelming protests and demonstrations forced him to submit his resignation in January 2020, against his wishes of course. Yet because there was no consensus on a replacement Abdul Mahdi remained as a caretaker prime minister until May 2020. During this period, his critics that are members of parliament claimed that corruption was at its highest level in his cabinet.[35]

After two aborted attempts to nominate a successor to Abdul Mahdi, Mohammed Tawfiq Allawi (holder of British citizenship) and Adnan al-Zurfi, (holder of US citizenship) mainly due to Iranian objection, the different parliamentary groups agreed on nominating Mustafa al-Kadhimi, the head of the Iraqi Intelligence Service, (another holder of British citizenship) to become the new prime minister. It was clear that Kadhimi's selection was based on US pressure and the tacit approval of Iran. Iran attitude could be explained as an attempt to mitigate its tension with the United States. Kadhimi's first promises were: to prosecute those who participated in the killing of the demonstrators and those who gave the order to them, to combat corruption, to comply with the demands of the protestors to improve services, and finally to insure that the carrying of arms will be restricted to the state armed forces.

Obviously, Kadhimi's job was not an easy one, and the challenges he faced were enormous. To start with, he was accused by groups of the PMF that he was a United States stooge. More dangerous, of being a culprit, while he was head of the Iraqi Intelligence Service (Mukhabarat), in the assassination of the Iranian General Qasem Suleimani and the Iraqi leading member in the PMF Abu Mahdi al-Muhandis. The two men were killed by a United States drone near Baghdad international airport 3 January 2020.

Although, Kadhimi's initial declarations were positively received by the demonstrators, but his actions did not match his words. It is obvious that the man is shattered between the United States and Iranian influence. All indications point to the fact that he is prone to align with the United States, but he accepted an invitation from Iran to visit Tehran, where he met with the Iranian supreme leader Ayatollah Ali Khamenie. In the meantime, Washington extended to him an invitation to come and meet with president Trump, something his predecessor Abdul Mahdi failed to do during his term in office. Perhaps it is too early to judge his actions, but up to the time of writing these lines he did not take any actions against those who were accused of killing the demonstrators, or against those who were accused of giving the orders to use force to kill the demonstrators or against those who carried out the killings and continued to assassinate demonstrators, political analysts, journalists and media men who criticized the state of lawlessness in Iraq, as well as the domination of the militias.

In the final analysis, it could be said that the nomination and selection of each prime minister since 2005 was controversial and unconstitutional. Of course, the US-Iranian differences over the nomination of any new prime minister were covered by the ruling Iraqi parties by talks about (the constitutional and unconstitutional procedures). But the irony is that all the nominations or selections were in fact unconstitutional. Following the first elections (2005) the Shiite coalition agreed on Ibrahim al-Jaafari as the new prime minister, the US administration objected, as it regarded him to be close to Iran. In the end Jaafari was (convinced) to step down in favour of Nouri al-Maliki. In the 2010 elections, Maliki's list did not get the majority of the votes, his opponent Ayad Allawi's list did. In any democratic system the head of the state would ask the leader of the winning list to form the government, once he fails then the second

winning list will be called to form the government or a coalition government. But Maliki used his influence to make the high court issue a
decision in his favour. According to this decision Malik approached the
Shiite and Kurdish parties, giving the latter big concessions in order to
support his nomination. During the third parliamentary elections (2014)
Maliki thought he could repeat the same thing, but this time the US
administration decided to get rid of him, thus, they blocked his attempt
for a third term, despite the fact that he managed to get the support
of the majority of the blocs inside the parliament. Due to US objection
to Maliki, the Shiite coalition agreed to choose Haidar al-Ibadi in order
to keep the nomination inside the Dawa Party. The election of 2018 was
another irony. Because of the sharp differences between the United States
and Iran, and to end the impasse which lasted for five months, the two
sides agreed to choose Adil Abdul Mahdi as a new prime minister. Abdul
Mahdi selection was a clear violation of the terms of the constitution.
He has neither been a nominee in the elections that took place that year,
nor was he a member of any of the coalitions inside the parliament (i.e.
not a member of the parliament). The same happened with the nomination of Kadhimi, who again did not participate in the elections nor
belonged to any list or coalition inside the parliament. While the constitution clearly states that only the biggest winning coalition has the right
to submit one of its members to the president of the republic to assign as
a prime minister. Of course, the parliament passed and approved all these
unconstitutional nominations due to external pressure (Iran and United
States).

IMPLICATIONS AND REPERCUSSIONS
OF THE OCCUPATION OF MOSUL IN JUNE 2014

Before the United States withdrew from Iraq in 2011, they signed a security agreement in 2008 with Iraq entitled the Status of Forces Agreement
(SOFA). According to this agreement and its related protocols, the American forces were given the freedom, without the consent of Iraq, to take
action to fight terrorism in and around Iraq.[36] However, this did not
prevent Washington from doing nothing to prevent the fighters of Daesh
from occupying Mosul and extending their presence to other areas in
Tikrit, parts of Anbar and Diyala in June 2014. Yet, the United States
was fast in taking effective military action against these brutal fighters
when they approached the borders of Erbil, the capital of the Kurdish

region. The intense bombardment by the US Air Force, and some other European countries, managed to drive these fighters away. It seemed that the US hesitated to take on the advancing Daesh forces for two reasons. Firstly, they said that the Iraqi government had not asked for their assistance; and secondly, they were looking for an excuse to blame the then prime minister, Nouri al-Maliki (2006–2014), and his failed foreign policy for what had happened. He refused to listen to US advice to change his sectarian policy that led to the alienation of vast segments of the Iraqi people, especially the Sunnis. What was not said was that the United States was not really concerned about what happened in Iraq. In fact, the USA, Europe, Turkey and other Gulf States supported Daesh when they were fighting the Syrian regime which they wanted to remove. They were also happy to see Daesh advance towards Iran's borders. However, their attitude changed when Daesh decided to invade the Iraqi Kurdish region and brutally beheaded American and European citizens. Only then did the United States lead a coalition to fight Daesh, but only from the air.

The Mosul setback revealed gross deficiencies which the Iraqi successive governments tried to cover up, or claimed they did not exist. The first deficiency was the fragility and meagreness of the so-called new Iraqi army formed by Bremer. The low-level investigation that took place in Baghdad months after the disaster revealed that the number of troops who were supposed to defend Mosul was grossly and fictitiously enlarged. Most of the recruitments never took place; they were merely names on paper, the salaries of whom were going into the pockets of their corrupt commanders.[37] Secondly, the government of Maliki was not affected by this disaster since it held none of the military leaders or commanders accountable for what happened. This position prevailed under the rule of Haidar Ibadi (2014–2018), Adil Abdul Mahdi (2018–2020) and the present Premier Mustafa Kadhimi (March 2020–).

Some Sunni leaders also believed that Maliki was clearly indifferent to the loss of the Sunni-dominated areas which he had always repressed because they opposed his sectarian policies. Thirdly, the KRG was also apathetic towards this military disaster and simply regarded it as part of the Shiite–Sunni struggle in Iraq. It could also be said that the KRG was, in reality, satisfied about the defeat of the Iraqi army, and regarded it as a golden opportunity to extend its sphere of power to the so-called disputed areas, especially Kirkuk. The KRG only realized the error of its thinking after Daesh forces reached the walls of Erbil and put the whole

Iraqi Kurdish region under threat. Yet, under these dangerous circumstances, the KGR tried to exploit the events in order to obtain, and sometimes actually received, direct military assistance and arms from the United States and European countries.

THE SECTARIAN POLICIES AND ITS HARMFUL EFFECTS

As already discussed above, the sectarian language and policy were very clear in the speeches and behaviour of the new politicians, as well as how the governments were formed. This policy was also evident in dealing with the overwhelming Sunni-dominated areas of Mosul, Anbar and Tikrit. The usually mixed areas in Baghdad and Diyala are not exempted. Sectarian militias carried out campaigns that resulted in area cleansing, for example, Sunnis were forcefully evacuated from the dominant Shiite area and vice versa. The same happened to Christian families especially those living in Baghdad. All these campaigns were carried on a sectarian and ethnic basis. Even the Kurdish parties did the same with Arab families living in the areas under their control, without any response from government institutions.

The sectarian and ethnic scheme adopted by the occupying administration succeeded in sowing discord among the Iraqis. The parties and people accompanying the occupation adhered to this scheme simply because they knew that they had neither any real support inside Iraq nor qualification and that it was only through relying on religion, sectarianism and factionalism could they remain in power. Thus, the newcomers concentrated on performing sectarian rites in the Shiite and Sunni areas, and at fanatic national events in Iraqi Kurdistan. The portraits of religious leaders, even Iranians, were extensively used during elections and religious events. The Shiite, Sunni Kurdish representatives were keen only on getting the ministries and positions that would bring to them billions of dollars. When the people finally became aware of this fact it was too late, as the corrupt politicians and parties had managed to accumulate huge wealth which they can use to buy support.

Since 2003, the successive Iraqi governments of Allawi, Jaafari, Maliki, Ibadi and Abdul Mahdi did not consider the protests as demands to correct wrong policies; rather they looked at them as attempts to bring down the government with all its privileges. Here again, sectarian rhetoric was used. Maliki, for example, considered the opposition to his rule and corruption as 'a Sunni revolt' against 'the Shiite's rule', or a war similar to the one took place more than 1400 years, between the army of Yazid against the army of Imam Husain (Grandson of Prophet Mohammad) which he claimed to represent.[38] From his point of view, he had the right to fight any opposition, especially if it came from the Sunni component.

It was not strange, then, that he ordered his forces to use excessive means to subdue the population of Mosul, Tikrit and Anbar when they were merely using peaceful means to protest. Indicatively, he was reported to have said to the then president of the republic, Jalal Talabani: 'Why don't you [the Kurds] take Mosul and rid us of its annoyance?'.[39]

Yet, Abdul Mahdi and his allies from the pro-Iran militias of the PMF regarded the protests against the inefficient administration, lack of services and widespread corruption, as a foreign-backed conspiracy to topple the regime. This 'plot' in their opinion justified the use of excessive force and random killing against the protesters in Baghdad and other southern cities.

As a response to the policies of alienation and marginalization, the Sunni groups and tribes felt that the Shiite-dominated coalitions were ingrates who ignored their victory in defeating al-Qaeda in 2006–2007. Their reaction, in turn, was also sectarian. They thought that the only way to end the Iranian supported Shiite domination and Maliki's government was by cooperating with regional Sunni governments and organizations. Even the supposedly secularist Baath leadership did not object to this way of thinking, and went as far as cooperating with the fanatic and terrorist Daesh fighters. They only realized their mistake after that organization physically annihilated their comrades and a large numbers of Sunni inhabitants in the areas they occupied.

Despite all these tragedies and divisions, the coalitions taking part in the political process showed no sign of remorse or attempt to rebuild the national unity of the country. On the contrary, even the tragedy of Mosul was exploited to increase sectarian and ethnic divisions. Immediately after the fall of Mosul and Tikrit, the Iraqi government, in response to a call from al-Najaf Marja'iya, formed the PMF, armed civilian militias. This force contained only Shiites and was also fully backed and dominated by Iran. Although, this force managed to stop the advance of Daesh forces towards Baghdad, and helped in liberating areas in Diyala and Tikrit, its brutal sectarian behaviour towards the Sunni inhabitants of these areas created further divisions. Instead of calling for the establishment of a real national army, the representatives of the Sunni population retorted by demanding the establishment of their own armed militia forces. Taking advantage of this situation the KRG practically annexed areas in their region, and escalated the disputes with the central government over financial issues. The lines of division were becoming more deep and entrenched.

In the midst of this depressing scene, a glimmer of hope appeared in October 2019 in the form of huge popular demonstrations in most cities, including Baghdad, against the continued corruption (there were similar demonstrations and protests in October 2015, especially in Basra). What characterized these demonstrations were as follows:

- They erupted in the southern Shiite-dominated provinces, the provinces from where the government parties claimed their legitimacy based on votes.
- For the first time since 2003 the demonstrations got the full support of al-Najaf Marja'iya. This support could only be regarded as a belated expression of the guilty conscious felt by the Marja'iya for either supporting or keeping silent about the corrupt governments in Baghdad.[40]
- The demonstrators maintained their peaceful character and orderliness and continued despite the brutal repression used by the authorities in some provinces.[41]

Similar demonstrations were also staged in Iraqi Kurdistan, and similar brutal means were used against them. Unfortunately, no similar demonstration was held in the Sunni-dominated areas. It may be that the latter did not dare to take such steps for fear of the extensive existence of the PMF in their areas. As it was said above, the repressive measures taken against these demonstrations (in 2015 and since October 2019), which were increased under Abdul Mahdi rule, claimed the lives of more than 1000 people.

The Future of the Integrated and Democratic Project in Iraq

It could be fairly stated that the unifying, national and democratic project in Iraq received a major blow as a result of the occupation and the deplorable sectarian and quota system that ensued. The foreign intervention, the policies of those who came with the occupation, and the sheer scale of corruption also played a major role.

As a result of 35 years of Baath Party domination, which included eight years of war with Iran and the 12 years of inhumane sanctions following the invasion of Kuwait, people had become indifferent to what was happening. Not only indifference and despair were clear in the attitude of the people but also a fair number believed that the American occupation would not only rid them of Baath rule but would also establish democracy and prosperity. Regrettably, some of the educated elite were also thinking the same thing.[42] The other regrettable phenomenon was that large segments of the Iraqi society accepted the sectarian, ethnic and factional policies and practised them. The secularist attitudes that had always characterized the society, especially in big cities, have now disappeared in the face of the invading militant religious, sectarian and narrow ethnical ideas. This may be explained by the fact that society had been influenced by the 'religious campaign' initiated by the late president in the 1990s,[43] and the impact the dire days endured by Iraqis prior to the occupation had on the people. Normally, the Iraqis loathed speaking about sectarian affiliations and their negative aspects. The Iraqi residential neighbourhoods were all mixed, and intermarriages, between different religions, was common. To ask about the sect, religion or ethnic background of any citizen was an insult not only to the person asked but also to the one who posed such a question. This situation was turned upside down after 2003; professing sectarian, religious and ethnic affiliations became more than a daily practice. What was striking was that those who spread and circulated these tendencies were people who had lived for more than 25 years in secular and democratic Western countries. Even more striking was that secular parties like the Iraqi Communist Party and the National Democratic Party accepted these tendencies and worked within them.

The other problem was the absence or weakness of any general national organization. The policies of the Baath Party, which was built on no tolerance for any difference of opinion, kept Iraq void of any national movement that could effectively oppose the occupation. What was available were only some nationalist figures that tried to establish national fronts, but lacked the means to be effective, as compared with the means made available by Iran, the United Statesand the Gulf countries to their sectarian adversaries. The best example here could be the National Iraqi Foundation Congress (NIFC), established in May 2004 in Baghdad. It included Arab nationalists, a representative of the Sadirists, Islamic figures, independents, former communists and Baathists, national democrats, Arabs, Kurds, Turkomans, Christians, and Sabians. Despite its popularity, it failed to maintain its activities, especially after it refused to approve the constitution or take part in the ensuing elections. It even failed to maintain the publication of its newspaper and future activities due to the difficulties put in its way by the American administration and the sectarian parties.[44] In the end, it was frozen and its leaders remained national names who refused to cooperate with the occupation and without any effective role on ground.

As for democracy, it could be fairly said that the occupation managed to implement a crippled version of it. Corruption and the stealing of public funds were the main features of the new system established after 2003. A previous vice premier, Baha al-Araji, admitted that between 2003 and 2014 around US$1 trillion was squandered on fake projects and grossly inflated arms contracts.[45] As the bulk of these figures went into the pockets of politicians and the budgets of the ruling political parties and coalitions, it is difficult to see how any elections could be fair and democratic, since any upcoming elections would bring back the same grim and corrupt faces.

The arrival of Haidar al-Ibadi to power as prime minister, following the elections of 2014, was an indication of an Iraqi and American desire to remove Maliki who had ruled unsuccessfully for two terms since 2006. Despite the unprecedented internal, regional and international support Ibadi received,[46] he failed, during his four-year term to take daring measures to combat corruption. It is true that his discourse was different from Maliki's, but he remained inactive because he continued to feel indebted to the same al-Dawa party as his predecessor, and to the same Shiite coalition, that had chosen him for the premiership. Both sides, (Dawa Party and the Shiite coalitions) feared any real reforms as they will surely affect a significant number of their members. Also, Ibadi has been part of all the governments that have ruled Iraq since 2003 and has never been known for opposing any of the measures (policies) taken previously. His other problem was that he continued to think that national reconciliation can be achieved through organizing all-national conferences or declarations. He has not integrated the idea that reconciliation can easily be achieved through real, speedy, effective and daring reform measures that would end sectarian policies, marginalization and corruption.

Abdul Mahdi was no different from his predecessors. During his short term in offices he failed to do anything positive. On top of that, he was the first premier since the occupation who ordered the killing of peaceful demonstrators, being in Baghdad or in the other southern provinces, including the ones that took place in the province he belonged to, Nasiriya. While one cannot judge the present prime minister, Kadhimi, because of his short term in office, but his promise to hold those responsible for the use of excessive measures against the demonstrators has not materialized.

The question today is whether there is a way to make amends for all these mistakes and to heal the terrible divisions afflicting present-day Iraqi society. The answer may lie in the anti-corruption demonstrations overwhelming Baghdad and the other southern cities (October 2015 and resumed with more impetus in October 2019). These demonstrations started as a protest against corruption; but soon the demonstrators increased their demands to include more general ones which include rejection of the sectarian policies and quota system, defending the rights of the displaced to return to their home towns, and releasing the unjustly detained. More importantly, is that the society is now showing itself to be transcending parochial sectarian thinking. It is true that these demonstrations have not yet achieved anything constructive, but some observers believe that if this movement continues it will surely enforce changes in the politics of the country. It was hoped that the then Prime Minister Ibadi would take strength from them and make daring and quick reforms. But, unfortunately, all his promises have proved to be void. Some say that as a weak person he did not have the courage to face his Shiite coalition. Others believe that there are suspicions of corruption hovering over him. In the end, his hesitation, (and later on his declaration that he will comply with the sanctions imposed on Iran), allowed his opponents and rivals to rally against him. This was clear in the decision of the parliament on 2 November 2015 that obliged Ibadi to seek the approval of parliament for any reform measure he wished to undertake, and in foiling his attempt to win another term.

Another serious wave of demonstrations erupted in Baghdad, Basra, Nasiriya, Diwaniya, Karbala and Najaf, in October 2019 (under Abdul Mahdi's rule), again in protest against the high level of corruption and the total lack of services, especially electricity and water supplies. These demonstrations and protests are still on (June 2021), under Kadimi's rule. It could be fairly said, that all prime ministers since 2005 have failed to deal with these protests or take any measure to combat corruption, ameliorate services or end the spread of uncontrolled militias, to calm or satisfy the demands of the protesters. In fact, the events in the cities where the demonstrations were taking place, especially Baghdad, Basra and Nasiriya, took a sharp turn of events when certain armed militias waged a campaign to abduct and terrorize the leading members of these demonstrations. Young men and women were abducted or assassinated in cold blood, while the government failed to arrest any of those responsible for these assassinations.

Successive prime ministers since 2004 are not the only people to be accused; parliament too should take a bigger share of the blame. Since it was established in 2006, parliament has proven to be a paradigm of corruption, inefficiency, and dedication to sectarian and factional affiliations. Moreover, a fair number of its members gained their seats either through rigged elections or the quota system.[47] The constitution bestowed all the powers on parliament to observe and hold corrupt officials accountable. But its conduct, throughout all these years, has shown that it never held anyone accountable and never sent any corrupt or failing official to court. On the contrary, its conduct has shown that it contained a large number of corrupt deputies who had stolen public funds, as well as covering up for the ones who were accused of it. Finally, all the probes it made were based on favouritism and conducted on a sectarian and ethnic basis.

IN SEARCH FOR SOLUTION

In searching for a solution to the multiple crises, two viewpoints transpire. The first takes the position that the problem has become so complicated that any talk of solving it internally has been rendered almost impossible. Those who took this position based their beliefs on two arguments, they include:

- The divisions between all the components of the Iraqi society and their vested interests.
- The degree of foreign interference and influence.

The second viewpoint stresses that a solution can come from Iraq and by the Iraqis, without any external or foreign intervention. It is likely that the first party that thought of solving the Iraqi problem through external involvement was the United States and Britain. Some believed that the two countries, when planning to invade Iraq, had carried out their plan efficiently, but that they did not have a clear idea about what to do next. Others believed that what happened in Iraq had taken place according to a well-thought out US plan. What the US administration was not expecting was the intense resistance the invading forces faced. The significant thing is that after finding themselves bogged down in the Iraqi quagmire and when all the information the US administration had about the invading forces being met by Iraqis holding flowers proved wrong,[48] they had to begin to think of finding a face-saving way out. After claiming Iraq as an occupied country in 2003, the United States suddenly declared in 2004 that it would hand over sovereignty of the country to the Iraqis through the UN. Then UN Secretary-General Kofi Anan responded positively and dispatched the veteran Algerian diplomat, Lakhdar Brahimi, to find a way out of the impasse. After the many meetings Brahimi had with different prominent Iraqi politicians and personalities, he reached the following conclusions:

- That the then GC appointed by Bremer had no popularity whatsoever, and adamantly refused to form a transitional government, as the council was demanding.
- That Iraqi public opinion held similar views about most of the personalities, parties and organizations that came with the occupation.
- That Iraq needed a government of efficient technocrats that should not include any member of the GC or representatives of the parties that came with the occupation.
- That the members of the transitional government should not be allowed to nominate themselves in the forthcoming elections after their service.
- That the political parties should take advantage of the transitional period to prepare their programmes for the next elections.
- He thought that the Iraqis had the merit and ability to govern themselves.
- It was not surprising that the parties cooperating with the occupation and the GC strongly attacked Brahimi's ideas in order to foil his mission. He was accused by them as being a stooge of Saddam Hussein and of being hostile to the Shiites.[49]

In the end, after claiming that they accepted his suggestions, it was the United States that frustrated Brahimi's mission. When the time came to nominate the transitional prime minister, the United States had a hand in the nomination of Ayad Allawi as prime minister, as well as with nominations for other important ministries. With a few exceptions, only Brahimi's nominations for ineffective ministries were accepted. In the end, nothing was achieved from Brahimi's scheme. Regrettably, Brahimi not only remained silent about American interventions and selections but also gave them his blessing in the report he submitted to UN in June 2004.[50] It should be noted that the views presented by Brahimi were relayed to him by the nationalist Iraqis he met in Baghdad and abroad, but he failed to uphold them. This prompted some Iraqi nationalist personalities to submit these ideas again and in detail.[51] Dr. Khair el-Din Haseeb was the first to put forward a plan of 21 points to end the occupation in 2005.[52] His initiative came after the failure to convene the different national Iraqi movements and personalities in conciliatory meetings. The main points of Haseeb's plan were as follows:

- The unequivocal and speedy withdrawal of the US forces and according to a short specific period of time.
- The declaration of a ceasefire by the Iraqi resistance.
- An agreement should be reached under the auspices of, and with guarantees from, the UN Security Council, and in consultation with the Iraqi resistance and other national forces that have not collaborated with the occupation, in selecting a prime minister for Iraq for a transitional period of no more than two years. The chosen prime minister should have the authority to select a cabinet from neutral candidates and technocrats, in a non-binding consultation with the UN representative in Iraq. The transitional prime minister and the ministers will refrain from nominating themselves in any elections hereafter. The cabinet will be endowed, during the transitional period, with all the legislative, executive and financial powers necessary to carry out their duties.
- The UN Security Council should be committed to preserving Iraq's independence, sovereignty and territorial integrity. The initiative should also cover reconstruction of the national army on a professional and patriotic basis, the transitional government's right to invite a limited number of Arab forces from the countries that had not encouraged or participated in the occupation of Iraq, to perform peacekeeping missions in Iraq; abrogating the constitution adopted by a rigged referendum and preparing, within one year, a law on

elections and a law on political parties. The transitional government should hold general elections within the second year of the transitional period, to elect two houses of parliament, one for the deputies and the other for senates, taking its guidelines from the provisional constitution drafted by the Beirut Symposium of July 2005, and in consultation with a large number of Iraqis inside and outside the country. The initiative also held the United States and Britain responsible for what happened to Iraq and obliged them to pay compensation in the form of grants for the damage they inflicted on Iraq and its population.

To reiterate these views a detailed programme, under the auspices of the Centre for Arab Unity Studies, was drawn up by Iraqi specialists—each one in his own field of expertise including economics, oil, constitutional law, elections, reconstruction of the army and national unity. Apart from the then obvious hostile reaction of the United States and other collaborating Iraqis to the plan, there were two reasons why this initiative did not get the attention it deserved. Primarily, it came very early, and at a time when there was a regional and international assumption that the United States would succeed in finding a suitable solution for Iraq.[53] The leaders of the resistance, for their part, felt that their successes on the ground would achieve better results.

Those who upheld the latter view, believing that the solution should come from inside and by the Iraqis themselves, did not deny a role for the UN. In this regard, one could mention two initiatives. The first, called 'The Project for a Comprehensive Iraq', was presented by the Association of Muslim Scholars in Iraq (AMSI), headed by Dr. Muthana al-Dhari, as 'The Suitable Solution to Rescue Iraq and the Region'. This initiative was put forward in Amman on 15 August 2015.[54] It was followed by a second one put forward by the Baath Party at a meeting in Doha in September 2015. This meeting, convened under the auspices of the UN Secretary General and the government of Qatar, with binding guarantees from Arab and international sides, claimed to have included all the Iraqi groups.[55] While the AMSI claimed that it had gotten the approval of the Baath leadership for their initiative, Baathist representatives did not attend the Amman meeting and denied their approval of it. In turn, the AMSI leaders did not attend the Doha gathering, of which they disapproved. In analyzing the two initiatives, it can be concluded that although the one proposed by AMSI did transcend sectarian rhetoric, and it was criticized on two accounts: Firstly, the initiative came from an all-Sunni religious body when most Iraqis, and after 13 years of religious rule, were not enthusiastic about such an example. The Iraqis were not prepared to see a major or central role for any religious body in ruling Iraq. The majority of the Iraqis wanted to see an initiative coming from a national, patriotic and secular coalition. The second aspect criticized was that the initiative only concentrated on the harmful Iranian interference in Iraqi affairs and never mentioned other harmful regional interference, which also nourished and encouraged sectarian division.[56] Finally, AMSI was called upon to revive the NIFC, which was more collective, and of which it was a part and to present its initiative under the name of the NIFC. However, in fairness, this initiative stressed its adherence to diversity and pluralism, it rejected political revenge, and it stressed that the tragedy of Iraq was the tragedy of a country and its people. It also said that it was inspired by the right to resistance, and to holding the demonstrations, popular uprisings and sit-ins that are taking place in Iraq. It also called for a consultative meeting for all the Iraqi groups opposing the present political project to participate in. Finally, it called on the international community to seize this opportunity to find comprehensive and realistic solutions to end the treacherous crises of Iraq,[57] but, once again, this initiative did not succeed in getting the needed support.

The initiative of the Baath Party, in fact, depended on the desire of the Qatari government to convene an all-Sunni conference. Unfortunately, the party complied with this call only to have an erroneous start right from the onset. Instead of calling for an all-Iraqi meeting, the Baath representative declared that the party was taking part in the Sunni Components Conference. This was confirmed by two other groups that belonged to the party, the Islamic Army and the Military Council when both declared that they would not take part in the conference because, according to their words, it 'disperses Sunni unity'. This discourse should have been rejected by a party that regarded itself as secular. It is true that the policies of the successive Iraqi governments were sectarian par excellence, but this should not be confronted in a similar manner and language.

Although, the party representatives declared that they had adopted large parts of the AMSI initiative, and that the AMSI agreed with it, AMSI rejected these claims and refused to attend the conference.[58] A close look at the Baath initiative revealed great similarity with that of Haseeb and the plan drawn by the Iraqi experts in 2005.

Nonetheless, what happened in Doha was puzzling. It seems that the efforts of the Doha conference to convene the Iraqi Sunni components resulted in two separate meetings being held. Thus, Doha's alleged intention to convene leaders of the Baath Party and some members of the present Iraqi government and parliamentarians, as well as all Sunnis, did not materialize. In the end, two separate meetings, both under the auspices of the Qatari foreign ministry, were held. The head of the Iraqi parliament who went to Doha did not attend any of the meetings due to criticism from Baghdad. The Baathists also refused to attend the meeting at which some Sunni Iraqi parliamentarians were present. The Qatari foreign minister continually mediated between the two conferences without any success at convening them in one meeting. However, the only positive aspect that came out of the meeting was that it managed to bring Baath Party representatives to meet with the ambassadors of the Gulf States (Saudi Arabia, Kuwait and the United Arab Emirates (UAE)), as well as the UN representative for Iraq and his deputy, which some scholars saw as amounting to a tacit United States approval.[59] This was the first time that these countries accepted the idea of sitting together with representatives of the Baath Party. An ultimate evaluation of the Qatari-supported initiative would show that, apart from the fact that it had come from an external element, it still only concentrated on one component of the Iraqi society; the Sunnis.

As far as the Iraqi government was concerned, the then Prime Minister Ibadi deplored the convening of the conference and described it as 'a breach of Iraqi sovereignty',[60] although, Qatar claimed that it had the approval of the Iraqi government. He also prevented parliamentarians and other members of his government from travelling to Qatar. Supporters of former Prime Minister Maliki gathered more than 100 signatures demanding the removal of the head (Speaker) of parliament, accusing him of attending the 'divisive Doha meeting'. Ironically, to avoid that prospect, the head of parliament returned to Baghdad via Tehran!

All these events confirmed the deep divisions within Iraqi society and strengthen the view that under Iraq's current circumstances, where one-third of the country is embroiled in continuous demonstrations and protests, and enduring daily explosions, killings, corruption, lack of services and a huge drop in oil prices, the Iraqi people will not be able to solve their problems alone.

In the final analysis, and from the personal point of view of the author, the main reason for the failure of these initiatives coming from parties with undoubted national loyalty was the desire of each of them to be the only party playing the leading role. Haseeb's initiative, for example, was disregarded mainly because the Baath Party felt that Haseeb was trying to benefit from popular support their party enjoyed inside Iraq, while in fact their party disintegrated and collapsed after the invasion in 2003. Others rejected it for pure sectarian reasons. The initiative of AMSI was aborted by other groups from the same Sunni component, believing that they did not have enough weight within it. They also claimed that AMSI, following the death of its leader, Sheikh Harith al-Dhari, had lost most of its credibility. In lieu of agreeing on a united course, as they were all aiming for the same objective and shared the same views about the problems facing Iraq, they differed and resorted to a sectarian discourse. Instead of gathering forces they sought the assistance of foreign countries and parties that encouraged sectarian tendencies. The other major deficiency in all these initiatives was that they did not take into consideration the developments that had taken place in Iraq since 2003; developments that included the occupation of Mosul and Anbar, the formation of the PMF, the dispersal of the army, the huge foreign influence in Iraq today, the refusal of the ruling parties, especially the Kurdish ones, to amend the much criticized constitution and finally the very much expanded federal system. All these changes, or realities, in addition to others, had created a new atmosphere that had been overlooked by the different initiatives. Also, all the parties that presented these initiatives did not have the internal support that could face the overwhelming Iranian influence, the strong United States presence and the role of the PMF. All these elements can be expected to fight against any attempt to curtail or put an end to their influence.

Under such complicated circumstances, some scholars have evoked two other ways to bring about a complete major change: military coups or sweeping popular revolutions. Both possibilities are hard to envisage due to the way in which the new army has been established and the lack of any popular movement that could lead a widely supported revolution. Even if one of the army commanders risked a coup d'état, he would still have to face two obstacles:

- The reactions of the many militias, especially the PMF, that have grown stronger than the army itself.

- The American, or regional powers (Israel and Gulf countries), reaction which would accuse such a move as being an illegal act against a democratically elected government,[61] while in reality they are against allowing Iraq to return as a major regional power.

Some scholars, however, still believe that democratic measures can still improve matters. But rarely have democratic methods succeeded in making improvements. Democratic procedures can succeed if the institutions of the state actually exist and could then be reformed. In such a case a powerful and genuine reformist might succeed, otherwise the anti-reform elements would be stronger and would defeat any reformer's attempts at implementing change. This is the case for Iraq.

Some sources recently spoke of a solution to the Iraqi impasse through another direct United States intervention, which could come about not from any love for the Iraqis but because of the possible five-sided alliance which included Russia, China, Iran, Syria and Iraq, of which the United States never approved.[62] Indications of this was shown in different ways. It took the forms of leaks by the American media that spoke of the United States' intention to replace Ibadi with another American citizen of Iraqi origin.[63] More significantly, was the United States insistence on removing Ibadi's successor, Prime Minister Adil Abdul Mahdi, (October 2018–May 2020), from office because of his subordination to Iran, the uncontrolled influence of PMF, and his attempt to sign a strategic agreement with China. He was replaced, upon United States pressure, by Mustafa al-Kadhimi, as Prime Minister (May 2020). Kadhimi is another holder of British nationality and known for his alignment with US policies. But how prepared will the US administration be in defending him, or how able would the newcomer be to enact major changes, which would certainly anger Iran and its many loyal powerful militias? This remains to be seen. More important, is the fact that if Kadhimi wanted to curtail the Iranian influence, he needs some real support, or able forces on the ground to support him and his decisions. How ready would the United States be to offer such a support, is something that remains questionable?

With the absence of a robust civil society organizations, popular movements or political parties capable of bringing about real change, the hope for political reforms remains suspended and weak, if not non-existent, for the near future. The regular general elections that took place after 2003 managed only to recycle the same corrupt, inefficient and undeserving people, something that added to the depressing mood engulfing the majority of Iraqis. Perhaps this is a pessimistic view, but it remains a realistic and not an imaginary one; yet above all, it represents the feelings of the majority of the Iraqi people.

To sum up, it should be stated that any solution to the Iraqi problem would have to be closely connected to solving the problems in the region, especially in Syria and the US–Iranian dispute. In other words, the outcome of these crises will have a direct effect on Iraq. To be more explicit, if the schemes or plans to divide and destabilize the countries of the region failed, then there would be great hope that Iraq will escape division and disintegration. On the other hand, if the US–Iranian dispute escalates or reaches military confrontation, then Iraq will become the battle ground and will certainly plunge into more chaotic situation.

Finally, one could say that the conditions in Iraq now are similar to that of some countries established following the period of direct colonization, countries that were ravaged by corruption and disregard for people's feelings, interests and rights. In these countries at that time, popular and nationalist movements were inspired to take control through revolutions. When such movements were non-existent, the national armies took the initiative to bring about such a change. Will history repeat itself in Iraq? And if such an event was to take place, will the change be a reformist patriotic one or would it once again turn the country into a corrupt military dictatorship and lead to the eventual repeat of the vicious circle of bloody military coups? Or could such a change lead to proper elections and democracy? In some Latin American, African, Asian and even European countries (Greece and Portugal), such a change and result have been achieved. There are, however, those who argued that the way the new Iraqi army was built does not qualify it to play such a role. Moreover, Iran, the Gulf States, Israel and the US will strongly oppose such a move simply because they all want to see Iraq remain weak and divided (although, it was rumoured recently that the United States is toying with such an idea as a way to curb Iranian influence). But by using the same example as the colonial periods, when the odds were identical, and similar initiatives fraught with difficulties, some third world armies, including Arab ones, led by young nationalist officers and supported by the masses, managed to make such a daring move and succeeded.

NOTES

1. The pilot was first lieutenant Hamid al-Dhahi. Later in the year another pilot, Munir Rofa, (Radfa in Israeli literature) smuggled an Iraqi Soviet made fighter Mig 21 to Israel.

2. Correspondence with the former head of the Iraqi counter-intelligence service (1981–1986), Colonel K. Shakir, August 2020. The same source mentioned that the meeting was attended by the deputy chief of the French Intelligence service, Picott, who was asked to use France influence among the African communities in the United States. Yitzhak Rabin, the Israel Prime Minister was also in Aqaba, but the Iraqi team refused to meet with him.

3. Ibid.

4. Ibid.

5. Ibid.

6. Ibid.

7. Ibid.

8. For details about this affair/deal, see: Lisa Klobuchar, *The Iran–Contra Affairs: Political Scandal Uncovered*, White Thomson Publishing Ltd, 2008.

9. Correspondence with K. Shakir, the former Iraqi counter-intelligence department.

10. The plan also spoke about dividing other countries such as Syria and Lebanon. Yinon wrote that Iraq's dissolution was even more important for Israel than that of Syria, and that Iraq was stronger than Syria. He wrote that in the short run it was Iraqi power that constituted the greatest threat to Israel. See http://cosmos.ucc.ie/cs1064/jabowen/IPSC/articles/article0005345.html/.

11. Ibid. Other Iraqi Arab politicians also established good relations with Israel before and after the invasion. See the reports in BBC News (20 September 2006) and albaghdadia (October 2015).

12. For full minutes of that meeting see: http://www.moqatel.com/openshare/Behoth/IraqKwit/8/doc11.doc_cvt.htm.

13. Fukiyama, Francis. 2006. 'Where do the Neo-conservatives Come From?' (Arabic). http://www.minculture.gov.ma/index.php?option=com_content&id=416:fukuyama-traduction-anouar-elmourtaji&Itemid=157.

14. Ritter, Scott, *Endgame: Solving the Iraq Crisis*, New York: Simon & Schuster, 2004. Blix, Hans, *Disarming Iraq*, London: Bloomsbury, 2004. 'Blair's Blind Faith in Intelligence'. 2010. *The Guardian*, January 28. http://www.theguardian.com/commentisfree/2010/jan/28/hans-blix-tony-blair-iraq. 'UN Weapons Inspectors Knew That Iraq No Longer Possessed WMD'. 2003. Information Clearing House, October 1. http://www.informationclearinghouse.info/article4869.htm.

15. Senate, 'Report of the Selected Committee on Intelligence on Post-war Findings about Iraq's WMD'. 109th Congress, 2nd session. September 2006. https://fas.org/irp/congress/2006_rpt/srptl09-331.pdf.

16. al-Assaf, Sawsan I., and Saad N. Jawad,*Iraqi Women Between the Democracy of the American Occupation and the Principle of Humanitarian Intervention (Arabic)*. Amman: Dar al-Jinan, 2013.

17. Zbigniew, Brzezinski, *Second Chance: Three Presidents and the Crisis of American Superpower*, New York: Basic Books, 2007, p. 137.

18. This neighbour fled Iraq in the 1990s, and settled in the United States with CIA help. He returned with the United States invading forces and settled in his father's house which was adjacent to mine in Baghdad.

19. In his initial reply he tried to put all the blame on the first (US civil administrator in charge of Baghdad) Ambassdor Barbara Bodine. Later on Bodine defended herself in an extended interview, and put the blame on the US administration which she said refused to put enough forces on the ground to ensure stability and normal life in Baghdad and other cities. https://m.youtube.com/watch?v=B5WGXi2w5R0.

20. Jawad, Saad N., and Sawsan I. Al-Assaf, 'The Higher Education System In Iraq and Its Future'. *International Journal of Contemporary Iraqi Studies* 8 (1), 2014, pp. 55–72.

21. Bremer, Paul, *My Year In Iraq: The Struggle to Build a Future of Hope*, New York: Threshold, 2006.

22. This is what was mentioned in the Iraqi constitution of 2005, which did not mention that Iraq was an Arab state and a member of the Arab League.

23. Shaban, Abdul Husain, 'Paul Bremer in the Scale'. http://www.ahewar.org/eng/show.art.asp?aid=1363 (Arabic) al-Hiwar al-Mutamadin, Bremer fi al-mizan. 2011, http://www.ahewar.org/debat/show.art.asp?aid=76ar721. See also Saad N. Jawad, Rai al-Youm, London, 09/08/2020. https://www.raialyoum.com/index.php/هل-حقا-ان-العراق-دولة-مصطنعة؟-او-انه-كيا/

24. For fuller details, see http://www.middle-east-online.com/?id=189193./.

25. Bremer, op.cit., p. 36.

26. So, Mr Bremer, Where Did All the Money Go?' *The Guardian*, 7 July 2005. http://www.theguardian.com/world/2005/jul/07/iraq.features11.

27. This was Ayham al-Samarrai' the first minister of electricity after the occupation. He was in detention and under interrogation for his corruption.

28. Both Jalabi and Shawkat are members of the same party.

29. Abdelhadi, Magdi, 'Israelis 'Train Kurdish forces'. BBC News, 20 September 2006. http://news.bbc.co.uk/1/hi/world/middle_east/5364982.stm.

30. 'Iraq War in Figures', BBC News, 14 December 2011. http://www.bbc.co.uk/news/world-middleeast-11107739.
31. Feldman, Noah, *What We Owe Iraq*, Princeton, NJ: Princeton University Press, 2004.
32. Zangana, Haifa, *The City of Widows*, Beirut: (CAUS), 2008.
33. The funny thing is until his nomination al-Maliki was using an alias name (Jawad al-Maliki), although he was a government official since his return to Iraq following the occupation.
34. See Chapter 4.
35. https://www.alsharqiya.com/ar/news/parliamentary-calls-to-investigate-what-the-abdul-mahdi-government-spent.   https://www.google.co.uk/amp/s/www.al-monitor.com/pulse/ar/originals/2020/01/iraq-economy-us-sanctions-abdulmahdi.amp.html%3fskipWem=1.
36. Saad N. Jawad, 'Agreement to Withdraw or Permission to Remain?' Bitterlemons International, 18 December 2008. http://www.bitterlemons.org/international/previous.php?=1&id=254#1039.
37. The term used now in Iraq to refer to these recruits or soldiers are 'ghost soldiers'.
38. This comparison was also aimed at reviving sectarian divisions based on incidents that happened more than a millennium before, and were the main reasons for dividing the Muslim world.
39. *al-Mada* newspaper, 14 December 2014. Baghdad.
40. Most of the Shiite politicians claimed that they had the full backing of the Marja'iya.
41. Some Shiite politicians accused the demonstrations of having been instigated by foreign powers and some even attacked the Marja'iya for the moral support it extended to the demonstrators.
42. More regrettable is that some similar Arab elites are still thinking this way after the Iraqi disaster.
43. Fawaz A. Gerges, *A History of ISIS*, New Jersey: Princeton University Press, 2016. pp. 61–62.
44. The NIFC was presided over by the late General Subhi abdul Hamid, with Sheikh Jawad al-Khalisi as its secretary-general, Dr. Wamidh Nadhmi as his deputy, Salman Abdullah as treasurer and the author as its spokesman. It also included the AMSI, the Sadirists, a splinter group of the Baath party and many independent personalities. Ironically, some members of it were treated in the same manner under the old regime because of their persistent calls for democratic change.
45. Araji said that this amount consisted of US$800 billion in oil revenues and US$200 billion in foreign assistance. Other sources put the figures between US$700 billion and US$350 billion. Reports in Arabic are available on the Albayan and Aljazeera websites. He was accused by his own leader, Muqtada al-Sadir, of huge corruption, and was detained in Sadir's

headquarters in Najaf for a while. It was rumoured then that he was freed after paying a huge amount of money.

46. As opposed to his predecessor, Ibadi was strongly supported by a large number of Iraqis, al-Marja'iya, Turkey, the Gulf States, the United States and European countries.

47. A number of deputies gained only tens of votes but were nominated to the parliament by their winning lists.

48. For this Senate report, see http://fas.org/irp/congress/2006_rpt/srptl0 9330.pdf/.

49. For this report in Arabic, see http://www.al-jazirah.com/magazine/080 62004/almlfsais4.htm.

50. For this account, see http://iipdigital.usembassy.gov/st/arabic/texttr ans/2004/06/20040608152432aywalhsib-le0.2970392.html#axzz3n uXmZH8B/.

51. Khair El-Din Haseeb, (ed.), *Planning Iraq's Future*, Beirut: (CAUS), 2006.

52. Ibid.

53. This view was expressed by one of the staunch supporters of the occupation when he said that it was a well-known fact that the United States makes mistakes at the beginning but after a short while it resorts to using its brains, reviews its policies and finds the best solutions in the end.

54. Full details are available in Arabic from the Aljazeera website.

55. This was reported by Al-Hayat newspaper, London, on 6 September 2015.

56. The reason for this was because Qatar was also supporting the initiative.

57. *Al-Hayat* newspaper, London, 6 September 2015.

58. It later appeared that a breakaway faction from the association attended the conference.

59. Lund, Aron, 'The Doha Congress: Negotiating a Return of Iraqi Baath Party? – Analysis'. *Euroasia Review and Analysis,* 2015. http://www.eurasiareview.com/06092015-the-doha-congressnego tiating-a-return-of-iraqi-baath-party-analysis/.

60. Ibid.

61. Note that the United States experiment in South Korea was quite the opposite as it allowed military coups, supported the efforts to building a strong industrial revolution and supporting genuine democracy, something it did not apply in the case of Iraq.

62. It was evident that Iraq's participation in this coalition was in accordance with an Iranian decision.

63. For detailed information on this in Arabic, see www.iraqkhair.com/.

CHAPTER 4

The Iraqi Constitution: A Solution or Continuous Predicament?

INTRODUCTION

The main aim of any constitution is to introduce a new social contract between the state and its citizens, to ensure the rights and liberties of the latter, and to make sure that the former will not encroach on them. Its other role is serving as the guarantor of the unity and sovereignty of the state. Consequently any constitution should arise from the needs and demands of the people and it should contain what they desire. The other axioms of drafting a constitution are that it should not be imposed by an external power, and it should be drafted, discussed and approved by the citizens involved.

Moreover, all international agreements, including The Hague and Geneva Conventions, do not give a foreign power the right to impose a constitution on an occupied country. By implication, the agents who cooperate with the occupier also do not hold the right to impose a constitution.[1] Despite this, the US occupying power in Iraq after 2003 annulled the existing Iraqi constitution, laws and regulations and issued its own code. Paul Bremer, the Civil Ruler of Iraq, issued 100 laws (obligatory orders) and introduced to the Iraqi Governing Council, which he had established himself in July 2003, the Transitional Administrative Law (TAL), which was approved as the new transitional constitution of the country. The TAL was written and imposed without the proper involvement of Iraqis.

© The Author(s), under exclusive license to Springer Nature
Switzerland AG 2021
S. N. Jawad, *Iraq after the Invasion*, Middle East Today,
https://doi.org/10.1007/978-3-030-72106-0_4

The US experiment in Iraq was not their first. It was preceded by other similar forays, notably in Germany and Japan following the Second World War.[2] In Germany and Japan, the US successfully changed the governments from dictatorships to democracies. Several elements of these two experiences stood out: the constitutions were drafted by indigenous people under the supervision of the US forces; the constitutional heritage, experience, and history of the two nations were not totally neglected; and the social fabrics of the two societies were not disregarded.[3]

In Iraq the practice was different. As Noah Feldman, who was instrumental in drafting the TAL (and later on the constitution) explained: the difference between the Iraqi case and that of Germany and Japan was that the US aimed to transform those two countries (Germany and Japan) into rich capitalist allies. The aim was not to build democratic states.[4] In Iraq, the US aimed to create not a nation state but a 'civic nation' with 'a viable identity of the centrifugal main elements of Arab Shiites, Arab Sunni and Kurdish religious and secular populations hitherto held together (supposedly only) by a succession of authoritarian states'.[5]

Thus, the US ignored the history of the Iraqi state and Iraqi identity, reducing the Iraqi state to a collection of Shiites, Sunnis, Kurds and other minorities. This idea or the vision of such a state was quickly adopted by the Iraqi parties and groups that accompanied the invasion and who would be made the new rulers of the country.[6] Therefore the new constitution emphasized the differences and divisive issues rather than focussing on the uniting elements of the Iraqi society. The drafters of the constitution overlooked the fact that 'the main purpose of constitution is to serve as a covenant that stitches diverse communities into something resembling a unified state. Such documents, when they are useful, serve as important symbols worthy of reverence by disparate groups'.[7] The United States constitution, for example, concentrated on unity and liberty despite the differences that existed between the different elements of US society.

The swift success of the invasion of Iraq gave the US a false sense of confidence that its control of the country would not be challenged. The equally swift and effective Iraqi resistance to the occupation was a surprise to US leaders. The resistance inflicted heavy casualties on the US forces—over 4500 soldiers were killed in Iraq between 2003 and 2012.[8] Deaths of contractors and soldiers from other coalition forces increased the number killed to over 6000.[9] These unexpected losses pushed US policymakers to adopt an early exit strategy. To justify this exit, the US planned a hasty timetable for Iraq to draft and approve a new permanent constitution, so it would be able to claim that democracy had been estab-lished in Iraq. Ignoring the failure of other rushed constitutions in Bosnia, Cambodia, East Timor, and Afghanistan,[10] the US hurried through the drafting of the Iraqi permanent constitution in only two months. This is the main reason for the constitution's many shortcomings and the numerous problems that have arisen afterwards.

This paper will examine how the new Iraqi constitution was drafted and approved. It will analyse the constitution's influence in solving, or adding to, Iraq's problems. It will explore whether the constitution is workable or in need of amendments, leading to the pressing concern of whether such amendments can solve the many problems created by the introduction of this document. Is there even a need for Iraqis to write a new Constitution to give them more time to think and discuss these issues between themselves? And ultimately, is such a bold step possible? This research will also explore and analyse the problems caused by the approval of this constitution.

HISTORICAL CONTEXT

Iraq has an ancient legal tradition. The Code of Hammurabi, completed in 1790 BC, is one of the oldest deciphered legal writings of significant length. From the ninth century, Iraq was governed by an Islamic code of law, which continued until it came under Ottoman occupation. In 1876 the Ottoman Empire introduced the first constitution for Iraq, dividing the country into the Wilayets (Vilayets) of Baghdad, Mosul and Basra. This constitution, which only lasted for two years, addressed relationship between the state and the citizen as well as the duties of the state towards different ethnic groups.

Following the occupation of Iraq by the British Army (1914–1918), the country was put under British mandate. As soon as the occupa-tion was completed, the three Iraqi Wilayets were subdivided into 14 provinces (now 18). The British High Commissioner became the only legislative and executive authority in Iraq. In 1921 a committee of British political officers was selected to draw up a new constitution for Iraq. The committee adopted (or consulted) constitutional models from New Zealand, Australia and elsewhere into a constitution for Iraq.[11] In 1923 they completed a draft which was given to an Iraqi committee to study. The Iraqi committee took almost two years to review the draft before approving it in 1925. This constitution, which was titled *al-Qanoon al-Asasi al-Iraqi* (The Iraqi Basic Law), contained 123 articles and continued to be effective until the Iraqi monarchy was overthrown in 1958. The constitution was amended twice, in 1925 and 1943.

The establishment of a republican regime in 1958 marked the end of a permanent constitution and the introduction of transitional (provisional) constitutions which lasted until the invasion of Iraq in 2003. The first provisional constitution was promulgated on 27 July 1958. It contained only 30 articles and the main innovations, apart from stressing the republican nature of the state, were the clauses that stated that Iraq was part of the Arab nation, Islam was the official religion of the state, and Arabs and Kurds were partners in the state.

In 1963 the first republican regime was toppled. The new regime introduced a new provisional constitution in 1964, which again was replaced in 1968 and 1970 by other provisional constitutions following coups. All three constitutions contained almost the same ideas and principles included in the first provisional constitution of 1958, but the 1964 and 1968 constitutions were prejudicial to the rights of the Kurds. In 1970, the Iraqi government signed a peace agreement with the Kurds, allowing them to enjoy autonomy, which necessitated an amendment to the constitution. In each of these constitutional iterations, or parallel to their proclamation, each republican regime stated its intention to draft a permanent constitution, and hold elections for a parliament and president of the republic, but none of these promises was kept.

In 1989, following the end of the Iraq-Iran war, the Baath government of Saddam Hussein declared its intention to draft a permanent constitution. A committee of Iraqi jurists, academics and specialists in constitutional law was formed for this purpose, headed by the Vicepresident, Izzat. Al-Douri. Deputy premier Tariq Aziz was assigned to supervise the work of the committee. The committee included eight members, two former ministers of justice, three university professors specialized in constitutional law, a deputy of the court of cassation, the head of the legal department in the foreign ministry and his deputy. But all hopes of having a representative constitution were dashed once the blueprint was published.[12] Many aspects of that proposed draft were positive, but to comply with the instructions of the Baath government the proposed constitution was designed to maintain the rule of the Baath Party and its ideology. The draft consisted of 179 articles. It was said that Tariq Aziz made some amendments that were not accepted by some members of the committee.[13] However, this constitution was never approved, or put to a public referendum due to the Kuwait crisis (August 1990) and the war that ensued in 1991. Thus the 1970 constitution remained in force until the regime was removed in 2003.

All the Iraqi provisional constitutions were generally secular and progressive, in the sense that they each contained basic political/human rights and liberties and avoided religious issues. Although all provisional constitutions mentioned Islam as the (official religion of the state) they also approved and esteemed the freedom of religion. In addition to granting Kurdish autonomy, the constitution of 1970 established Kurdish as an official language, together with Arabic, in the Kurdish areas, it spelled out the fundamental rights of citizens and provided for a general election for a national assembly. However, election did not take place until 1980, which was the first in the republican era. It was repeated again in 1984, 1988, and 1992. The principle of equality, the right to free education and a fair trial and freedom were all clearly stated in the 1970 constitution.[14]

But in general, Iraqis felt indifferent. They knew very well that constitutions were mere pieces of paper that ultimately had little power to bind their leaders. Despite the fact that people's basic rights were in general not respected, the government was free to cancel or amend the constitution whenever it wanted, while the people did not have any say in the process. Apart from the short period during the first republican regime (between 1961 and 1963), and under the Baath party rule (1968–2003) where there were other political parties virtually working openly, there were no effective opposition parties in Iraq. Under the Baath rule the Iraqi Communist Party (which operated openly between 1969 and 1978), and the Kurdistan Democratic Party (1970–1974) were allowed to act freely after years of underground activities, but were not allowed to challenge the Baath Party. In fact, they joined fronts headed by the ruling Baath party. The few civil society organizations that were allowed to work openly were controlled by the same party. Iraqis understood that their rights were denied by the regime, regardless of the wording of the constitution. The judiciary was not free and for most of the time, the country was living in a state of emergency, which meant the suspension of normal laws and the establishment of special courts.

THE TRANSITIONAL ADMINISTRATIVE LAW (TAL)

One of the main US allegations given to justify the invasion of Iraq was that the country lacked democracy. This issue made the occupying administration promote the idea of the need for a new constitution allegedly (to establish democracy) in Iraq. Although the occupying power had no right to change the constitution (or any laws in occupied territories), and was only obliged to issue rules to protect the occupied territories; the US administration cancelled the then-existing provisional Iraqi constitution and issued a new provisional document.

Between 2003 and 2005 Iraq was ruled by two sets of laws: the laws issued by the US civil administrator in Iraq, Paul Bremer, who arrived in Baghdad in May 2003 and headed the Coalition Provisional Authority (CPA), and the Transitional Administrative Law issued by the same authority. Bremer had no previous knowledge of Iraqi history, politics or society, but immediately started to issue orders and regulations (ultimately around 100 in total), which were regarded as laws, (some of which are still effective in Iraq today).[15] These included banning the Iraqi courts from considering claims against US soldiers or security contractors (thus granting them complete immunity), appointing a national security adviser, appointing a US advisor for each ministry, regulating the media, dissolved the Iraqi armed forces and disbanded the Baath Party. All these (laws) resulted in the disenfranchisement of hundreds of thousands of Iraqis. Bremer also took full and undisputed control of all Iraq's financial resources and assets.

Bremer also formed the Governing Council (GC) which included 25 people selected according to their sect, ethnic background, and, most importantly, their loyalty to the US. This was the first time in the history of Iraq that appointments were made on sectarian and ethnic bases. If the leaders of the Kurdish parties were excluded, only five members of the GC were living in Iraq before 2003. Sixty-five per cent of the GC held other nationalities, (including the leaders of the Kurdish parties). In most cases, merit and qualifications were not taken into consideration. The GC was asked to form a committee to draw a provisional law to replace the cancelled provisional constitution, and submit it to the GC for approval within a specified timetable.[16] It was said that two drafts were presented to the GC,[17] but in the end the one presented by Bremer was the one approved. The new law was known as Transitional Administrative Law for Iraq (TAL). The GC members approved TAL with only minor modifications.

The Shiite members of Council's main objection were that the new law did not refer to Islam as the official religion of the state. On their insistence, Article 7 was included.[18] 'Sect' was mentioned in the TAL a number of times (Articles 12 and 20 for example). This divisive word had never been used in previous Iraqi constitutions and its use was rejected by a large number of Iraqis. The only Iraqis who were happy to use the term were those taking part in the political process. It is important to add here that constitutions drafted for disunited, countries, or the ones that were threatened with the risks of disintegration, concentrated on points of unity rather than division. The US constitution as an example, in an attempt to create a united country, stressed the importance of unity. The fact that 'sect' was mentioned in Iraq's constitution became a strong argument for those demanding an expansion of the quota system and more dangerous the calls of other federal regions like the one in Iraqi Kurdistan.

The TAL did contain some new, and somehow, positive elements. Article 30 established that 30% of the Iraqi parliament must be women (68 of 275 deputies, later on the number of deputies were increased to be 325). This percentage was later reduced to 25%. Article 11 declared Iraq to be a bilingual state, Arabic and Kurdish.[19] Finally, Article 4 declared Iraq to be a federal state and Article 27b prohibited armed militias that acted out of the control of the central authority.

The TAL also set out a detailed and binding timetable for the GC to issue a permanent constitution. Clauses 60 and 61 stated that the new National Assembly, which was not elected but was appointed by Bremer himself, should draft a permanent constitution before 15 August 2005, and that the draft of the permanent constitution should be presented to the Iraqi people for approval in a general referendum no later than 15 October 2005. It also stated that if the permanent constitution was approved in the referendum, elections for a new elected government would be held no later than 15 December 2005 and the new government should assume office no later than 31 December 2005.

It was clear that the occupying power was determined to show the world as well as the growing Iraqi resistance that it intended to establish democracy in Iraq by the end of 2005. It was also obvious that the US was planning an early exit. Some Iraqi political observers regarded this timetable as hasty, fearing it would result in an ill-considered constitution. But calls for the divulgence of the discussions revolving around the drafting, and to delay any phase of this plan were rejected by the GC, and most importantly by the CPA, which became the main partner in directing and conducting the consultations. The special committee to draft a permanent constitution was formed only in mid-June 2005, meaning that such a vital document had to be completed in only two months!

The drafters of the TAL, and later the permanent constitution, were determined to weaken the central government and strengthen the provinces, or the regional entities (Article 52). There was also clear favouritism towards the Kurdish parties. For example, Articles 53, 54, and 58 acceded to Kurdish demands and further weakened the central government. Furthermore, the authority of the Kurdish regional administration was extended de facto though not de jure to provinces of what was termed as 'disputed areas', such as Kirkuk, Diyala and Mosul (Nineveh), in addition to the three recognized Kurdish provinces, Dahuk, Erbil and Sulaimaniya.[20] Other Iraqi provinces were given the right to establish their own federal status, but Baghdad and Kirkuk were barred from doing so.

The oil-rich Kirkuk province became, as always, a very difficult issue. Historically, Kirkuk was not predominantly Kurdish. Although successive Iraqi governments since 1964 tried to change the demographic composition of the province by settling some Arab tribes in it, yet other Arab tribes had long inhabited this area. Both the Arabs and the Turkomans of Kirkuk have troubled historical relations with the Kurds. Some northern parts of the province are predominantly Kurdish, southern areas are Arab, and the centre is Turkoman.[21] Yet following the 2003 invasion and the domination of the Kurdish parties in the province, the Kurdish regional government moved Kurdish families of Syrian and Turkish origin into Kirkuk, claiming that they had previously been living there. These moves have been consistently opposed by the Turkoman and Arab inhabitants of Kirkuk.

In short, as Jonathan Morrow observed, 'the TAL process… was notoriously, if unintentionally, hasty and secretive, and was heavily influenced by US political interests'.[22] The TAL was written by US nationals assisted by two expatriate Iraqis holding US and British nationalities, and who had not lived in Iraq since they were young children.[23] None of the drafters was an expert in constitutional law. The document itself was written in English and was poorly translated into Arabic[24] and passed (or in the words of Andrew Arato, was 'imposed')[25] to the appointed GC for approval. However, the CPA, and most of the advisers who took part in the process insisted that the constitution was Iraqi-made.[26] There was considerable pressure within Iraq for Iraqi involvement in the process. Most notable among the calls was a Fatwa (a ruling on point of Islamic law) issued by Ayatollah Ali Sistani in June 2003, in which he said, 'Those forces [the coalition or the CPA] had no authority to write a constitution for Iraq'.[27] He added that 'these forces [or authorities] do not have the authority to appoint the members of the constitution writing council. There is no guarantee that this council will produce a constitution that responds to the paramount interests of the Iraqi people'.[28]

Thus the CPA's plan to use mainly US advisors to write the Iraqi constitution was foiled by Iraqi opposition and Bremer was put in a bad corner. To avoid this embarrassing situation, he adopted a new plan by which he tried to make the TAL look like it was an interim constitution written by Iraqis and approved by them. He handed the translated copy of the TAL to the GC and the appointed national assembly, asked them to select a committee to discuss and approve a permanent constitution in just two months.

Drafting and Approving the Permanent Constitution

Before speaking about the process of drafting and approving the new permanent constitution, one should answer, or indeed decipher, the issue of who wrote the first draft of the constitution. It was said that in 2004 the US government asked a young American lecturer at NYU, Noah Feldman, to draw a draft for an Iraqi constitution.[29] There is no confirmation from the US administration or from Dr. Feldman himself about that, although he admitted that he was an advisor. We also know about two other influential persons, Larry Diamond and Peter Galbraith, (both wrote books about their role in such a capacity). A previous US ambassador to Croatia, Galbraith claimed to have volunteered to assist the Kurdish team in the drafting committee,[30] while Diamond wrote extensively about his (advisory) role in the process of writing the constitution.[31]

The late Edward Said, who was known for being well informed about what takes place inside the US decision-making circles, said something different. He wrote at that time the following: 'It was recently announced in the US press that a 32-year-old assistant lecturer of law, Noah Feldman, at New York University, would be responsible for producing a new Iraqi constitution. It was mentioned in all the media accounts of this major appointment that Feldman was an extraordinarily brilliant expert in Islamic law, had studied Arabic since he was 15, and grew up as an Orthodox Jew. But he has never practiced law in the Arab world, never been to Iraq, and seems to have no real practical background in the problems of post-war Iraq. What an open-faced snub not only to Iraq but also to the legions of Arab and Muslim legal minds who could have done a perfectly acceptable job in the service of Iraq's future. But no, Americans wanted it done by fresh young fellow, so as to be able to say, "We have given Iraq its new democracy"'.[32]

The Iraqi government, however, claimed that it carried out the work alone. The Governing Council appointed a committee of 55 people to write the draft, it started work on June 13, 2005. The members were divided according to the quota system: 28 from the Shiite coalition lists; 15 from the Kurdish lists; and eight from Ayad Allawi's *al-Iraqia* list, (which mostly consisted of Shiites); a Christian, a Turkoman, a Communist and a Sunni were also added. One month later, after strong objections from the Sunni community, the GC added 14 Sunni members to the committee.

The committee lacked any constitutional law experts or representatives of civil society organizations (especially women's groups) and the committee's discussions were held behind closed doors, thus ignoring public opinion.[33] To counter criticism of the lack of legal expertise, the committee claimed that it nominated a board of law advisors to the committee. This claim was never substantiated. If there was such advisory committee the names of these advisors were never disclosed. The only board of advisors the Iraqis knew about were in reality comprising mostly foreign experts appointed by the American side: the CPA or the US embassy in Iraq.

As explained later by one of its members who was the repertoire of one of its sub-committees responsible for writing the minutes: (The modus operandi of the drafting committee, was like this, the head of the sub-committee, who was Ahmad al-Safi al-Najafi, the representative of the religious *al-Marja'iya* of Najaf, and sometimes his deputy Hadi al-Hakim, after opening the session, he would present a set of clauses brought by him, asking the members to discuss and approve them. Members of the committee only discussed or suggested minor or secondary issues, only to give the constitution an Islamic-Shiite tinge).[34] The most important issue is that nobody asked the head of that committee where he brought those clauses from, and who had actually wrote them.

A few days after their appointment, two Sunnis members of the drafting committee and one of their advisors were assassinated near a restaurant in Baghdad. These men were well known for their strong objections to the proposed draft.[35] A few days later another Sunni committee member was kidnapped and disappeared ever since.[36] As a result, after only a few days of taking part in the discussions, the Sunni representatives suspended their participation in the committee, demanding action against the killing of their colleagues. Although they all returned to the committee ten days later, they were in fact greatly intimidated. On 8 August, this committee was suspended and the discussion was continued largely by Shiite and Kurdish groups, with no real Sunni representation.[37] Altogether, the Sunni members of the committee were involved for only three to four weeks.

It was clear from the discussions inside the committee that each group was concentrating on its own limited objectives, and the broad outline drafted in TAL was not discussed. The Shiite religious members were mainly concerned about establishing Islam as the state religion and securing the right to perform Shiite ceremonies. It seemed that they regarded the insertion of these issues as official recognition of their existence and their majority. The Kurdish members had clearer ideas about what they wanted and had a team of US and European experts supporting them.[38] They succeeded in preventing any discussion of the TAL; hence maintaining the broad sense of federalism, their rights to control their federal entity, to claim Kirkuk as part of their federal region and to confirm their share of the wealth of the state. On the other hand, the Sunni members were concerned about the Arab identity and the unity of the Iraqi state.

It seemed that neither the Shiites nor the Sunnis were aware of the divisive nature of most clauses, and those who were aware were too weak to impose their point of view. Hence there was no discussion of the provisions that would later become highly contentious, such as the broad federal system, the exploitation of oil and gas and the weakness of the centre of the country in dealing with the regions.

Iraqis in general were unaware of the document's detail as no version was issued publically. The author worked with a small group of constitutional law experts and academics to create some awareness of the equivocal or problematic issues in the draft, and to enlighten the public about the new constitution. Based only on the very few press reports that were issued, members of the group dared to speak about the dangers of the divisive clauses, but these critics were hounded by the police and unknown militias. Others were detained for much less covert reasons, simply because of their opposition.[39]

After several meetings of the constitutional committee, the main points of difference were as follows:

1. The nature of the state and the extent of the federal system

Kurdish members of the committee insisted that Iraq should be a federal state and demanded that the official name of the state should include the word 'federal'. The Sunni Arab members refused to accept this terminology and insisted that Iraq was not made up of a collection of different entities as the legal term 'federal' indicates. They wanted to use the word 'united' instead of 'federal'. The Shiite members did not object to 'federal,' as the clause that gives the Kurds the right to a federal entity could also be extended to other provinces. They hoped that this would allow them to establish a Shiite southern federal region.

2. The role of Islam

This matter was the main concern of the Shiite members who mostly claimed to be religious and members of conservative religious parties. Their aim was to write a clear clause into the constitution that declared Islam as the state religion and the source of all legislation. They also wanted it to mention their religious sectarian practices and authority, *al-Marja'iya al-Diniya*, the Shiites Higher Religious Authority in Najaf and elsewhere, as an independent and revered body that had a significant role in modern Iraq. The Kurds and some members of *al-Iraqia* Party wanted to have a secular constitution which did not mention religion.

3. The relationship between the federal (decentralized entities) and the central government

The Kurds wanted a broad federal system in which the federal entity would have powers that superseded those of the central government.

They were encouraged by the broad authorities in all fields (economic, political, education etc.) bestowed on the Iraqi Kurdish Region by TAL's. They even insisted on stating all the controversial clauses that were stipulated in TAL into the new constitution. The Sunni members wanted an effective central government with only broad autonomy given to Iraqi Kurdistan.

4. The identity of the Iraqi state

The Sunni Arabs wanted to include a clause stating that Iraq was an Arab state and part of the Arab nation. This was vehemently opposed by Kurdish members who regarded their part of the country as part of their own divided Kurdish nation. Other minorities wanted their ethnic or religious groups mentioned, while some Shiite members wanted to include the Iranian nationality as a component of the Iraqi people. Language was also contentious and the Kurds insisted on official recognition of Kurdish in a bilingual state.

5. The issue of Kirkuk and the so-called (disputed) areas

Oil-rich Kirkuk province was regarded by the Kurdish parties as part of the Kurdish region. They wanted it to be included in the Kurdish federal entity and described the city of Kirkuk as the capital of Iraqi Kurdistan.[40] The Sunni and Shiite Arabs refused to concede this point, as they regarded Kirkuk as a mixed province.

6. The De-Baathification law

The US removed all Baath Party members above a certain level from state organizations. The Arab Sunni members thought that the law was enforced excessively and that sometimes it was used to silence any opposition to the Shiite and Kurdish domination of the government. They also argued that in democracies nobody should be alienated from participating because of their political views.

7. Sharing the wealth of the country

The Kurds wanted a clause allowing their federal region to explore and control any wealth within its borders, and to pay only a share of the proceeds to the central government. The Sunnis argued that, as in all other federal systems, the central government should have the authority to manage national wealth, negotiate the ways of exploring these resources, and disburse a fair share to all parts of the country.

These disputes were not restricted to the constitutional committee of 69 members but soon involved the US administration and policy-makers from neighbouring countries. The US was especially impatient in its interventions. The US Ambassador to Iraq, Zalmay Khalilzad,[41] urged the committee to finish by 15 August 2005, as stipulated in TAL.[42] Several early meetings of the (Leadership Council)[43] took place at the US Embassy. By 10 August, the United States was strongly expressing its views on substantive constitutional issues. On 12 August, in efforts to accelerate the drafting process, the US Embassy circulated its own draft constitution in English.[44]

Finally, a draft constitution, consisting of 139 articles only, was submitted to the National Assembly on August 23, 2005 (one week behind schedule). The Sunnis raised a great outcry, objecting strongly to its hasty promulgation. To overcome this problem and to avoid its rejection by the overwhelming Sunni provinces in the referendum, the American mediators intervened again and proposed addition of a new article (140) that allows amendments of the constitution. This became later on article 142 of the present constitution.

What is perilous here is that the proposal to include this article was made after the draft was adopted by the National Assembly and rati-fied by a national referendum, which means that the inclusion of such an article was illegal. This was the first attempt to forge the constitution. The move was in fact a hoax that deceived the Sunni representatives, who either naively or advisedly overlooked the fact that it is almost impos-sible to amend the constitution once it was adopted and ratified, as the Kurdish parties had an ironclad right to veto any amendment. According to the draft itself, any amendment could be foiled if it was rejected by three provinces, which means that the three Kurdish provinces are enough to block any amendment. On account of the objections of the Kurdish parties to the idea of adding this article, the American side added five more articles, after the constitution was ratified by a national referendum with its 139 articles. Besides the fact that this process was illegal, the added articles, which were subtly favoured the Kurdish parties and region, had negatively impacted national unity, especially as these articles were neither discussed, endorsed or certified by the Constitutional Committee or National Assembly. Nor were they included in the draft that was put forward to the people in the referendum. This was the second forgery. The third act of forgery was carried out during the vote counting, especially in the province of Mosul (Nineveh).

The draft was finally put to a referendum on the date stipulated in TAL, 15 October, and according to the official results, it was approved by 78.59% of the voters. This result was strongly contested by many Iraqi politicians, especially Sunnis.[45] Officially it was announced that only the provinces of Salah al-Din (Tikrit) and al-Anbar (Ramadi) voted against the draft. Yet Initial unconfirmed results suggested that a third province, Nineveh (Mosul), also voted against it.[46] But it was announced that the negative votes did not amount to two-thirds of the voters, and thus could not prevent the draft's passage,[47] and that was the third and most dangerous forgery. Some Iraqi Sunni leaders claimed that other provinces such as Diyala, al-Muthana and al-Qadissiya (the last two having Shiite majorities) also voted against the Constitution.[48] Those who opposed the draft argued that the delay in announcing the results of the referendum (more than 10 days) and failure to open referendum centres in opposition areas suggested that the results were manipulated. In the case of Mosul and after realizing that the votes refusing the draft were becoming higher, the Iraqi authorities stopped the counting and ordered the transfer of the ballot boxes to Baghdad to do the count. Later the former head of the Iraqi parliament, Dr. Mahmoud al-Mash'hadani, spoke out publicly about the rigging of votes in Nineveh (Mosul).[49] Other Iraqi politicians said the same. Yet, despite the objections to the results of the referendum, the constitution was declared as approved by the majority of the voters.

THE IMPACT OF THE CONSTITUTION

It is essential to examine the constitution to assess its viability and suitability for helping to unite and improve Iraq. The constitution has some positive and progressive clauses. These include: No law should be drawn that contradicts the principles of democracy and the rights and liberties of the citizens; the people are the source of power and its legitimacy;

the submission of the armed forces to civil authority; the prohibition of torture; the independence of the legal system; and the importance of civil society organizations. Almost all of these rights existed in previous constitutions, but observers thought that it was possible they would gain real meaning in a democratic environment. Unfortunately, the experience proved it didn't.

The constitution also contained negative and divisive content. Rather than helping to solve many of Iraq's problems, it contributed to them and even created more serious ones. The main problematic issues are as follows:

1. The Preamble

   The constitution contains an unusually long preamble (330 words), a sectarian and divisive political communiqué par excellence, which bears no relationship to the constitution itself. As the Shiite members of the constitutional committee failed to include the role of their religious leadership (*al-Marja'iya al-Diniya*) in the constitution, its role and status were emphasized in the preamble. This gave immediate focus on Iraq's old (buried) differences and tragedies, rather than concentrating on fraternity and unity. It seems that the idea of this preamble was taken from the US constitution, as it starts with the words 'We the people of Mesopotamia, [not Iraq] the homeland of the apostles and prophets, resting place of the virtuous imams, cradle of civilization, crafters of writing, and home of numeration…'. But while the US preamble contained only 51 words, and stressed unity, freedom and prosperity, the Iraqi version had no mention of freedom.[50]

2. The role of Islam[51]

   Article 2 established Islam as the official religion of the state and as the fundamental source of legislation. But Point A of the First Paragraph of the same article stated that 'No law that contradicts the established provisions of Islam may be enacted'.[52] While there may be no harm in stating Islam is the official religion of the state, as the overwhelming majority of the population are Muslims, Point A rendered all the positive aspects that were mentioned in Chapter 3 (The Liberties, Articles 14–46) meaningless. In reality, practice, and with the domination of the conservative religious parties, institutions and personalities, any liberty could be cancelled if a religious institution claimed that it contradicts Islamic beliefs, as we have seen in many cases in Middle Eastern states.

Sectarian affiliations had never been mentioned in any Iraqi constitution, as the aim of previous governments was to strengthen the sense of unified identity. The 2005 constitution mentioned sects at least twice apart from the preamble, (Articles 41 and 43). Article 43 went so far as to mention one sect's specific practices (rituals) in affirming the freedom of 'Practice of religious rites, including the Husaini [Shiite] ceremonies'.[53]

In line with this sectarian-conservative religious attitude, Article 41, which allowed the recreation of the Shiite and Sunni personal status courts, is troublesome. It describes Iraqis according to their religious sects and beliefs in dealing with their personal status, a problem that old laws had managed to prevent through a unified personal status law since 1959.[54]

3. Relations between the central and regional governments

The constitution stated that in the event of contradictions between central and local laws of any regional administration, authority is conferred on the local administration, perhaps the only time such a hierarchy has been established in modern constitutional history. Immediately after approving the constitution, the Kurdish federal region issued its own local constitution which included many clauses that contradicted those of the central government, especially in the field of exploiting national and regional wealth, such as oil. Article 115 of the Iraqi Constitution states: 'The priority goes to the regional law in case of conflict between other powers shared between the federal government and regional governments. Article 121, 2 states: 'In case of a contradiction between regional and national legislation with respect to a matter outside the exclusive powers of the federal government, the regional authority shall have the right to amend the application of the national legislation within that region'. In the absence of clear articles defining the powers of the federal central government the region was left free to do whatever it wanted.

Article 126 states that 'Articles of the Constitution may not be amended if such amendment takes away powers from the regions that are not within the exclusive powers of the federal authorities, except by the approval of the legislative authority of the concerned region and the approval of the majority of its citizens in a general referendum'. In other words the drafters awarded the Kurdish region an iron-clad veto.[55] The Shiites were also indirectly allowed such rights because they were sure of the domination of their sect over most of the southern provinces.

4. The armed forces

Article 9 was also left loose and divisive as it does not speak about the authority of the state to establish one unified army. Although it described the Iraqi armed forces as one body, it also stated that 'this body is composed of the components of the Iraqi people with due consideration given to its balance and its similarity without discrimination or exclusion and shall be subject to the control of the civilian authority' (Article 9, 1, A). In Paragraph B it stated that 'The formation of military militia outside the framework of the armed forces is prohibited'. Yet in practice, the Ministry of Defence has no authority whatsoever over the Kurdish armed force, the *Peshmerga*, which is officially regarded as part of the Iraqi military totally financed by the central government.

Following the occupation of Mosul (June 2014) a new armed militia (The Popular Mobilisation Forces PMF) was established to stop the advancement of the terrorist fighters of Daesh (ISIS) towards Baghdad. Immediately the PMF were fully adopted and sponsored by Iran. Finally, the PMF was declared to be legal forces, put under the command of the commander of the armed forces (in name only), and fully furnished by the Iraqi government, (salaries, armaments etc.). But in reality, these forces or regiments (67 groups legally approved by the Iraqi parliament and more unregistered but fully active), remained unconstitutional which similar to the Peshmerga, as they contradict the article that says the Iraqi armed forces are the only body that is allowed to carry arms. More dangerous is the policies adopted by some previous governments (in particular that of Nouri Maliki and Adil Abdul Mahdi) which made the PMF overshadow the Iraqi armed forces, (this was mainly because of their fears from possible military coups). In many cases, some members of PMF were appointed to command some regiments or administrative sections of the Iraqi army.

5. Foreign affairs

In any federal system the foreign affairs of the state normally falls under the authority of the central government. However, Article 121, 4, states: 'The regions and governorates shall establish offices in the embassies and diplomatic missions, in order to follow up cultural, social and developmental affairs'. In reality, some of these offices became more influential than the main diplomatic mission itself, especially in some that were headed by ambassadors representing the two main Kurdish parties.[56] Another problem was raised when the Kurdish Regional Government started to initiate agreements with foreign countries without the approval of the central government.

6. Kirkuk

This issue is perhaps the most problematic. The approval of the permanent constitution legally meant the abolishing of TAL, but the (illegal) article 143, inserted on the insistence of the Kurdish parties, reinstating two articles from TAL, Article 53(A) and Article 58, in the new constitution. Article 53 of TAL (A) stated: 'The Kurdistan Regional Government is recognized as the official government of the territories that were administered by that government [Kurdish] on March 19, 2003 in the governorates of Dahuk, Erbil, Sulaimaniya, Kirkuk, Diyala and Nineveh [Mosul]'. While article 58 of TAL dealt with the issue of Kirkuk and what it called the (disputed areas) in other regions, the census, immigration by previous governments and a referendum in order to determine the people's willingness to join the Kurdish region.

The added(unconstitutional) article (140) of the constitution stated: 'The executive authority shall undertake the necessary steps to complete the implementation of the requirements of all subparagraphs of Article 58 of the Transitional Administrative Law,' and that 'The responsibility placed upon the executive branch of the Iraqi Transitional Government (stipulated in Article 58 of the Transitional Administrative Law) shall extend and continue to the executive authority elected in accordance with this Constitution, provided that it accomplishes completely (normalization, a census and concludes with a referendum in Kirkuk and other disputed territories to determine the will of their citizens), by a date not to exceed the 31st of December 2007. Thus one can understand the continued great tension between the central government and the Kurdish Regional Government (KRG) and between the latter and the population of Mosul and Diyala, as the KRG regards parts of these two provinces as (disputed areas), while it regards the oil-rich Kirkuk province as an integral part of Iraqi Kurdistan. Contrary to what was stipulated in Article 53 of the TAL, before the US occupation in March 2003, Kirkuk was not under the authority of the KRG, nether were any parts of Mosul and Diyala.

7. Natural resources

The issue of exploring and exploiting natural wealth, especially oil, has also been highly divisive. The constitution left this matter loosed as well. It was not accidental that the oil and gas-rich regions, Basra, Missan and Anbar, were demanding federal status. In fact, some provinces, especially Basra, started to defy the central government over many issues, and the latter was unable to respond. Their main complaint is that the natural wealth of their provinces is being handed to the other areas, especially the Kurdish region. According to the constitution the KRG receives 17% of the national budget with the right to fully exploit the oil revenues in the Kurdish region,[57] while other provinces receive far less (for example the governor of Thi Qar province, another area demanding federal status, complained that his province receives only $10 million, less than 1% of the budget). In order to achieve greater equality, the central government drafted a new law for oil and gas by which it planned to remove the special privileges of the KRG. Before the law could be put to parliament, the KRG announced its rejection and threatened to withdraw from the federal government, thus stymying the bill.

8. The identity of the state

Arab Sunni members of the constitutional commission were insistent that the constitution should mention that Iraq is an Arab state and part of the Arab nation (75–80% of Iraqis are Arabs). This was adamantly refused by the Kurdish members. Ultimately, Article 3 stated: 'Iraq is a country of multiple nationalities, religions, and sects, it is a founding and active member in the Arab League and is committed to its charter, and it is part of the Islamic world', again stressing the Islamic and sectarian nature of the state. The Shiite members of the commission, who always criticized the Arab countries for supporting Saddam Hussein and the Arab League for not taking any action against the atrocities committed by his regime, allied with the Kurdish members in the drafting of this article, leaving the Sunni representatives in a minority and disappointed.

9. Terrorism

The article about combating terrorism (Article 7, 2) was so loose, broad and ill-defined that it could be used to condemn anybody who opposed the political process—a strategy that had been used before. The Sunni members in the drafting committee objected to this article. The articles about (uprooting) the Baath Party (de-Baathification Law) also pose a similar danger (Article 7, 1). It is true that Article 135 exempted a fair number of members of the old Baath Party from being held accountable for their membership, but this matter was left to the Higher Commission for De-Baathification, which had the power to determine who would be excluded. The *al-Iraqia* list of Ayad Allawi, which included a fair number of Sunnis, complained that many of its political candidates had been disqualified by decisions issued by this commission.

10. The issue of double nationality

The constitutionallowed Iraqis to hold two nationalities, but stipulated that whoever is appointed in a high sovereign or security position should relinquish the other nationality (Article 18, 4). But no Iraqi official obeyed this regulation. Most of those officials condemned for corruption have fled the country and settled in the other country where they were naturalized. Since 2003 all the presidents of the republic, almost all prime ministers and a big number of ministers and ambassadors were holders of foreign nationalities. The biggest scandal was that some ambassadors were holders of the nationality of the country they were assigned to, i.e. they were citizens of the states in which they were appointed as an envoy. This would raise a question about their loyalty, is to the country they represent or to the state they have taken the oath of allegiance to. In other words, if a clash of national interests occurred between Iraq and the country the ambassador is legally a citizens, which party will the ambassador serve?

11. On their part Iraqi women were also dissatisfied with the constitution as it stipulated the annulment of the progressive personal status law of 1959 with all its advanced and progressive amendments (Article 41).[58]

12. Researchers in the field of higher education complained that the constitution indirectly restricted their researches and academic

projects. Article 9, E, states the following: (The Iraqi Government shall respect and implement Iraq's international obligations regarding the non-proliferation, non-development, non-
production, and non-use of nuclear, chemical, and biological
weapons, and shall prohibit associated equipment, materiel, tech-
nologies, and delivery systems for use in the development, manufacture, production, and use of such weapons). Science departments of the Iraqi universities are complaining that their labora-
tories are short of equipment necessary for their projects for fear
that their work may be seen as helping in developing prohibited
weapons.[59]

13. Finally, the language used was incredibly weak and problematic,
raising concerns about the ability of the body that drafted or translated the constitution.[60] The senior Iraqi politician, Ali Allawi,
noted that the constitution was 'utterly alien in construction and
phraseology from the Arabic language and the Iraqi experience'.[61]

ATTEMPTS TO AMEND THE CONSTITUTION

When US negotiators felt that the proposed draft was going to be rejected
by the predominately Sunni provinces, they suggested inserting a new
clause to encourage the Sunni representatives not to vote against it.[62] This
added clause[63] stated: 'The Council of Representatives (parliament) shall
form at the beginning of its work a committee from its members representing the principal components of the Iraqi society with the mission
of presenting to the Council of Representatives, within a period not
later than four months, a report that contains recommendations of the
necessary amendments that could be made to the Constitution, and
the committee shall be dissolved after a decision is made regarding its
proposals'.[64]

The second paragraph stated: 'The proposed amendments shall be
presented to the Council of Representatives all at once for a vote on
them, and shall be deemed approved with the agreement of the absolute majority of the members of the Council'. The third paragraph stated:
'The articles amended by the Council of Representatives pursuant to item
"Second" of this Article shall be presented to the people for voting on
them in a referendum within a period not exceeding two months from
the date of their approval by the Council of Representatives. And finally,

the fourth paragraph stated that 'The referendum on the amended Articles shall be successful if approved by the majority of the voters, and if not rejected by two-thirds of the voters in three or more governorates'.

Because of the inclusion of this article the Sunni groups participating in the political process, especially the Islamic Party (IP) headed then by Tariq al-Hashimi, advised the Sunni community, a day before the referendum, to vote in favour of the constitution. This decision received much criticism, especially from the Sunni community. It was not clear what made the leaders of this party change their minds so drastically and at such short notice, but it seemed that this was due to the pressure exerted on them by the US embassy, as well as their desire to be in the new government.[65] It is also possible that some other sorts of temptations, and threats, were offered to them to vote for the constitution.

As soon as the constitution was approved demands for its amendment was made. The first response was from the Sunni members of the constitution committee who rejected the constitution, saying that they had not agreed to the terms and calling for international support to block it.[66] In February 2006, anticipating the formation of a committee to review the constitution, an unofficial Sunni group of academics and politicians articulated demands which included: relaxing Article 142; suspending the implementation of federalism; giving central government ownership of natural resources; repealing De-Baathification law; and preventing any region annexing Kirkuk.[67]

Although the Iraqi parliament had established a committee to review the constitution, it did not convene. In September 2006 another committee was established, but this one was already illegal because the first paragraph of Article 142 permitted only four months to propose the amendments and this time had elapsed. At any rate, the committee did not convene until December 2006. It initially included 27 members, with two more added later to represent small ethnic minorities. It decided that decisions should be made only after a consensus was reached. This committee was given four months to present its suggestions.[68] In May 2007 the committee presented 51 amendments, although it has been suggested that there were actually 70.[69] It decided that there were 3–5 amendments on which it could not agree, and that it needed input from the heads of the major political blocs in the parliament to reach a conclusion.

In November 2008, Prime Minister Nouri al-Maliki joined in criticizing the Constitution and stressed the need for its amendment. He said, 'the Constitution was drafted in a hurry and in an atmosphere where the quota system was overwhelming'. He added that 'because of the fears of the past some articles were included which restricted the powers of the centre, both for the time being and the future... Decentralization should not be dictatorship and what we fear is that the federal region is confiscating [abducted] the state'.[70]

In 2011 the second largest group in the parliament, *al-Iraqia*, joined in calling for the amendment of the Constitution. Their reasons were different to al-Maliki's; they wished to curb the prime minister's powers.[71] Only the Kurdistan coalition, the parties of Jalal Talabani and Massoud Barzani, continued to call for full adherence to the Constitution and they made their participation in any governing coalition conditional on upholding it.[72]

Despite all these criticisms and demands, the Iraqi constitution was not amended. This was because of two factors. First: it has proven to be impossible to amend the most controversial issues. For example, no amendment can touch the powers of the regions in general and the Kurdish region in particular. Article 126, 4, clearly states: 'Articles of the Constitution may not be amended [the Arabic version states "cannot be amended"] if such amendment takes away from the powers of the regions that are not within the exclusive powers of the federal authorities, except by the approval of the legislative authority of the concerned region and the approval of the majority of its citizens in a general referendum'.

Yet most of the problems that Iraq is witnessing are because of the struggle between the central government and the Kurdish federal entity and the way prime ministers continue to dominate Iraqi politics. The Iraqi political scene is in a state of impasse, as the Kurdish regional government is not prepared to relinquish any of its powers, in the field of the armed forces, the economy, or in claiming territory, and because of the failure of the different governments to find a way to reconcile with the other groups, as well as the intransigence of the other parties of the political process.

Second, the sharp division and differences among the Iraqi political blocs and parties taking part in the political process have hindered the amendment process. Ironically, all the conflicting parties refer to the Constitution when they want to support their demands. The Constitution can be used to support opposing demands because it is so vague.

Finally, nobody, until lately, realized or discovered that five very critical articles were added to the text after it was approved in a national referendum and passed by the parliament. Practically all these amendments are illegal and should be removed from the document, or at least they should be put again for another referendum. The Kurdish Parties, the main beneficiary of the added articles are not only keeping silent about this issue but they insist that the government should implement them. Ironically the KRG), taking advantage of the debacles of the Iraq armed forces in the fighting with the terrorist Daesh fighters, sent its Peshmarga into oil-rich province of Kirkuk and annexed it by force to the Kurdish region. It justified this armed action as an implementation of article 140 which the government failed to do! At any rate, the many problems engulfing Iraq are sidelining this critical matter.

THE CONSTITUTION'S CONTINUING DAMAGE

Considering the myriad confusions and divisions underlying the Constitution's drafting process, it is not surprising that the document has created more problems than it has solved. The Constitution has been a major factor in maintaining the chaotic situation that pervaded most of Iraq. More than eighteen years after the invasion, and following four rounds of elections, Iraq is still one of the most dangerous and corrupt countries in the world.[73] The security situation is fragile and municipal services like electricity, sewage, and clean water are almost non-existent. The food ration that Iraqi families received since the sanctions were imposed on Iraq in 1990 is barely for the population. All the governments formed after each election was incomplete, (for example, most of them did not include ministers for defence, interior and national security, this was mainly because of the quota system pursued by all the governments, and the sharp differences between the parties participating in the political process).

The ambiguity of the most sensitive articles in the constitution continued to have a negative influence on Iraq. For example, after the 2010 election, the largest party, *al-Iraqia*, felt it had a mandate to form the government. This was disputed because Article 76, 1, does not make it clear whether the largest party or the largest coalition has the right to form a new government. It took the federal court several months to respond and it decided against *al-Iraqia*. This decision would have been less contentious had the President given the winning party the chance first to form a government. Instead, Nouri al-Maliki, the incumbent Prime Minister and leader of the second-placed Dawa Party refused to leave office and asked the head of the federal court, who was a member of his electoral list, to interpret Article 76, 1. In the end, the Judge ruled in favour of al-Maliki. Another problem occurred following the elections of 2014. Although Maliki's coalition won most of the seats in that election, the US embassy in Baghdad objected to him having a third term, and brought pressure on the leaders of the different coalitions to choose another member from Maliki's Dawa party. It was agreed then to name Haidar al-Ibadi as the one to form the new government. All Maliki's objections, complaints and threats to sue the president of the republic for that unconstitutional decision went unnoticed. Following the elections of 2018, a bigger breach of the constitution was committed when the winning parties and coalitions failed to agree on an acceptable nominee as a new prime minister. After months of indirect haggling, mainly and indirectly between the USA and Iran, it was agreed that Adil Abdul Mahdi should form the government. Abdul Mahdi was neither a member of the parliament nor a member of any of the winning lists. He did not even take part in the election. Yet when the latter was forced to resign one year later by the overwhelming popular protests, the parliament accepted another US favoured nominee, Mustafa al-Kadhimi, who again was neither a member of parliament nor a member of any of the winning lists. This conduct, and many others, showed the amount of respect the US and the parties participating in the political process had for the constitution.

The second feature of Iraqi politics following the approval of the constitution was the many bones of contention that emerged between the central government and the Kurdish regional leadership. In the end, the KRG began to behave as a de facto independent entity paying no attention to the central government. This was manifested by the region receiving foreign dignitaries, who avoided, or in fact, snubbed the central government.[74] The central government criticized such visits and insisted that they should have been arranged through Baghdad and with the capital's prior knowledge. Despite the tension caused by the visits between Iraq and the countries the visitors belonged to, and between the centre and the KRG, however, the latter was not deterred. On its part the Kurdish regional officials rejected this criticism, claiming that they had behaved according to the Constitution.

Another problem relates to the absence of a law to regulate the exploration of oil. Baghdad and Erbil have been at an impasse on the issue for the past years, or to be more precise since the approval of the constitution. The central government claimed that it is the sole power with the right to sign oil concessions in Iraq, according to Article 112, 1, while the KRG says it holds this right, according to the same article. Ironically they are both right because of the ambiguity of the article, which granted the federal government authority to explore the 'present fields', but gave the regional government the right to explore and sign agreements for any new fields. The Kurdish Regional Government has managed to sign a number of oil concessions with foreign companies since 2005, but these have led to tough confrontations with the central government, which eventually suspended the exportation of oil extracted from wells in Iraqi Kurdistan. In the end, and because of the high volume of corruption that overwhelmed the Kurdish region (and the central government), as well as the high priority given to the interests of the ruling families and that of the leaders of the Kurdish political parties, the process of signing oil concessions with foreign oil companies, resulted in the Kurdish region becoming indebted to these companies. The debts are estimated to be between $27 billion and $36 billion, which the region is now unable to pay and wants the central government to settle. While the central government claimed that the region is indebted to the national budget, as it failed to transfer or pay to the Iraqi treasury its share of the proceeds (billions of dollars) for the oil exported by the region.

Finally the Constitution contained more than 60 articles that required new laws to be activated. In the 16 years since the Constitution was approved, Parliament has not issued many of these laws. Thus many important issues are still left pending, such as: the political association's law; the law about the freedom of peaceful demonstrations and free public meetings; the personal status law; the law to establish the union council; the law to regulate the sharing of national resources and the law detailing the powers of the regions. Above all the intense differences between the different blocs and lists in the parliament remained the main obstacle to civil discourse or progress. Attempts to implement these new laws could threaten the country's already fragile political foundations.

CONCLUSION

A permanent constitution is a very important document for any sovereign society, and governments usually draft them over a long period of time. Yet Iraq had no such luxury, being forced to draft its foundational document in only two months. In October 2005, Iraqis went to vote on a permanent constitution they had not seen, read, studied, debated or drafted.[75] Strangely is the fact that they voted on an incomplete draft.[76] They did so, perhaps naively, thinking that it would bring them the peace and prosperity they desperately desired. They followed the instructions that their political and religious leaders gave them, and the majority did not realize that this document would be another source of misery. Moreover, the vast majority of Iraqis did not know that they were ruled by a forged constitution, a constitution different from the one they voted for.

For the Iraqis, the permanent constitution remained controversial. The debate continued about who drafted it and the divisive and ambiguous nature of most of its articles. Reading through the Iraqi Constitution is like walking through a minefield. The drafters left too many loose ends and loopholes which threatened the unity, if not the existence, of the state. The Kurdish Regional Government had often threatened to secede from Iraq if the key articles, they included in the constitution in their favour were not implemented. Ironically, as was mentioned above, some of these articles are illegal as they were added after the approval of the document.

The insistence of the drafters of the Constitution on keeping the central government weaker than the regional authorities has caused a serious problem for the state. In all federal systems Foreign, Defence and Monetary affairs remain in the hand of the central government, only in the Iraqi federal system are these affairs challenged, and in many instants, confiscated by the Kurdish Regional Government. Because of the failure of successive central governments to make the Kurdish region abide by the terms of the constitution, other provinces began to collect taxes, smuggle oil and form armed militias that are out of the control of the central government. Attempts to establish federal entities along the lines of the KRG (although have hitherto failed), are increasing, mainly because of the big advantages the Kurdish region is enjoying, as those in favour of making the provinces a federal part claim. As long as the weak central governments fail to make the Kurdish region act as an integral part of a federal state, the demands of other provinces, especially the oil and gas-rich ones will continue to increase.

The problem of Kirkuk and the so-called disputed areas is still pending, despite the stipulation that a census was to determine the region's future by the end of 2007. The elections of 2010, 2014 and 2018 proved that the Kurdish parties did not have a majority in Kirkuk, Mosul and Diyala, but these areas are still dominated by the presence of the Kurdish forces.[77]

The Constitution, given its broad deficiencies, has garnered almost no respect from the government which it is supposed to guide. This situation is evinced by the government's reaction to the peaceful demonstrations across Iraq in 2011, 2018 and 2019, sometimes known as the Iraqi Spring. This movement was organized to speak out against corruption and to demand an improvement of basic services. Yet, in blatant violation of the constitutional clauses that granted the protesters this right to free speech, the protests were brutally suppressed by government forces and Kurdish regional forces. The existence of some special prisons, which are not under the authority of the Interior Ministry or the Justice Ministry, but rather are run directly by armed militias in the Kurdish region and rest of Iraq, posed another related problem, although government officials claimed that their actions are justified by Article 7, which gives the state the right to combat terrorism. The broad and loose nature of this article has allowed the government and the Kurdish regional authority to encroach on any opposing voices.

The hasty way the Constitution was drafted, the many external interventions, the absence of real Iraqi constitutional experts, the weakness of the central government and the sharp divisions undermining the country have all contributed to the precarious situation in Iraq.[78] Calls to amend the constitution are increasing, especially from the Arab coalitions, yet all these calls, including the one to revive the committee established in 2005 to look into the amendments have been strongly opposed, especially by the Kurdish parties.[79] To correct all these mistakes and solve the existing problems a consensus should be reached by the different blocs that dominate the Parliament. Even the Kurdish Regional Government's refusal to consider amendments and the accompanying threat of secession should be mitigated, especially following the US administration's clear indication that a Kurdish independent state in Iraq is out of the question.[80] But the reality is that it will be extremely difficult to convince those who found the greatest advantage from the current legislation to drop it in the hope of establishing a united, settled, and more secured country. Of course, the disrespect for the law and regulations in the Kurdish region are similar and will be discussed in Chapter 5.

The US claimed that its objectives for occupying Iraq, apart from the unfounded claims of protecting against weapons of mass destruction (WMD), were first to remove a hostile dictatorial regime and replace it with one that complies to US plans for the region, second to rebuild Iraq into a democracy where human rights are respected, and third to make Iraq into a democratic model that its regional neighbours could emulate and envy. But now, after more than eighteen years of occupation and heavy US influence across the spectrum of Iraqi politics, it is hard to reach any other conclusion that these goals have all failed. The deep structural, legal and political failings of the Iraqi Constitution have contributed greatly to this failure (not to mention of course the grave mistakes committed by the US occupying administration).

Mahmoud al-Mash'hadani, previous speaker of the parliament, and member of the (commission to write the constitution) from the Sunnis component said in a TV programme (the referendum on the constitution was rigged, and we the representatives of the Sunni component were threatened by the Americans and forced to approve it. They told us that the constitution will be approved, and we [the Americans] will make sure this result will happen, your only choice [the Sunnis representatives] is to accept it as it is and call upon your followers to vote for it. As compensation, they suggested adding an article about amending it following its approval. This was done by adding an article after the approval of the constitution).[81] Other members of the constitutional committee spoke lately about being unaware of the articles added after the approval of this vital document.

Finally Eighteen years after the US invasion, and following four rounds of elections, Iraq remained one of the most dangerous, unstable and corrupt countries in the world. One could fairly say that not only the ill-conceived US experiment to remake Iraq has failed, but also the deep structural, legal and political failings of the Iraqi Constitution, for which US officials and Iraqi politicians bear full responsibility.

NOTES

1. Andrew Arato, *Constitution Making Under Occupation: The Politics of Imposed Revolution in Iraq*, Columbia University Press, 2009, p. 54. See also Article 43 of the 1907 Hague Convention which states, "... [The occupant power] shall take all steps in his power to establish and insure, as far as possible, public order and safety, while respecting, unless absolutely prevented, the laws in force in the country." Ibid., p. 24.
2. The US was involved in other direct and indirect political experiments in South America but most of these attempts were rejected by the people of these countries.
3. In Japan for example the new constitution preserved the Emperor's spiritual position as well as regarding him as the symbol of national

unity. In fact Arato argues that the new Japanese constitution was in reality an amendment of the Meiji Constitution of 1889. See Arato, p. 33. In Germany the new constitution depended in parts on the Weimar constitutions that were written in 1919, and followed German constitutional tradition since the foundation of the Reich in 1871. See: http://en.wikipedia.org/wiki/Basic_Law_for_the_Federal_R epublic_of_Germany#Drafting_process.

4. Noah Feldman, *What We Owe Iraq: War and the Ethics of Nation Building*, Princeton University Press, 2004, p. 7.
5. Arato, p. 3.
6. It is worth noting that when the British occupied Iraq in 1914 they saw the three old Ottoman Vilayets (Wilayets) Mosul, Baghdad and Basra, which had always been ruled from Baghdad, as a coherent one nation. See Majid Khadduri, *Independent Iraq: A Study in Iraqi Politics from 1932 to 1958*, Oxford University Press, 1960; and Reidar Visser, Historical Myths of a Divided Iraq, *Survival*, Vol. 50, no. 2, April–May 2008.
7. Zackary Elkins and Tom Ginsburg, *The Iraqi Draft Constitution in Comparative Perspective*, Centre for the Study of Democratic Governance, University of Illinois, no date. Accessed at www.comparativeconstitutions project.org.
8. See the following: http://icasualties.org/; http://antiwar.com/casual ties/; http://www.bbc.co.uk/news/world-middle-east-11107739.
9. http://antiwar.com/casualties/.
10. Arato, op. cit., p. viii.
11. The committee members had all lived in Iraq since 1914 and knew the country well.
12. Raad al-Jida, op. cit., pp. 23–24. The members of that committee were Dr. Munthir al-Shawi, professor of constitutional law and former minister of justice, Akram al-Douri, a jurist and former minister of justice also, professor Raad al-Jida and professor Salih Jawad al-Kadhum, booth specialists in constitutional law, dr. Riyadh al-Qaiysi and Dr. Akram al-Witri, head and deputy of the legal department in the Foreign Ministry and Judge Awni Fakhri deputy of the court of cassation.
13. Raad al-Jida, op. cit.
14. For the differences between the content and application of the constitutions, see Sabah al-Mukhtar, The Rule of Law in Iraq, in Eugene Cortan and Mai Yamani (eds.), *The Rule of Law in the Middle East and the Islamic World*, I.B. Tauris, 2000, pp. 76–80.
15. L. Paul Bremer and Malcolm McConnell, *My Year in Iraq: The Struggle to Build a Future of Hope*, Simon & Schuster, 2006.
16. Bremer and the US ambassador to Iraq told the GC end of November 2003 that it should present and approve a provisional law before 29 February 2004. It took the GC one month to form the committee for this

purpose, and the meetings were postponed for long times. See Atta Abdul Wahab, Sirat Amal Siyasi, al-mouasassa al-Arabia lil dirasat wa al-nashir, Amman, 2008, pp. 51–52.

17. The late Atta Abdul Wahab, then a rotating member for Adnan Pachachi, member of the GC, stated that he was asked by Adnan Pachachi, then the interim head of the GC, to draw a draft for a (provisional constitution). Abdul Wahab says that he endeavoured to do that, but when his draft was presented to the GC, Massoud Barzani presented another one. (It seems that Barzani's version was the one that was given to him by the CPA and his American advisors.) Abdul Wahab also said that because of the short time the GC was given to discuss the drafts, and because of the (fatigue) the GC members felt, due to the rush to meet the deadline stipulated by CPA, the draft of Barzani was approved sometimes without deep discussions. Atta Abdul Wahab, op. cit., pp. 49–52. It should also be added that only one or two members of the committee were qualified to discuss such an issue.

18. Article 7 states, 'Islam is the official religion of the State and is to be considered a source of legislation. No law that contradicts the universally agreed tenets of Islam, the principles of democracy, or the rights cited in Chapter Two of this Law may be enacted during the transitional period. This Law respects the Islamic identity of the majority of the Iraqi people and guarantees the full religious rights of all individuals to freedom of religious belief and practice.' Coalition Provisional Authority, *Law of Administration for the State of Iraq for the Transitional Period*, 8 March 2004, p. 3. Accessed at http://www.refworld.org/docid/45263d 612.html.

19. In fact the Kurdish language was acknowledged as the second language of Iraq since 1970 (The March Autonomy Agreement), and teaching of Kurdish was made obligatory all over Iraq, but following the collapse of the Kurdish revolt in 1975 lessened the application of this experiment.

20. This term was badly used, because these areas were not disputed ones, but there was no established way to prove who were the majority of the inhabitants.

21. This is a strikingly mixed region. The Kurdish national movement wishes to use the census of 1957 to determine Kirkuk's future. This census did not consider nationality (or race), but only determined the language of the inhabitants. Through this criterion the percentages of those who spoke Kurdish, Turkish and Arabic were given. The census showed that the percentage of the Kurdish speakers in Kirkuk City was 33.53%, while that of Turkish speakers was 37.62%, and Arabic speakers was 22.53%. In the whole Kirkuk Province the figures were 48.24, 21.44, and 28.19%, respectively. In 1970, according to the agreement which granted autonomy to the Kurdish region, the northern sub-districts of Kirkuk which had

a Kurdish majority were taken out of Kirkuk and attached to the Kurdish autonomous area, hence reducing the Kurdish percentage in the province.

22. Jonathan Morrow, *Iraq's Constitutional Process ll: An Opportunity Lost*. USIP, No. 155, November 2005.
23. Arato, op. cit., p. 140. See also Peter Galbraith, *The End of Iraq: How American Incompetence Created a War Without End*, Simon & Schuster, 2006, p. 139.
24. Ali Allawi, *The Occupation of Iraq*, Yale University Press, 2007, p. 222.
25. Arato, p. 140.
26. See for example Feldman, *What We Owe Iraq*; and Larry Diamond, *Squandered Victory*, Owel Books, 2005.
27. Feldman, p. 40.
28. Arato, p. 99.
29. Noah Feldman, born 1970, was in 2003 a lecturer at NYU. He Speaks Arabic and a specialist in constitutional law. In 2003 he was a lecturer at NYU, now at Harvard. He served as senior constitutional advisor to the Coalition Provisional Authority in Iraq, and subsequently advised members of the Iraqi Governing Council on the drafting of the Transitional Administrative Law or interim constitution. In 2004 he published his own book. (What We Owe Iraq: War and the Ethics of nation building), in which he outlined how the (new Iraq) should be built. On top of that he admitted that he was a consultant to the drafting committee, http://www.law.harvard.edu/faculty/nfeldman/bio graphy.php.

    See Feldman, *What We Owe Iraq*. Peter Galbraith was a US career diplomat who advised the Kurdish parties and later earned lucrative commissions for his role in oil deals. (See Michael Rubin, Norway exposes Peter Galbraith Scandal, *The Corner*, 10 October 2009.)
30. In his writings, especially his book The End Of Iraq, Peter Galbraith spoke about how he advised or more correctly encouraged the leaders of the Kurdish parties to state their exaggerated demand, especially in the field of sharing the wealth of the country and how to make the Kurdish regional authority have powers more than the central one. Later on he netted at least $100 million as commission from the Kurdish regional government following the signature of oil deals between the Kurdish Regional government and foreign oil companies. He also advised them to state in the constitution that if three provinces rejected any amendment it will fall, the Kurdish regional government controls three provinces, Dahouk, Erbil and Sulaimaniya. For details see Peter W. Galbraith, *End of Iraq*, Simon & Schuster, NY 2006, Chapter 8.
31. Larry Diamond, Larry Diamond, Squandered Victory, Macmillan 2005.
32. Edward Said, The Arab Condition, *al-Ahram Weekly*, 22 May 2003.
33. Morrow, pp. 3 and 8.

34. Dhia al-Shakarchi, https://m.ahewar.org/s.asp?aid=657514, https://m. ahewar.org/s.asp?aid=657375&r=0. The man admitted afterwards that he was obliged to leave the committee after five sessions only because he was forced by the head of the committee to write minutes contrary to what was discussed.
35. Dr. Mijbil Issa Ibrahim and Dhamin al-Obaidi.
36. Dr. Hasib al-Obaidi, a political scientist.
37. Morrow, pp. 9 and 12.
38. Arato, p. 142.
39. Dr. Mundher al-Shawi, member of this group, a constitutional law professor and a former minister of justice, was imprisoned and released later on the condition that he left Iraq and never again interfered in matters concerning the constitution. The group's members felt intimidated following Dr. al-Shawi's arrest and their work was stopped.
40. Massoud Barzani told Paul Bremer, Kirkuk is the Jerusalem of the Kurds (Quds al-Akrad), Bremer answered him that one Quds is enough we don't want another one.
41. Ali Allawi, p. 404.
42. For an account of the deep involvement of US officials in the process see Ashley S. Deeks and Matthew D. Burton, Iraq's Constitution: A drafting history, *Cornell International Law Journal*, Vol. 40, 2007. See also Morrow, pp. 9 and 14. Morrow describes the pressure exerted by the Secretary of the State, the Secretary of Defence and the President himself, and their refusal, together with the UK government, to extend the timetable.
43. The (Leadership Council) comprised the heads of the major Iraqi political coalitions who participated in the Constitutional Committee.
44. K.B. Yousef, *Did the US Intervention in the Iraqi Constitution Help Make It Illegal?* http://deafwalls.wordpress.com/2009/03/17/did-the-us-intervention-in-the-iraqi-constitution-help-make-it-illegal/.
45. Morrow, p. 3.
46. Charles Tripp, *A History of Iraq*, 3rd edition, Cambridge University Press, 2006, p. 301.
47. http://www.alwasatnews.com/1146/news/read/500479/1.html. The Independent High Electoral Commission-Iraq explained that Nineveh's vote was 55% against and thus did not constitute the 2/3 votes needed to reject the constitution. http://www.iraqiparty.com/news_item/567/. A similar finding was made about the result in Diyala province. See also, Morrow, p. 3.
48. See the declaration of the Sunni leader Salih al-Mutlak: http://almoslim. net/node/42080.
49. Interview with *al-Rashid*, Iraqi TV channel, 15 July 2012. Also Mahmoud al-Mashhadani, interview with al.-Sharqia TV channel, bil harf al-wahid, Tuesday, 09/04/2013.

50. The preamble of the US constitution read (We the people of the United States, in Order to form a more perfect Union, establish Justice, insure domestic Tranquility, provide for the common defense, promote the general Welfare, and secure the Blessings of Liberty to ourselves and our Posterity, do ordain and establish this Constitution for the United States of America).

51. For discussion of the considerable time and argument the committee spent on this issue see Deeks and Burton.

52. The Second Paragraph of Article 2 states, 'This Constitution guarantees the Islamic identity of the majority of the Iraqi people and guarantees the full religious rights of all individuals to freedom of religious belief and practice such as Christians, Yazidis, and Mandian Sabians'.

53. Such ceremonies endangered the lives of those who practice them, and this clause also meant that all state institutions would be paralysed for days while these ceremonies were being practised (as happens in Iraq today). Universities, schools and government institutions, even Iraqi embassies abroad, suspended their activities in order to observe the Husaini ceremonies.

54. This clause was strongly rejected by women organizations as it stipulated the cancellation of a very progressive personal status law which was issued in 1959 and its advanced amendments in later years.

55. Arato, op. cit., p. 87.

56. See Nouri Al-Maliki's complaints, al-Bawwaba, 23 October 2012, http://www.albawwaba.net/news/111971; and Yaniv Voller, *From Rebellion to de facto Statehood: International and Transnational Sources of the Transformation of the Kurdish National Liberation Movement in Iraq into the Kurdistan Regional Government.* Ph.D. thesis, LSE, 2012.

57. This percentage also caused big controversy. To start with the percentage was initially worked by the UN during the Oil for Food agreement when Iraq was under international sanctions in 1996. It was calculated according to the percentage of the Kurdish population in Iraq, and it was put accordingly at 11%. The first interim government of Ayad Allawi, raised this share to 17%, without justifying this decision. Later on Prime Minister Maliki, in order to win the support of the Kurdish parties for his quest for a second term following 2010 elections, bestowed on the government of the region other privileges which made the region's share jump to 25%. Even the southern provinces that produced most of the Iraqi oil production did not receive such privileges.

58. For details about this issue see; Sawsan I. al-Assaf and Saad N. Jawad, *Iraqi Woman; Between the Democracy of the Occupation and the American Principle of Humanitarian Intervention*; (Arabic), al-Jinan publications, 2012, pp. 119–120. See also the report, *Searching for Peace in Iraq*,

compiled by Sawsan I. al-Assaf, Ali Dahir Ali, and Kai F. Brand-Jacobsen, issued by NOVA Innovacio Social, 2012, pp. 90–91.

59. This issue should remind us of the (barbaric) behaviour of the UN inspectors in the 1990s, when they entered all Iraqi scientific colleges destroyed laboratory equipment and burned books and materials they said that they could help Iraqis to manufacture WMD.

60. Article 46, for example starts with the words *La yakoon*, whereas the correct legal term is *La yajoze*. For the weak legal composition of the constitution see Zuhair K. Abbod, A viewpoint of some of the Iraqi constitution articles (in Arabic), http://www.mokarabat.com/s833.htm, also Abdul Husain Shaaban, *The mines of the Iraqi constitution* (in Arabic), http://www.mokarabat.com/m763.htm.

61. Ali Allawi, p. 222.

62. Muamar al-Kubaisi, op. cit.

63. It was supposed to be article 140, but when five other article were added it became article no. 142.

64. For the full text of the constitution see *Iraqi Constitution*, Ministry of Interior, The Republic of Iraq, 2006, www.iraqinationality.gov.iq/attach/iraqi_constitution.pdf.

65. Arato, op. cit., p. 244.

66. Ali Allawi, op. cit., p. 401.

67. Jonathan Morrow, *Weak Viability: The Iraqi Federal State and the Constitutional Amendment Process*, USIP Special Report, July 2006, http://www.usip.org/files/resources/Morrow_SR168.pdf.

68. http://www.alquds.co.uk/data/2007/06/06-08/05m36.htm.   The committee was chaired by Shaikh Humam Hamoudi, the same person who led the constitutional committee in 2005.

69. http://www.ebaa.net/khaber/2007/06/09/khaber004.htm.

70. Ibid.

71. http://www.albawwaba.net/news/62374/.

72. See the full memorandum of the Kurdish coalition in: Sawsan I. Assaf and Saad N. Jawad, op. cit., pp. 326–328.

73. Saad Jawad and Sawsan al-Assaf, *Iraq Today, the Failure of Reshaping a State*, LSE IDEAS Blog, 4 June 2013. http://blogs.lse.ac.uk/ideas/2013/06/iraq-today-the-failure-of-re-shaping-a-state-on-sectarian-and-quota-lines/.

74. Such as the visit made by the Jordanian and Turkish foreign ministers in September 2011 and August 2012, respectively.

75. Larry Diamond, Consensus and Iraq's Constitution, *Los Angeles Times*, 15 October 2005.

76. Arato explains how deadlines passed without the completion of the draft and how deliberations continued even while the constitution was voted on. Arato, pp. 240–242.

77. Seeing that the Kurdish Regional Government holds most of the advantages over Baghdad, (as against the failure of the central government to do anything constructive), other southern and western regions are already demanding a status similar to the Kurds. At least five provinces are asking to be federal entities: Basra, Missan, Nineveh, Anbar, Salah al-Din. The first three have large oil and gas reserves, yet they have not been granted the same privilege as the KRG to collect revenue, although they are encouraged by the loose conditions anticipated in the Constitution. The related articles stipulate that one third of the members of any council of a province could submit a demand for a federal status before going to a referendum.
78. Jonathan Morrow, op. cit., p. 21, accurately remarks that the deficiencies in the constitutional process are having an immediate and violent effect on the lives of the Iraqis.
79. *Al-Mada* newspaper, (Baghdad), 3 September 2011.
80. For example in October 2012, according to *Al-Sharq al-Awsat* newspaper, quoted by the *Iraq Electronic Journal*, (Amman) no. (308), 30 October 2012.
81. See note 49 above.

CHAPTER 5

The Kurdish Dilemma in Iraq: A History of Lost Opportunities

The Kurdish problem has been, and remains, the biggest challenge facing Iraq and threatens its existence as a state and unified entity. All Iraqi regimes have tried to find solutions to this problem but have failed. However, they are not the only side to blame. Different Kurdish leaderships shared this failure.

In fact the persistence of the Kurdish problem in Iraq has puzzled many observers. They could not explain why such a problem always erupts in a country that, since its inception as a modern state in 1921, has recognized the distinctive Kurdish identity and the cultural, rights of the Kurdish people. On the other hand, the Kurds living in the other parts of Greater Kurdistan (Turkey, Iran and Syria) are not recognized as a nation and are even denied the right to maintain their own identity. At no point in time did any Iraqi constitution or regime deny the existence of this people or deprived them of their political rights as equal citizens with their fellow Iraqis. Also, the Kurds' cultural rights, such as speaking their own language, wearing their national costumes and listening to their own music, were always respected.

On the political and social levels, the majority of Arab and Kurdish nationals participated in all political and social activities as one Iraqi people. The Kurds were always members of, and sometimes held leadership positions, in most of the country's opposition political parties and organizations, state institutions and ruling political parties; they have

S. N. Jawad, *Iraq after the Invasion*, Middle East Today, https://doi.org/10.1007/978-3-030-72106-0_5

served as senior officials in the government under both the monarchy and the republic. Indeed there were governments that limited the Kurds' political activities, especially if they were regarded as oppositions to the central authority, but no law or constitutional provisions were promulgated to deny their existence or take their rights away. Following the 1958 revolution, all Iraqi constitutions stated the fact that the Kurds were partners with the Arabs and other minorities in the Iraqi homeland. Even if these constitutions were not always respected, the principle remained. On the other hand, the Kurds demonstrated their desire to be part of the State of Iraq since the beginning of national rule (1920) despite attempts by Britain, the mandated power at the time,[1] and Turkey to incite them to the contrary,[2] each for its own interest. Under the monarchical regime, Iraq witnessed some tribal rebellions but because Britain, the major influential power in Iraq was in alliance with that regime at that time, British forces usually assisted or participated in quashing these rebellions.

The so-called Kurdish revolt which erupted in 1961 was in reality a mere protest or an outcry by feudal landlords against the implementation of the Agrarian Reform Law (issued in 1958) in their areas. Unfortunately, the government dealt with it in the wrong way. In the end, it was exploited by Mulla Mustaf al-Barzani and the KDP turning these tribal rebellions into national revolt. Ironically, the Kurdish revolt was staged against the regime of the late General Abdul Karim Qasim, who legalized, for the first time in the history of Iraqi Kurds, political parties (the Kurdistan Democratic Party), professional unions and newspapers. Qasim also allowed the then deported and displaced Kurds, headed by Mulla Mustafa Barzani, to return to Iraq and to their mountainous homes. Yet General Qasim let a golden opportunity to isolate the tribal, feudal Kurdish elements slip out of his hands when he failed to differentiate between those who resorted to arms to defy the government and to the implementation of progressive laws and those who were leading peaceful political activities. It was an irony that the feudal landlord managed to instigate the peasants, whose interest was the agrarian reform that was made, to carry arms to defend the interests of their feudal masters. At the beginning of the armed revolt, the KDP issued a statement denouncing it as tribal feudalist movements and declared its full support for the republican regime. Qasim, unfortunately, considered the party to be an accomplice to the rebellion. He dissolved the party and issued an order to arrest its secretary-general. In other words, he dealt with the party that was very influential among the educated and urban, which was one of the first organizations to support the republican regime, the same way he did the tribal feudal elements who staged a rebellion depending on the support of Iran. Failing to convince Qasim that they were against the rebellion, and noticing that the police and security institutions were hunting the leaders of the party and its cadres, the party's politburo decided to join and adopt the tribal rebellion, giving it some nationalist-political slogans that expanded it. It was said at that time that even Mulla Mustafa was waiting for Qasim to seek his assistance to crush the tribal feudalist rebellion, as he did in 1959 with a similar rebellion (Lolan rebellion instigated by the Shah of Iran in an attempt to destabilize the new republican regime). But Qasim did not do that, instead he accused Mulla Mustafa of being the one who was leading the new rebellion, and sent the Iraqi air force to bomb Barzan, Mulla Mustafa's home village.[3] The rebellion, which was turned into a political, national and cultural revolt, also left the door wide open to increased foreign and external intervention.

All the solutions suggested to deal with the Kurdish problem have failed. The solutions put forward by successive governments were divided into two types, the first one, which was used more frequently, was the military one. This solution not only failed but also resulted in bloodshed and destruction. It also did more harm by widening the gap between the Arab and Kurdish communities. There were many reasons that caused this failure; paramount among them were foreign intervention, disorganization and poor management of the Iraqi armed forces and the political instability that overwhelmed Iraq since 1958.

The second type (paradigm) took the form of peaceful solutions that were put forward every now and then, mainly when a major military campaign failed. This solution failed for several reasons, including the lack of mutual trust and confidence between the two sides, the government and the leaders of the Kurdish parties. It also failed because both sides were addressing the problem with the logic of weakness and strength. When each side, felt weak or needed time to strengthen its position, gave concessions and reconciled, only to find that the other side had hardened its position and increased its demands, and vice versa.

In general, the central authority since the beginning of national rule in the 1920s to this day cannot accommodate or accept the idea of a decentralized authority in Iraqi Kurdistan, while the Kurdish parties, especially the main ones, the Kurdistan Democratic Party (KDP) led by the late Mulla Mustafa Barzani (and his son Massoud after him), the PUK led by the late Jalal Talabani (followed by his wife and son Haval) and the Gorran movement (Change Party, formed by the late Nawshirwan Mustafa, and now led by Omar Said Ali), were all not prepared to accept any authority in Iraqi Kurdistan other than one that absolutely guaranteed their complete domination. One could also add the penetrating foreign and external influences, especially on the Kurdish political parties. Unfortunately, these parties always believed, and still do, that only by relying on external support can they achieve what they wanted, regardless of their past and bitter experience in this field. Throughout their history, they were promised external assistance and support by foreign powers, only to be abandoned and left alone to face a gruesome destiny (as was the case with Britain, then the Soviet Union, Iran, Turkey, the United States and Israel). Sadly, to this day, the Kurdish leadership is still ready to give all kinds of concessions to foreign parties and are not willing to reconcile with Iraqi governments. Perhaps the best example for this attitude is what the late Mulla Mustafa told the late Shah of Iran in March 1975 when the latter informed him that he was going to stop any support to the Kurdish armed revolt and movement, a decision that led to the collapse of the Kurdish revolt. Mulla Mustafa's reply was 'We are your people and as long as you are satisfied with the Algiers agreement, and believe that it is in the interest of Iran our motherland, we have no objection to it, we are at your disposal if you tell us to die we die or to live we live. We have been sincere to you and will continue to be so in the future'.[4] On its part, central governments have often been unwilling to speak to the Kurdish people directly, or treat them as politically equal, or try to propitiate them alongside the state.[5] Examples of what has been said above abound.

The purpose of this paper is not to discuss the evolution of the Kurdish issue or dilemma in Iraq; rather, it is to highlight the missed opportunities to find a lasting peaceful solution. The paper will also clarify how those heading Iraq and the Kurdish national movement, as well as external powers, have manipulated and exploited the issue for their own interest, only to keep Iraq weak and divided.

First: The Historic March Manifesto 1970

The 11 March Manifesto (agreement), which approved for the first time in Iraq, and the Arab world, the principle of autonomy, remains the most important and historic shift in dealing with the Kurdish issue in Iraq. Whether one disagreed or agreed with the policy of the Arab Baath Socialist Party in Iraq, the fact remains that this party should take the credit for daring to initiate and approve the principle of autonomy for Iraqi Kurdistan, which was until then, looked at in the Arab way of thinking as a taboo and as a step to separating or dividing the country. There were other parties, such as the Iraqi Communist Party, that while out of power spoke about this principle, but such a decision that is taken and implemented by a governing party was something bold and unprecedented. This is based on many facts, perhaps the most important one is that this principle was totally rejected by the Iraqi layman, the Arab world and the different Iraqi regimes. It was even regarded by some as creating 'another Israel' inside Iraq.

On the Kurdish side, although the intellectual wing of the Kurdish movement in Iraq had since the beginning of the 1950s put forward the slogan 'the voluntary unity between the Kurdish and Arab peoples in Iraq', and followed up in 1962 by the slogan 'democracy for Iraq and autonomy for Iraqi Kurdistan' as the main objective of the Kurdish armed movement, but all signs indicated that the Kurdish leadership, with its intellectual and tribal segments, did not really endeavour to achieve these goals. For example, the Kurdish parties have never cooperated with the other parts of the Iraqi national movement, parties and personalities to achieve democracy in Iraq. There is also much historical evidence indicating the readiness of the various Kurdish leaders to align and cooperate with dictatorial, military and repressive regimes in Iraq once these regimes agreed to respond positively to the demands that strengthened the hegemony of these leaders in the Kurdish region. Also, on several occasions, the Kurdish leaders abandoned the Iraqi national movement and cooperated with the totalitarian Iraqi regimes to obtain immediate benefits.[6] It was also noted that the majority of Kurdish cadres, especially the educated and intellectual ones, who were members of the larger Iraqi popular parties, were quick to withdraw from these parties and go to the exclusive and narrow Kurdish national parties.

As for the goal of autonomy, there is ample evidence that the Kurdish parties, especially the KDP, had no clear idea of this goal and were only using it to embarrass successive governments. Perhaps what happened in 1969, when the Baath leadership was trying to reach a peaceful agreement with the leadership of Mulla Mustafa, proves this point. After positive indications from the Baath Party government since it returned to power for the second time in July 1968, a delegation representing Mulla Mustafa came to Baghdad to negotiate with the Iraqi government. They met with former president Saddam Hussein (vice president at the time), who asked the Kurdish delegation to put forward their demands. The head of the delegation began to count the KDP requirements as follows:

- To release the Kurdish prisoners, to reinstate the Kurdish official employees who were fired from their jobs because of their support for the KDP.
- To compensate those who suffered because of the war in Kurdish areas.

But most important of all was the demand that the government should abandon cooperation with the Kurdish parties or elements that were hostile to the leadership of Mulla Mustafa Barzani, remove their representatives from the government and replace them with candidates nominated by Mulla Mustafa himself. Saddam Hussein's response was that these issues were secondary and did not constitute a permanent or long-term solution to the problem. He added that what the Iraqi leadership wanted was a solution based on autonomy. This suggestion confused and perplexed the Kurdish delegation and they could not discuss it, the only thing they managed to say was to ask to return to Iraqi Kurdistan to consult with their leaders.[7] It was then said that Mulla Mustafa sent a high-level envoy to the Shah of Iran to consult with him—or to take his approval. Some said Mulla Mustafa went himself.[8] The Shah's response was that the Baathists were lying and that the best way to catch them in their lies was to accept the offer and watch them go back on it.

However, the Baath leadership did not renege, they went on to declare autonomy in March 1970 as the basis for the solution, which was to be ultimately fulfilled in four years. In March 1974, when the time came to implement the autonomy plan proposed by the government, the KDP rejected it, even though the Iraqi leadership had published the law a year before it was to commence, they handed a copy to the KDP and asked national figures, political parties, legal experts and academics to discuss it. Several public hearings and discussions were conducted over the plan and were broadcasted in the media, but the Kurdish leadership rejected it. Instead, the KDP submitted another plan that was, in turn, rejected by the Iraqi government. The KDP was told the only alternative available to it is by discussing and giving its opinion, suggestions or amendments to the government's proposals. As the negotiations between the government and the KDP reached a deadlock, the Kurdish leadership asked the government to delay the date of commencement of the autonomy plan, which was 11 March 1974. This idea was refused by the government on the pretext that it did not want to be considered or looked at by the Kurdish people as an authority that did not honour their promise! The government again asked the KDP to reconsider its proposition carefully and give an answer. The KDP not only rejected this ultimatum but also declared that it was completely severing its relationship with the central government. It withdrew its ministers from the cabinet and further escalated by asking all Kurdish employees and prominent figures in Baghdad and other Iraqi cities to leave their jobs and join the 'Kurdish revolution'. It is interesting to note that the Iraqi authorities did not prevent any Kurd from travelling towards Iraqi Kurdistan.[9] In the midst of all this, no official statement came from the Kurdish side that spoke about the shortcomings of the plan or the desire of the Kurdish side to preserve autonomy. Of course, the official plan showed a clear government endeavour to ultimately and totally control the Kurdish region. However, the KDP then was not powerless or unable to hinder or force amendments for such a plan. The Party felt that it had the means and power (big and heavily armed Peshmerga, as well as regional and international support) to exert pressure on the government to amend the suggested plan. Unfortunately, on its part, the government felt that it had enough power to impose its plan, which envisaged the creation of an autonomous region that includes the three all-Kurdish provinces of Erbil, Sulaimaniya and Dahuk only, with clear central authority domination. As intransigence from both sides spiralled, the KDP deployed its armed Peshmerga fighters to control strategic populated cities and towns in Iraqi Kurdistan. At that time, the government's only response was to issue a warning to the KDP that it should avoid escalating and instigating actions. It also gave the Kurdish leaders an ultimatum of two weeks to 'return to the united national path' and accept the announced autonomy plan for the Kurdish provinces, which was promulgated on 11 March 1974. At the end of the ultimatum (April 1974), the well-armed and well-drilled Iraqi military units moved into the areas controlled by the Peshmerga. During the remaining months of that year, the Iraqi army managed to regain control of areas that were left by the Iraqi government since 1962.

Foreseeing the defeat of the elements he was using to exert pressure on the Iraqi government, the then Shah of Iran decided to get involved directly in the fighting by using his sophisticated military arsenal in supporting the Peshmerga (this was added to the logistical and armament support from Israel and the United States).[10] All these elements intervened to prevent the Iraqi armed forces from completing their mission of defeating the Peshmerga and crushing the Kurdish revolt. The war, which the Iraqi government expected to finish before the end of the summer of that year protracted, as it became a direct confrontation between the Iraqi army on the one hand and a big number of Iranian units as well as big Israeli teams of consultants on the other.

Having in mind the experience of 1963, when the protracted war in Iraqi Kurdistan played into the hands of the Iraqi army to topple the Baath party after its first short tenure in office, the Baathist leadership decided not to let their party face a similar fate.

In order for the Baathist regime to soon end this problem, the government decided to come to terms with the Shah of Iran to stop his support for the KDP. After some secret negotiations, brokered by President Houari Boumediene of Algeria, Iraq and Iran signed the Algiers Agreement (March 5, 1975). According to this Agreement (Treaty), Iraq conceded to the long Iranian demand to share the Shatt al-Arab waterway in the south as a price for Iran to stop its support of the Kurdish movement.

Most of the Kurdish leaders always find that it is more expedient to cooperate with foreign and external elements to keep successive Iraqi governments at bay than to show any sign of coming to terms with the government, it was now the turn of the Baathist leaders to resort to the same tactic by making concessions to foreign powers (Iran) even if that meant sacrificing half of Iraq's only waterway to the Gulf, Shatt al-Arab. It saw this as a better alternative, one that would guarantee quicker results, than giving concessions to Iraqi Kurdish parties. Immediately after the signing of the Algiers Agreement between the two countries, Iran withdrew all its military units and armaments from Iraqi Kurdistan and stopped its support to Mulla Mustafa Barzani and his Peshmerga. Within a few days, the Kurdish armed movement totally collapsed. Neither the USA nor Israel were able to do anything to save Mulla Mustafa, as the Shah told them that he was not ready to jeopardize his agreement with Baghdad by allowing any support to go through Iran. Funny enough, only at that stage did the Kurdish leadership send an urgent appeal to the Iraqi government, seeking dialogue and accepting the autonomy law introduced by the government the previous year. Some KDP politburo members even defected to the central government, blaming Mulla Mustafa Barzani for all the intransigence of the past and for following the orders of the Shah and Israel. In fact, this group of defectors joined another smaller number that defected at the beginning of the confrontation in March 1974. Barzani, his family, the rest of the KDP leadership and a small number of the Peshmergas sought refuge in Iran. They were disarmed by the authorities there and settled in camps on the condition that they would never be active politically. Later on, the Barzani family took refuge in the USA and the UK. In 1979 Barzani died in Iran, and the leadership of the KDP went to his two sons Idris and Massoud. Following the death of Idris in 1982, Massoud remained the sole leader of the party.

Following the collapse of the Kurdish revolt, it was the turn of the Iraqi government to misconceive the situation. Although, it has not backed away from the principle of autonomy, in its celebration of a victory the government missed a historic opportunity to establish peace on a permanent and solid basis. Seeing the total collapse of the Kurdish revolt and the huge number of Kurdish fighters surrendering and handing over their weapons en mass, instead of pursuing a policy of forgive and forget, or no victor no vanquished, it resorted to the policies of punishment, deportation and exiling Kurdish activists and their families to the southern provinces of the country. Another opportunity was lost, as similar ones would be lost later.

What has been said above is for the purpose of clarifying the fact that almost all parties (internal or external elements), including Arabs and Kurds, that dealt with the Kurdish dilemma were not often serious or sincere about finding a lasting solution to it. Neither were they interested in the wellbeing of the people, be it Arabs or Kurds. Successive governments have been talking about a peaceful solution but in the sense of total dominance of the central authority. The Kurdish parties and their leaders have been talking about their desire to achieve Kurdish national rights, but in reality, their intentions were to guarantee their full and unchallenged domination over the region, to keep it away from any central authority, while putting the interests of foreign and external elements over those of the Iraqi people, Kurds and Arabs. More importantly, was the mistake made by the Iraqi government then of never thinking of starting a dialogue or making any overture towards the Kurdish elements that sought refuge in Iran to win them over. Neither did it try to bring them back to their country to prevent Iran or any other power hostile to Iraq from using them again, something that will happen later on.

Second: The Iraq-Iran War and the Revival of Armed Kurdish Activities

The Islamic revolution in Iran (1979), soon followed by the Iraq-Iran War (1980–1988), were the two events that represented a golden opportunity for the Kurdish parties taking refuge in Iran. Taking advantage of the military, financial and political support provided by the new Iranian Islamic regime, the two main Iraqi Kurdish parties, the KDP headed by Massoud Barzani, son of Mulla Mustafa Barzani, who assumed the party's leadership following the death of his father in 1979, and the Patriotic Union of Kurdistan (PUK), which was founded and headed by Jalal Talabani, as opposed to the KDP, were soon to renew their activities inside Iraqi Kurdistan. The two parties harnessed the services of their fighters (whose numbers began to escalate after it had fallen significantly and reached a few hundred following the collapse of 1975) to fight alongside the Iranian forces and against the Iraqi army, especially in the battles that took place around Iraqi Kurdistan. Despite the fact that the actions of the two Kurdish parties had hurt the feelings of the Iraqis in general, and the Kurds in particular, because they saw in them a collaboration with the state that abandoned them five years ago, the then Iraqi government accepted to open the door for negotiations with the hope of reaching an agreement and understanding with any Kurdish faction that wished to do so. Of course, this was done not because the government was willing to reach an understanding but because the Iraqi forces were facing a difficult time during the war and the Kurdish fighters were hurting the Iraqi troops in the north of Iraq. It was mostly Jalal Talabani who tried to take advantage of the weak position of the Iraqi government. He accepted an invitation from the head of the Iraqi intelligence service, Barzan al-Tikriti, half-brother of late President Saddam Hussein, and secretly came to Baghdad in 1983 holding direct negotiations with the Iraqi government.[11] Then he made these visits public, by giving an interview to a Lebanese magazine (considered to be the mouthpiece of the Baath Party), stressing that the talks were moving well towards an understanding between the two parties. In the article, he went as far as declaring that Saddam Hussein was the arbitrator (moderator) and not the enemy or opponent.[12] But one year later, when Talabani thought the Iraqi forces could be defeated in that war, he changed his approach, left the negotiations and sided again with Iran. (Talabani may have felt relieved to do so at the time. His behaviour could be considered as a belated response, rather revenge, to a similar behaviour of the Baathist Iraqi leadership towards him in 1970, when the Baath government sold him down the river in favour of Mulla Mustafa in order to sign with the latter the March Agreement, despite Talabani's unlimited cooperation with the Baath regime when it came to power in 1968.) Talabani also revealed later on that, during the discussions that took place inside the leadership of the PUK, it was agreed that the Party should accept the initiative extended to it by the then Iraqi government not to reach a lasting agreement but to get monetary and armed assistance from the government, as such assistance had been stopped by the Iranian government.[13] In other words, the PUK was not at all serious about solving the Kurdish dilemma, while the Iraqi government was only interested in decreasing the pressure it came under during the war.

It should be noted that since mid-1982, there were some indications that the Iraqi regime was weakening and on the verge of collapsing. The Iraqi army had significant military setbacks; it had to withdraw from the lands it occupied initially inside Iran and was generally on the defensive facing massive, intense and repeated attacks by Iranian forces trying to invade Iraqi territory. These attacks were carried out with the strong support of Arab governments like Syria and Libya, as well as the Kurdish armed militias of Talabani and Barzani. The two sides also managed to establish bases in remote areas of Iraqi Kurdistan. They added to their military activities some political ones like establishing coalitions (fronts) with other Iraqi parties opposing Baath rule, such as the Iraqi Communist Party, a splinter faction of the Baath Party loyal to the Syrian Baath party, and some nationalist and Islamist parties. Still, some Iraqi communist and Arab nationalist leaders rejected the decision of their parties to align with Iran against their country. Some of them even split or abandoned their parties over the issue, but this did not affect the approach, which continued until the end of the war. Eventually, the war ended with a clear Iraqi victory in mid-1988, when the Iranian leadership at the time was obliged to 'gulp a cup of poison', in the words of Mr. Khomeini when he accepted the ceasefire.

Instead of investing this victory to take a courageous decision to open a new page (fresh start) with the Iraqi opposition, especially the Kurdish parties, the Iraqi leadership, unfortunately, kept on branding them as traitors and stooges, barred them from coming back to Iraq and left them on the other side of the borders waiting for future opportunities to fight the Iraqi army. This idea of leaving opposing parties, factions or personalities abroad and ready to be exploited by powers hostile to Iraq was, and still is, an eternal problem in Iraqi politics.

Third: The Experience of Kurdish Rule Away from the Central Authority Since 1991

The erroneous or catastrophic decision to invade Kuwait (August 1990), followed by the insistence on not withdrawing from it despite all the efforts exerted by countries, organizations and international figures to spare Iraq a destructive war, led the United States and Britain, with urging from Israel, to form an international coalition to oust Iraq by force. This move, was endorsed by the UN, culminated in a devastating war waged on Iraq (January 1991), which ended not only with the ousting of the Iraqi armed forces from Kuwait but also the destruction of Iraq's military forces and infrastructure. It is no secret that the main objective of this campaign was to destroy the huge military power Iraq enjoyed after the war with Iran. The Iraqi defeat was an opportunity not to be missed for Iran. Immediately, it sent its troops, together with the Iraqi militias that it was sheltering, into Iraqi cities bordering Iran from north to south. The Barzani and Talabani parties did not hesitate to invest this golden opportunity to storm villages, towns and even some large Kurdish cities such as Sulaimaniya and some of Erbil's outskirts, believing that the Baathist regime was over. But this belief proved to be erroneous and premature. With its remaining military power, the regime in Baghdad managed to regain control of all Iraqi cities, including the Kurdish ones. The militias of the two main Kurdish parties once again turned to guerrilla warfare against Iraqi military forces.

On 8 April 1991, the European Union issued a resolution imposing a no-fly zone in northern Iraq to protect the Kurds. On April 10, the United States issued a resolution banning military operations in the no-fly zone. It seemed at that time that President Saddam Hussein had concluded that these decisions were to be used as an excuse to destroy the remaining Iraqi military capabilities through a war of attrition. Thus, he decided to withdraw Iraqi military forces, as well as government civil administration, from the three Kurdish provinces of Sulaimaniya, Erbil and Dahuk, leaving them to the two rival Kurdish parties, the KDP and the PUK. As a result of the influence of the two parties in the Kurdish provinces, the KDP dominated Erbil and Dahuk, while the PUK controlled Sulaimaniya.

Despite the withdrawal of the government administration in the summer of 1991, the central authority showed readiness for a dialogue with the two Kurdish parties based on the initiatives and mediation of

Iraqi Kurdish figures. As a result of these mediations, and to take advantage of the weak position of the Iraqi regime, Massoud Barzani and Jalal Talabani alternated in visiting Baghdad to discuss with the Iraqi government ways to modify the autonomy plan proposed in 1974, into 'a real and expanded autonomy', in the words of the Kurdish leaders. It was said that the negotiations went well, so in August 1991 the two parties were supposed to sign a final agreement to amend the Autonomy Law of 1974 but they declined at the last minute and refused to sign. Massoud Barzani, who headed the last delegation that month, was reported to have said, that it was excellent and represented the ambitions of the two parties and the Iraqi Kurds after going through the final version of the new agreement. However, Barzani added that, as a matter of courtesy, he should present the new agreement to Talabani so that they would come together to sign the final agreement.[14] Then he left and never returned. Instead of coming to Baghdad to finalize the agreement, the heads of the two Kurdish parties went to Turkey and then summoned to Washington. They were told by the United States that they should not sign any agreement with Baghdad because this would represent a lifeline for a regime the United States still wanted to topple through sanctions, blockade, and international, regional and internal isolation. So the Peshmerga of the two parties took advantage of the US support, taking control of many areas in Iraqi Kurdistan in a clear show of defiance to the Iraqi government.[15]

For their part, the leaders of the Kurdish parties tried to justify their withdrawal from the dialogue by saying there were two main points that had not been satisfactorily resolved. The first was the problem of annexing Kirkuk to the autonomous region, and the second was that they wanted the agreement or solution to be based on federalism rather than autonomy.[16] The Iraqi government, however, denied this, insisting that the agreement was complete and approved by the two Kurdish parties; it attributed the parties' refusal to sign it to the role of external elements, especially the orders issued by the US administration. Ironically, the United States did nothing to stop the series of internal fighting between the two Kurdish parties since 1992.[17] In 1996, the Patriotic Union of Kurdistan (PUK), backed by Iran, succeeded in invading the areas of the Kurdistan Democratic Party (KDP), especially the city of Erbil. These intensive and bloody internal fighting caused the death of thousands of innocent civilians and militia fighters from both sides. As a result of successive debacles, Barzani was compelled to appeal to the central authority and to President Saddam Hussein personally to save him and his party from a tragic fate. Accordingly, units of the Iraqi armed forces stormed Dahuk and Erbil in August 1996, expelled the (PUK) fighters and pursued them until they were driven out of their main stronghold in Sulaimaniya into Iran. The Iraqi forces then withdrew again from Iraqi Kurdistan, handing over all the Kurdish provinces to Barzani's party (KDP). However, a while later, Talabani (PUK) fighters managed to gain control of Sulaimaniya, only to bring the situation back to what it was before the fighting, the (PUK) in total control of Sulaimaniya, with the (KDP) controlling Erbil and Dahuk. Accordingly, each party formed its own administration, a situation that is still going on now. (It seems that the Iraqi government at that time was satisfied with that situation, which did not allow any party side to have supremacy or total control of the region, fearing that this could lead the party that achieves this to harden its position towards the central government. It wanted them both weak and divided.) On their part, the two Kurdish parties continued to demonstrate the depth of their mutual animosity and the impossibility of reaching an understanding or any sort of unity for the benefit of the Kurdish people, which they claimed to stand for. This fact raised the question: if the two parties were unable to unite or, at least, reach some sort of understanding under such difficult circumstances in their region, why were they fully coordinating abroad under foreign patronage? In other words, why did the differences between them not take centre stage in the meetings of the so-called Iraqi opposition abroad under the auspices of the USA, UK and Israel while there was no coordination between them in Iraqi Kurdistan? This question will be raised again and more after the occupation and under the federal solution. Indeed, this could only be answered or attributed to the external influence that external influence could exert on the two parties, while the interests of the Kurdish people, in general, meant little to these politicians.

While the two Kurdish parties have withdrawn from negotiations with the Iraqi government, their leaders and other Kurdish individuals living abroad actively joined the so-called 'Iraqi opposition' abroad. Sensing the weak position and disorganization of this opposition, as well as its need for a 'safe shelter inside Iraqi Kurdistan', and with the backing of the foreign sponsors, the two Kurdish parties exerted unlimited influence on the leaders of this opposition to accept the idea of federalism as a solution for the Kurdish dilemma. Although, it was obvious that such a matter was not in the hand of the opposition figures and was, in fact, beyond their ability to approve, the Kurdish parties insisted on including this matter in all the minutes of the meetings that took place at that time, only to raise it after the occupation as an obligatory agreement that should be respected and implemented.

Ironically, during that time, and despite the fact that the two Kurdish parties refused to sign an agreement with the central government, the relations between the Iraqi Baathist government and the leadership of the two Kurdish parties remained somewhat cordial; the two parties continued to send positive signals to the Iraqi central government, especially the Barzani wing, at the same time their coordination with the US-led international coalition set to topple the Iraqi regime of Saddam Husain, and with Iran, was continuing at very high levels.

When the oil-for-food formula (scheme) was approved by the United Nations in April 1995 (accepted by Iraq only in May 1996), Kurdish provinces were allocated 11% of Iraq's revenue of oil exports to be handed by the two Kurdish parties directly. Because of this financial independence, US protection and the financial difficulties that Baghdad was suffering from (because of the economic and inhumane sanctions imposed on the country and the heavy debts caused by the Iraq-Iran war),[18] the influence of the central authority in the Kurdish provinces was further weakened. However, this did not prevent the families and leading figures of the ruling Arab and Kurdish parties from cooperating commercially to benefit from the oil-for-food plan, which allowed them to accumulate considerable financial profits. In other words, political differences between the two sides did not prevent them from conducting business-like mutual cooperation or exchanging secret visits for monetary gains. In the meantime, the relations sometimes took the form of exchanged and continued consultations between the regime and the Kurdish parties, especially with the leader of the KDP Massoud Barzani. In fact, these cordial relations and the continued consultations between the regime and the KDP were what made some circles in the occupying coalition think that the then hiding president Saddam Hussein was sheltered by Barzani in Iraqi Kurdistan after the fall of Baghdad. (One of the leaders collaborating with the occupation told the writer this personally.) Also, it was reported that the last head of Saddam Hussein's intelligence service (Mukhabarat) was sent by the former Iraqi president to meet with Massoud Barzani before the occupation of Baghdad to coordinate with him on some issues. Barzani also made several statements before the occupation denouncing the planned attack on Iraq at the same time his coordination with the coalition forces was at its highest level.

The KDP decision to maintain dual relations, with the Iraqi regime and with external powers planning to topple it, can be explained as part of the pure Machiavellian policy the Kurdish parties have been pursuing in order to obtain the highest number of gains, (Kurdish party leaders refused to describe this policy as opportunism, they rather said it was the result of so many experiences in which they were betrayed which made them no longer trust any party!!) Of course, this is not true because they mostly gave precedence to their external relations over their relation with the different Iraqi central governments. Thus, the relations of the Kurdistan Democratic Party with the central authority in Baghdad at that time can be looked at or described as a safety valve to ensure the regime's support in case its rival, the Patriotic Union of Kurdistan, dared to attack its territories again with Iranian support. As for the party's American, Western and Israeli relations, it could be described as a desire to ensure that it would not be deprived of the advantages of the expected regime change.

Indeed the late PUK leader Jalal Talabani was thinking in the same manner, after realizing that his attempt to control all Kurdish provinces by defeating and expelling the Barzani (KDP) party from Iraqi Kurdistan had failed, due to the role played by the regime in Baghdad; he tried to approach Baghdad hoping to win it to his side. But it seemed that the Iraqi leadership at the time had completely lost faith in him. However, Talabani continued to try resorting to all sorts of stratagems which can only be described as opportunist, ludicrous, wily and above all manifesting an unveiled agenda. This was clear in the letter he sent to the Iraqi government on July 10, 1998. Talabani sent the letter to the Vice-President of the Revolutionary Command Council, Izzat Ibrahim al-Douri, the second man in the political echelon at the time. The content of the letter showed the crocked way Talabani was using to re-establish his party's relation with the then Baath regime, a style that was not unfamiliar or new to Talbani's behaviour. He started the letter by describing how proud he was of the intimacy and brotherly relationship he had with al-Douri, and how he treasured this relationship. What was strange rather, was the reason he mentioned that obliged him to send this friendly personal message, which he hoped that the Iraqi leadership will give it the deserved attention and scrutiny. Talabani claimed that what attracted his attention and roused his worries was the situation that resulted from the Turkish-Israeli alliance which he described as strategically dangerous and would harmfully target the region for the next century. Consequently, he hoped that he would find a way that will address this threat to withstand and defend the region in order to thwart and defeat this hostile design through common struggle. Then he said that the first reason that made him write this letter was that (this alliance is made up of two main parties, Turkey, which posses the keys to water resources in its hands and the other, Israel, which holds the atomic bomb in its hands and posses broad, manifold and advanced (Octopus) relations with America, Europe and in other countries). Then he added 'I regret to say that a Kurdish party, which is an ally of yours [the Iraqi government] and enjoys your financial, media, military assistance, namely al-Barzani, is a caudal and subordinate partner to this alliance'. He added that he was sorry to see the Arab leaders being indifferent and paying no due attention to the dangers of Zionism, and how he (the Iraqi Kurd) has written and warned about this Turkish-Israeli danger, which he called the greatest and premier danger. He concluded that this danger would affect the 'Arab, Kurdish and Iranian', nations, who should overcome their contradictions and differences to form an alliance to confront it. Then he turned to talking about the method that should be used, in his opinion, to face this danger, which revealed the real reason behind sending the letter. He called on the Iraqi government to start a serious dialogue with his party only (not to solve the Kurdish problem, but to confront this danger). As for why he chose 'Al-Douri' in person, Talabani wrote because he considers him [al-Douri] a Muslim brother, he then added: as a trustworthy Muslim I ask you to answer frankly the following questions:

- Do you now want a serious dialogue to solve the Kurdish issue?
- Or you simply want a dialogue to normalize the situation in Iraqi Kurdistan and the relations between the two sides?
- Do you want a dialogue to discuss the pending issues between us?

Talabani then ended his letter with very cordial words, describing his fairly long letter as a heart to heart conversation with a dear brother. Finally, he said 'I hopes that wisdom will prevail (triumphs) over intransigence, brotherhood over hostility and the original [authentic] Iraqi feelings over chauvinism and sectarianism'. Then he told al-Douri that he (would be grateful if you would kindly extend my warm regards and my highest respect to Mr. President [Saddam Hussein] and the other comrades in the Baath leadership) (A copy of the original letter with Talbani's hand writing is with the author). Indeed this letter was not expected to fool the Iraqi Baath leadership for the following reasons: First, they were well aware of Talabani's pervasive tactics, second, they were not expected to believe his concerns about the Israeli's danger and designs for the region simply because they possessed first-hand information about his good relationship with the Jewish entity, and how he and his father-in-law, Ibrahim Ahmed, were the first to establish contact with Israel in the 1960s, third, the Baath regime's past experience with Talabani convinced it that his main attempt was simply to gather the regime's support against his arch-rival Barzani and not to find a viable solution to the Kurdish problem, and lastly, they were not expected to be scampered by Talabani's pious way of talking and his referral to Islamic brethren as they knew well enough that, as a secular man, religious feelings do not dictate his actions. For these reasons, the Iraqi leadership did not give this message any importance. It did not accept dealing with Talabani until the fall of the regime.

This incident again gives an example of the way some of the Kurdish leaders were thinking and what their real interests were and how much they cared about the Kurdish national feelings. It also showed that what determined the relationship between the Kurdish parties and the government, and vice versa, was the concept of strength and weakness for each party. This method or belief continued to rule the relationship between the two sides, even if it were all taking place at the expense of Iraq or national unity.

Fourth: The Occupation, Federalism and a Permanent Constitution

All the nations that occupied Iraq, along with the political parties, coalitions and people who came with them behind their tanks, claimed that the action, as a 'liberation', represented a new beginning for a democratic Iraq, despite the fact that it was a brutal, destructive and bloody occupation that not only lacked a clear mandate from the UN but also resulted in the total destruction of the country's vital infrastructure. They also claimed that Iraq would be a model that would be envied and begrudged by all the countries in the region and even the world. However, what happened was the complete opposite. Many leaders of the parties that ruled following the occupation admitted later that they had committed a terrible mistake by changing the former regime in the way they did, i.e. through invasion and occupation. In fact, most of them retracted and began to refer to the action as 'occupation' and spoke about 'the unforgivable mistakes committed by the occupiers'. Only the Kurdish parties and leaders continued to describe what happened as 'liberation'!

Since the two main Kurdish parties suspended their contacts with Baghdad in 1991, they became active parts of the so-called 'opposition abroad', which was, in fact, a collection of uninfluential groups and personalities mostly created, managed and funded by the American, British, French, German, Israeli and Iranian intelligence services, with the exception of a very few ineffective personalities who were motivated by national-patriotic desire to establish real democracy in Iraq and endeavoured to spare the country a devastating war.

On the Kurdish side, and despite the fact that the two main parties (KDP and PUK) were fiercely engaged in internal war in Iraqi Kurdistan, they were meeting and collaborating under the US-Western-Israeli-Iranian umbrella, not even daring to show their differences at these meetings. Yet they made the northern territories of Iraqi Kurdistan they controlled an advanced base for the coalition forces and the expected starting point for the coming invasion of Iraq, (Kuwait was the starting point of invading Iraq from the south). As soon as the decision to invade and occupy Iraq was taken in March 2003, the two Kurdish parties quickly declared their full support for it, with promises to provide all necessary logistical support for the invading forces.

As soon as Baghdad was invaded and occupied, a flow of Kurdish groups, armed Peshmerga and Kurdish civilian opportunists overwhelmed the Iraqi capital, trying to exploit the prevailing chaotic situation. The leaders of the two parties directed their Peshmerga to seize houses of former officials and make them headquarters of their parties and to take control of other public buildings, such as government departments, schools, institutes and colleges. This behaviour, as well as the spread of Kurdish militants in the streets of Baghdad, provoked and morally insulted the inhabitants of the capital who felt really powerless to confront these militias. In fact, this conduct (of occupying public and official buildings) was followed by US forces, the other coalition forces, the different armed militias that came from Iran and people who were working in the opposition abroad who returned with the invasion tanks. It was clear that the biggest and most influential forces on the Iraqi streets, apart from the US-led coalition forces, were the armed militias of the two Kurdish parties, as well as the armed militias that came from Iran together with the militias of religious parties that were trained there as well. This was due to the destruction of the Iraqi state and the disbanding of the army, together with all types of security forces and police.

Right from the beginning, it was clear that the actions and approach of the Kurdish leaders had three objectives. First, they wanted to hinder any attempt to build a unified, strong Iraq; their real intentions were to weaken Iraq as much as possible in order not to let any new central government stand in the way of Kurdish ambitions to create a separate Kurdish entity. Second, they wanted to gnaw as many territories as possible from the areas around the three all-Kurdish provinces in order to enlarge the Kurdish region at the expense of the Iraqi state. Third, they wanted to create a feeling inside Iraqi society, in particular, and inside the new governing circles and the US administration in Iraq that these adjacent lands, especially the oil-rich province of Kirkuk, were predominantly Kurdish and were ceded by previous Iraqi governments. All these were initial or preparatory steps to finally creating an appropriate and positive atmosphere to declare an independent Kurdish state in the north of Iraq. It seemed that the United States and Israel were bolstering (directly, in the case of Israel, and indirectly for the United States) these objectives. Both sides did not conceal their approval, and many decisions were taken by the occupying administration to back that. It should be remembered that Israel spoke as early as 1981 (during the intensity of the Iraq–Iran war) about the need to divide Iraq into three separate states: the Kurdish in the north, the Sunni in the middle and west and the Shiite in the south. This design was repeated directly by top US officials in the first years of the occupation, and indirectly by insisting that there was no state called Iraq and that Iraq was an artificial amalgamation of Shiites, Sunnis, Kurds and other smaller identities such as the Christians and Sabians. Other measures taken by the US civil (unchallenged) governor of Iraq Paul Bremer indicated that this administration was sharing the aims and hopes of the Kurdish political parties. Thus, the three parties—the US administration in occupied Iraq, the leading Kurdish personalities and Israel—began working towards this result by supporting the Kurdish side and showing that it is the strongest of the main Iraqi components. To bolster the position of the Kurdish parties, the civil administrator Paul Bremer transferred huge sums of money seized by the invading forces from Iraqi funds to them, and his decision to dissolve the Iraqi armed forces did not include the Kurdish Peshmerga forces and its institutions. Note that Paul Bremer mentioned in his memoirs that the new Iraqi leaders, especially Barzani, Talabani, Ahmad Chalabi and Abdul Aziz al-Hakim, either urged him to expedite the dissolution of the Iraqi armed forces or congratulated him when he took that disastrous decision.[19] Moreover, while Bremer deliberately dealt with Iraqi Arabs on a sectarian basis, dividing them into Shiites, Sunnis and Christians rather than as Arabs, he considered the Kurds as one unified entity and as Kurds, despite the fact that they had the same sectarian and religious differences.

The other supporting measures provided by the US administration in Iraq to the two Kurdish parties were represented by:

1. The formation of the Governing Council using sectarian, ethnic basis and quotas, in which the Kurdish parties enjoyed greater influence. It should be noted that at that time most members of the Governing Council were protected by armed bodyguards from the Kurdish Peshmerga!

2. The declaration of the Transitional Administrative Law (TAL), which was considered a constitution for the occupied country until a permanent constitution was to be drawn up. In this law, the areas claimed by the Kurdish parties, other than the three all-Kurdish provinces, were listed as part of the Kurdistan region of Iraq and termed 'disputed areas' . The province of Kirkuk, together with other northern parts of the three other Iraqi provinces bordering the Kurdish ones, namely Mosul (Ninawa or Nineveh), Salah al-Din (Tikrit) and Diyala, were all regarded as disputed areas. Then a paragraph was added to the Law stating that these articles mentioned in TAL (concerning the disputed areas) cannot be removed or amended even when a permanent constitution is to be written and approved for Iraq, and that was what happened.

3. In drafting the permanent constitution, which was mostly identical to the main provisions of the TAL, the KDP delegation to the drafting committee hired a group of international jurists and experts to help in outlining a draft that would be favourable to the Kurds, and this was done by planting mines and pitfalls in the draft that would eventually give the Kurdish region more powers than the central authority. For example, the Constitution states that:

   a. 'In any future dispute between the Iraqi constitution and the regional constitution of the Kurdish region, the latter will prevail'. In other words, the regional constitution has supremacy over the central one. b. 'The central government has the right to control and administer old or existing oilfields in the Kurdish region, but all new wells, discoveries and international investments would belong solely to the regional government'. c. 'The Iraqi state is a federal one and not a unified (united) entity'. d. 'The Iraqi state is obliged in a limited time to carry out a national census in the disputed areas to determine the wishes of its inhabitants whether they want to join the region or remain with the central government'.

In the meantime, the two Kurdish parties clearly interfered with the demographic composition of these areas, particularly Kirkuk, by transferring large numbers of Syrian and Turkish Kurds living in Europe to them.[20] Certain Iraqi-Kurdish ambassadors in Europe supplied these new citizens with Iraqi identities and passports and shipped them to Iraq.[21]

4. The government headed by Ayad Allawi (2004) increased the share of Iraqi Kurdistan out of the national budget and from oil imports from 11%, as approved by the United Nations in 1995 (based on the percentage of the Iraqi population), to 17%, with the state being obliged to bear (pay) the salaries of the Peshmerga and the employees of the region (Incidentally, the former Iraqi Prime Minister Adil Abdul Mahdi was the finance minister who collaborated with the then prime minister to increase this share.) In 2010, former Prime Minister Nouri al-Maliki, in order to get the support of the Kurdish parties for a second term, made other financial and political concessions to the Kurdish Regional Government. If one is to calculate the revenues of the region, i.e. customs revenues, which the region refuses to transfer to the central treasury, and oil revenues from oil exported by the regional government from oilfields in the north, either officially or through smuggling (which by the way goes mainly to the ruling Kurdish families), as well as the salaries the central government pays from the central budget, the share of the region could easily exceed 25% of Iraq's national annual budget.[22]

With all these privileges and more, the differences continued to escalate between the central authority and that of the region, whose government was and still is controlled by the KDP. It is interesting to note that, at any crisis or dispute between the two sides, the threats of secession was always present and voiced by the Kurdish leaders from both parties. The previous president of the region Massoud Barzani and his son Masrour, present prime minister of the regional government, and the one who ran the security apparatus in Erbil and Dahuk, continued to make provocative statements like 'Iraq is an artificial state' and 'there was no country named Iraq except in the minds of some politicians'.[23] Such statements confirmed that the majority of the Kurdish leaders did not believe in the existence of a country called Iraq, let alone think of building it as a stable entity, federal as they demanded and obtained, or restoring it as an influential regional and international entity.

In June 2014, the so-called Islamic State of Iraq and Syria (ISIS), a terrorist organization, managed to invade and gain control of the second-largest province of Iraq, Ninawa (Mosul). The new Iraqi army, formed by Bremer from the militias of the parties loyal to the occupation, did not stand up and resist this attack; rather they fled in a humiliating manner. This encouraged ISIS to advance and occupy other western provinces, al-Anbar (Ramadi) and Salah al-Din (Tikrit), until its fighters reached the outskirts of Baghdad. In total, ISIS occupied almost a third of Iraq. This prompted the religious authority in the city of Najaf, Grand Ayatollah Ali al-Sistani, to declare the Jihad, which resulted in the formation of what came to be known as the Popular Mobilization Forces (PMF) (al-Hashid al-Shaabi), which managed, with the help of Iran, to push ISIS forces away from the vicinities of Baghdad (It took the combined Iraqi forces—the newly organized army and the PMF—more than three years to drive ISIS out of these provinces.)

However, two events that took place at the time of ISIS advances and successes could be very enlightening concerning the relations between the Central and Regional authorities.

First, the then Iraqi Prime Minister Nouri al-Maliki issued a statement saying that the success of ISIS terrorist fighters was partly due to the support they enjoyed from the Kurdistan Regional Government headed by Barzani and his sons. He believed this support facilitated the occupation of Mosul.[24] The US magazine, Newsweek, supported this claim later on.[25] Second, taking advantage of the military debacle that was suffered by the Iraqi army, Barzani issued an order to his Peshmerga to take control of Kirkuk, declaring it an integral part of the Kurdish Regional Government. Thus, instead of defending Mosul and cooperating with the central government to prevent the fall of the city into the hands of ISIS, Barzani took advantage of the calamitous position of the central government to claim Kirkuk. Moreover, Barzani ordered his Peshmerga to proceed to take control of other territories that were regarded by the constitution as disputed areas. More alarming was Barzani's aggressive and defiant declaration in which he said that the areas taken over and annexed to the Kurdish region were 'liberated by blood and would not be returned to the central authority under any conditions'. He also claimed that his decision practically implemented a clause in the constitution [140] which the central government failed to execute (without a national census). At the same time, the other main Kurdish party, the PUK, lowered the Iraqi flag and hoisted the Kurdish flag only over the official buildings and the centre of the province of Kirkuk; it also suspended all relations with the central government. This move was followed by an armed operation by PUK Peshmergas, which resulted in taking full control of all the oil facilities and installations in Kirkuk. Also, it was rumoured that Kurdish officials in the region from both parties, with other Turkish officials on the other side of the border in Turkey, were involved in smuggling oil extracted from not only the northern Iraqi oilfields but also from areas and wells that were dominated by ISIS terrorist fighters.[26] It was natural that under such a situation the claims of the Kurdish party leaders about the non-existence of a state called Iraq became louder and regular. Instead of seeking to solve these differences through negotiations, the Kurdish leaders promoted the ideas of separating Iraqi Kurdistan, according to their justification and argument, which said, 'Since we [Kurds and Arabs] failed to live as partners we should separate as friends and be good friendly neighbours'.[27] What widened the gap between the two authorities was the decision of the central government to block the share of the region from oil exports. The central authority argued that the Kurdish regional authority was exporting, for its own ends, big shipments of oil directly from the northern oilfields. The central government also added that these revenues, together with the custom revenues collected by the regional authorities from the border checkpoints in Iraqi Kurdistan, were never transferred to the Iraqi treasury. In the end, the central government claimed that these exports and revenues constitute more than the share and quota allocated to the region by the Iraqi budget.

FIFTH: REFERENDUM FOR INDEPENDENCE AND THE GREAT LOSS

In the summer of 2017, while the Iraqi armed forces were engaged in fierce battles against the ISIS terrorist fighters to liberate Mosul, Massoud Barzani declared that he would carry out a referendum for the separation of Iraqi Kurdistan. There were allegations and indications that the idea of the referendum carried out on the 25 September 2017, despite widespread local, regional and international objections, came as a result of the external advice mainly from Israeli. To confirm these allegations, Barzani's idea was immediately supported by Israeli officials, and statements were issued openly declaring Israel's support for the independence of Iraqi Kurdistan. Furthermore, Israel also urged European countries and the United States to support this step.[28] In addition, a group of foreign advisers surrounded Massoud Barzani before and during the referendum, encouraging and advising him to move forward and not to back down. This group was described by Barahm Salih, a leading Kurdish politician and presently the Iraqi President of the Republic, as mostly corrupt and exploitative.[29] These advisers[30] included people who benefited from oil and other deals signed by foreign companies with the Kurdish regional government after 2003, such as Israel's Zionist activist Bernard Levy,[31] Zalmay Khalilzad, the former US ambassador to Iraq, Bernard Kouchner, France's former foreign minister, and one of Israel's most vocal supporters; Peter Galbraith, author of (The End of Iraq),[32] a former US ambassador, who was regarded as the godfather of most oil deals signed by foreign companies with the region making millions out of these deals. (Later he was sued and sentenced in Norway for some of his fishy roles.)[33] Additionally, he was bragging that he was behind the insertion of all the articles that were regarded as pitfalls into the Iraqi constitution while he was a member of the consulting team to the Kurdish delegation in the drafting committee; hence his book made this infuriating declaration in its title. Other prominent players included Iraqi Arabs and Kurds, such as Fakhri Karim Zangana, a former communist leader, who after 2003 founded a newspaper called al-Mada, and a Cultural Foundation empire under the same name, as well as Kamiran Qaradaghi, the former director of the office of President Jalal Talabani, and one of the most vocal people calling for the need to 'dismantle Iraq' in his own words.[34]

Talks about the referendum began to escalate when the Iraqi army and federal police forces started to reorganize their units and prepare for the liberation of the areas occupied by ISIS. The battle was initiated in October 2015 (the United States wanted to postpone this military action to 2017). After the quick liberation of the provinces of Salah al-Din and Anbar in 2016, the battle to liberate Mosul, the last and most difficult bastion of ISIS, began in October 2016. Despite the ferocity of the battle, its massive destruction and the large number of victims and casualties, civilian and military, the Iraqi forces liberated the city of Mosul a year later, in 2017. In spite of statements issued by the leadership of the Kurdistan region in support of this process, the Peshmerga forces did not participate effectively or as required to accomplish this victory. On the contrary, the leaders of the Iraqi Kurdish region issued many warnings to the Iraqi advancing troops against approaching the areas controlled by the Peshmerga. Moreover, statements were issued by the region that said, 'Because of the failure of the central authority to implement Article 140 of the constitution, which stipulated a referendum in the "disputed areas", the Peshmerga applied material measures to implement this article and annexed these areas to the region. Of course, the government felt helpless due to the fierce battles in and around Mosul. It appeared that the new conduct of the army, its different performance, its new fighting spirit and leaders who seemed determined and willing to restore the reputation of their institution, had frightened Barzani, his sons and his advisers, who had realized that their expansionist policy outside the region would not be tolerated indefinitely. To support this position, one could quote Massoud Barzani who told a Western diplomat that asked him to postpone the referendum, "I cannot. I have a chance that will not come again. Baghdad is weak but growing stronger, and then it will be too late".[35]

Despite calls from the central government to abandon the idea of the referendum, Barzani insisted on conducting it, as much as he insisted on carrying it out not only in the all-Kurdish provinces but provocatively in the newly annexed 'disputed areas'. Noting that many countries and organizations (such as Turkey, Iran, the European Union and the US administration, though shy) had joined in calling for the cancellation or postponement of the referendum, Barzani's only reply to these appeals was that he was ready for a 'postponement' if the Iraqi government resumed paying the region's share of oil revenues. He then made another peculiar statement in which he said that if the government agreed

to dialogue and internationally guarantees commitments he would 'postpone independence for two years'! This meant that to him the question
of independence was irreversible.[36]

It appears some foreign advisers had suggested to Barzani that there
were more than 80 countries that would back the outcome of the referendum immediately, with other countries to later follow suit and change
their negative position or, at least, remain neutral.[37] (This was confirmed
by his foreign and Iraqi advisers.)[38] Also, Barzani used these claims to
propitiate the dithering Kurdish parties and personalities who were still
thinking that the time was not suitable for such a move. Indeed this
suggestion or statement made many reluctant Kurdish leaders change
course and support him. In fact, the reluctance of Barzani's opponent
to approve his position was not baseless. At that time, Barzani's adversaries were put in an awkward, critical and indeed embarrassing position
for three reasons. First, they felt that the Iraqi, regional and international atmosphere was not encouraging, if not altogether hostile towards
this move. Second, they were pretty sure that such a step (referendum)
if successful would strengthen Barzani's dominance in Iraqi Kurdistan
much more than it already has and make him the unchallenged leader
of the region, as well as all the Kurdish people. Third, they feared that
if they continued to oppose the referendum they would be accused by
the Kurdish people of standing against a long sought after and historical
objective of the Kurdish national movement and people. So they decided
to accept Barzani's decision, albeit reluctantly.

The Iraqi government, on its part, justified its refusal of the referendum on three major bases. First, it claimed it was contrary to the
Constitution and that there was nothing in that document that justified
or authorized it. Second, all the Kurdish political parties accepted this
document and the highest percentage of votes in favour of it were registered in the three Kurdish provinces, meaning that the political parties
and the majority of the Iraqi Kurds accepted one federal and unified Iraqi
state. Third, there was nothing in the Constitution that referred to the
right of self-determination as advocated by Barzani. Barzani said in his
response that the constitution had been violated by the central government more than once—this was in reference to the implementation of
Article 140, which stated that the Iraqi government should take all the
necessary measures to carry out a referendum to determine the future
of what was termed as (disputed areas).[39] He added that the Kurdish

members of the constitutional committee deliberately used the term 'federal state' in case the Kurds decided to secede from Iraq.[40] Of course, the government responded by counting the times the Kurdish regional administration had violated the constitution.

It is also important to recall that Barzani's insistence on the referendum was due to the deep political division inside the region at that time, a division based on his insistence on remaining as president of the region despite the expiration of his legal term of office and the exceptional and unconstitutional extensions made in his favour. Because of this issue, Barzani resorted to expelling the speaker of Kurdistan parliament and prevented him and other ministers, members of the Gorran party, from entering Erbil before he finally suspended the work of parliament.

What slipped the minds of Barzani and his supporters was the fact that, although independence was, and still is, a legitimate right of all people, such an action required some preliminary steps or prerequisites. Firstly, it must not be done in a manner that harmed the Iraqi state, in whose constitution the Kurds had overwhelmingly voted in favour of, as it treated them as equal citizens, or the interests of the majority of the Arabic people of Iraq. Secondly, an independent Kurdish state remains a difficult choice, if not impossible for the time being, for several reasons which include: (a) The international community (with the exception of Israel) was, and still is, against the fragmentation of the region any more than it was already torn apart. (b) Barzani, like his late father Mulla Mustafa Barzani, did not take into consideration the notion that the international community, for its own interests, was always keen to cooperate with the central authority of Iraq (being an oil-rich country) rather than support a fraction of it. Yes, there were many countries, especially regional ones that were keen to keep Iraq weak and embroiled in its internal problems to make sure that it would not present a threat to them. But dismantling the state was not what they wanted, for they knew very well that such a move could affect the unity of their own territories. (c) Almost all regional powers supported the Kurdish armed movements and organizations because they wanted to prevent Iraq from regaining its powerful regional status, not because of the blue eyes of the Kurds. Such regional elements included some of the Arab Gulf states. There are some evidence and leaked information suggesting that a Gulf state, the United Arab Emirates, donated $25 million to the Kurdish regional government headed by Barzani to cover the costs of the referendum. One Arab researcher told the writer that when he blamed the ambassador of this Gulf country to an Arab capital, telling him that this work could lead to the division of Iraq, the ambassador simply replied, 'And what is wrong with that? If this happens it can lead to the division of Iran as well, and this is what we aim for!'[41] Other Arab Gulf officials for certain sectarian reasons said the same. The other serious statement was issued by the former US ambassador to Iraq, Zalmay Khalilzad, one of Barzani's advisors who was present during the referendum. In an article published in the influential Washington Post, he asked, in fact urged, the US government to modify its position and not oppose the referendum because, from his point of view, the Iraqi Kurdish political parties are more loyal allies than the Iraqi ruling parties.[42]

On 25 September 2017, the referendum was held; the results as was expected were overwhelming in favour of secession. Yet, there are many observations about this result. First, the referendum was not preceded by an official census to determine how many people were eligible to vote. It was said by the Kurdish administration that there were approximately five million people who were entitled to vote. This figure, according to the available statistics, was incorrect. Then it was said that nearly three million people cast their votes. This figure also cannot be correct since, as is widely known, the total number of Kurds in Iraq is estimated to be between six and seven million; even if the number is higher (say ten million), it is impossible that half of them were eligible to vote. The other observation was that the results were announced as a total figure and not according to the votes of each governorate, yet there is enough evidence that voting in Sulaimaniya and some of its cities, such as Halabja, were either very weak or negative.[43] Moreover, in the province of Kirkuk, Turkmen and Arabs, who make up two-thirds of the inhabitants, boycotted the referendum. There is also evidence that large numbers of non-Iraqi Kurds took part in the vote, especially in the province of Kirkuk, after being supplied with Iraqi documents by the Kurdish administration and certain embassies abroad headed by Kurdish ambassadors. Finally, according to a Carnegie report, the heavy-handed Kurdish security measures terrorized people in certain areas and forced them to vote 'Yes'.[44]

Sixth: Reactions of the Iraqi Government, the Neighbouring Countries and the World

Perhaps Barzani and his supporters were surprised more than anything else, by the cool and unexpected response of the then Prime Minister Haider al-Ibadi to the outcome of the referendum. Although, Ibadi issued a firm official statement in which he rejected the referendum and its consequences, he wisely decided against resorting to force to stop the process, even in the disputed areas. Meanwhile, he kept repeating that he would apply the articles of the constitution and the laws of Iraq in his response. He then took a series of calm decisions that embarrassed and bewildered Barzani and his administration, putting them all in an awkward position. These decisions included the closure of all borders linking Iraqi Kurdistan with the outside world and imposing a no-fly zone over all of Iraqi Kurdistan, thus, preventing any local or international flights from landing or taking off. He then ordered the Kurdish regional government to hand over all Kurdish international airports and border custom checkpoints to the central authority. All the countries of the world responded positively to these decisions and promptly stopped all flights and cargo shipments to Iraqi Kurdistan. On top of that, both Iran and Turkey, on their parts, closed their borders with Iraqi Kurdistan, thus, almost suffocating the Kurdish region. Then the Iraqi premier fired the governor of Kirkuk, who was a major element in escalating the tension in the province and disturbing the relationship between the region and the central government. The governor refused to step down, and Barzani immediately declared his full backing for the governor, a man he previously criticized. The prime minister then announced that he would send the federal forces to reclaim the disputed areas that had been taken over by the Peshmerga illegally. He asked the Kurdish forces to evacuate these areas peacefully, but Barzani refused to comply.

Regionally and internationally, no country has defied the decisions of the Iraqi central authority. Turkey and Iran, the two major countries bordering Iraqi Kurdistan, had both categorically warned the Kurdish regional administration against holding the referendum and unambiguously declared that they were rejecting its results and any move to use them as a foundation to establish an independent Kurdish state on their borders. At this stage, Barzani's agenda was thwarted by his inability to defy the central government, press ahead with the referendum's results and impose his conditions on the basis of his referendum. The painful blow directed to Barzani was when the Iraqi federal forces entered Kirkuk without fighting and recovered it from the Peshmerga forces on October 17, 2017. Of course, it should be said here that this was achieved through Iranian efforts and interventions, which convinced the leadership of the PUK, whose Peshmerga groups controlled most areas of the province, not to engage in fighting with the advancing government forces. This event prompted Barzani and his sons to accuse the PUK of treason. The governor of Kirkuk (a member of the PUK), after failing to incite the people of the province to take up arms and resist the 'Iraqi invasion' as he put it, fled to Erbil.[45] The fall of Kirkuk prompted the Iraqi armed forces to advance and retrieve all the disputed areas previously occupied by Barzani's Peshmerga on his orders. In a matter of days, the Iraqi forces reached the borders of the province of the three Kurdish provinces of Erbil, Sulaimaniya and Dahuk. The sudden collapse and retreat of the Peshmerga was another shock for Barzani. It was said that some elements inside the Kurdish administration had made great efforts to request, and plead with, the central authority not to advance further and storm the three Kurdish provinces, especially Erbil. In their appeal they called upon the central government not to 'foil the federal experiment',[46] as the petitioners put it. There was no evidence, however, that the central government had any intention of doing so. To make Barzani's position even worse, widespread demonstrations, especially in Sulaimaniya, flared up, demanding the regional government to pay their suspended salaries for the last six months or more. The demonstrators, mostly government employees, claimed that the revenues of the oil exported from Iraqi Kurdistan by the Kurdish regional authorities, together with the customs duty income from Kurdish border checkpoints, were sufficient to cover all the salaries of the employees of the region. Widespread anti-corruption demonstrations followed in most Kurdish towns.

It was now Prime Minister Ibadi's turn to fail in seizing this golden opportunity to establish a direct link with the Kurdish society, especially the working people, by providing them with their unjustifiably delayed salaries, especially in the areas where the demonstrations were raging and where the opposition to Barzani's referendum was clear. Ibadi's justification for this hesitation was that there was a big number of what is known in today's Iraq as 'ghost employees', i.e. names mentioned in the paying lists but are nonexistent in reality. Despite the validity of this claim, which is incidentally a phenomenon that has reached all the departments of the Iraqi state since 2003, he should have ignored it temporarily to show the people of the region that the central government was aware of their sufferings and ready to tackle them. A month or so later, the prime minister agreed to pay these salaries, but again the method was wrong. On top of the delay, he chose again to hand the money to the Kurdish regional administration to pay the salaries without any supervision from the central government, thus, presenting the administration with an opportunity to claim that it was the one that made the government concede and transfer the salaries (It was said later that the Kurdish administration did not pay the full salaries to the employees in the region; it paid half and kept the rest unaccounted for.)[47]

On the other hand, Ibadi continued to insist that the presidency of the Kurdish region should clearly declare the results of the referendum null and void if the regional administration wanted to resume normal relations with Baghdad. His request was ignored by the Kurdish administration for the simple reason that it saw it as a humiliating step, although, all the leaders of the region, bar Barzani and his sons, made it clear that the referendum was a mistake and a wrong action. Ibadi, however, could have achieved what he wanted indirectly by demanding that the regional government, which began issuing successive appeals to open a dialogue, announce officially, and in a documented way that Iraqi Kurdistan is an integral part of the State of Iraq, and that the intention of separation does not exist, something that was continuously repeated by most of the Kurdish leaders of the province with the exception of Barzani and his sons.

As a result of the failure of the referendum, Massoud Barzani resigned his post as the president of Iraqi Kurdistan Region, handing over his powers to Kusrat Rasul whom he appointed after the crisis to avoid any call for new elections. This was yet another illegal and unconstitutional decision by Barzani that could be added to his previous insistence on remaining as president of the region, despite the expiration of his term, together with all the exceptional extensions he bestowed on himself. He, however, retained the presidency of the KDP and the leadership of the Peshmerga forces, two moves that showed he had bowed to the storm but was still planning to return when the opportunity arises. What supported this conclusion was the repeated comments and statements issued by him and some of his aides that said the region would restore control of Kirkuk and the other disputed areas. As one KDP leading figure announced, 'The Peshmerga will wrest Kirkuk and the other disputed areas that were lost to the enemies [the Iraqi army] at the earliest opportunity'.[48]

Once again it appears that Mr. Barzani is still trying to play with the time factor in the hope that he will have another suitable opportunity, depending on internal, regional or international circumstances. He had not only failed to admit his mistakes but also failed to absorb what had happened correctly. He missed the main lesson which said that, with all the weakness of the Iraqi state, which of course cannot be indefinite, and no matter what the circumstances were, neither Iran nor Turkey, the two most influential countries in the region that encircle most of Iraqi Kurdistan, could accept a Kurdish state on their borders. The same goes for Syria, the third country that has borders with Iraqi Kurdistan, despite its difficult circumstances. Generally, the countries of the world always preferred to deal with the State of Iraq, benefiting from the investment opportunities this oil-rich country offered, rather than dealing with a small part that is geographically confined and surrounded by parties hostile to it; thus, they rejected the idea of establishing a new small state. It should be remembered that this way of thinking is not peculiar to Barzani and his sons but was, and still is, shared by most Kurdish party leaders. This was also the reason behind the failure of his father, Mulla Mustafa, in 1975, who could not imagine at any moment that the then Shah of Iran would abandon him and agree with an Iraqi government, and that the United States or Israel would not endeavour to save him if such an agreement materialized. Yet, the old Soviet Union, which backed Mulla Mustafa for some time when Iraq was not on friendly terms with Moscow, signed in 1972 a broad treaty of friendship with Iraq and was keener to uphold this treaty, which provided it with projects and influence in the region than to antagonize Iraq by defending the Kurdish movement. Finally, another fact that slipped the mind of Massoud Barzani was that the full support and backing to his ultranationalist objectives and hope for independence extended to him by the USA before 2003 was mainly because the Americans were keen on destabilizing the regime of the late president Saddam Hussein and that things changed after the USA occupied Iraq. The occupying forces were no more ready to accept a major challenge to the new Iraqi regime, which they had established and which was actually under their total domination. In other words, before 2003 the United States was extending support to Barzani because they wanted him to make life difficult for the regime of Saddam Hussein and weaken it, not because of the blue eyes of the Kurdish parties. But after 2003, and with their occupation of the whole of Iraq, this desire was overtaken by events.

As a result of his bitter experience with the referendum, Barzani lost almost everything, including his unchallenged position and all the privileges he enjoyed as ruler of a de facto independent state, the freedom to do whatever he wanted in Iraqi Kurdistan, with no real opposition even from the other Kurdish parties (even if there was any, he usually managed to subdue it), the way the countries of the world treated him as an uncrowned king, with official international delegations and foreign dignitaries converging in the regional capital Erbil without seeking the permission of the Iraqi capital, Baghdad and, finally and most importantly, the freedom to export oil worth billions of US dollars[49] (all revenues were deposited into a special account under his family's name in Turkey according to some sources).[50] Not only did he lose all these privileges, but he was also isolated internally, regionally and internationally. Only the arrival of the new Iraqi prime minister (end of 2018), Adil Abdul Mahdi, an old friend and colleague of his, saved Barzani from total collapse. Yet, once again, Barzani failed to take advantage of this opportunity to mend his relations with the other Kurdish political parties; instead, he took decisions that indicated his continuous intention to dominate the Iraqi Kurdish region irrespective of the rights and desires of the other political parties to share power with the KDP. At the end of May 2019, he designated his son-in-law and nephew Nigervan Barzani (son of his late brother Idris) as the new president of the Iraqi Kurdish region and his son Masrour as the new prime minister of the region, which revived the struggle with the other Kurdish political parties in Iraqi Kurdistan.

Seventh: What About the Future?

After all that has been said, what about the future? The question of looking into the future with regard to the Kurdish question may be a difficult one, especially in light of the volatile internal, regional and international situation. It may prove more difficult in view of the predominant thinking or belief among official Iraqi Kurdish and Arab leaders that at any moment something unexpected could happen that would enable any side to exploit and appear as the victor over the other. In fact, this has happened many times in recent history. Mulla Mustafa, who was exiled in the 1940s and lived for eleven years as a refugee in the Soviet Union, escaping death many times, was able to benefit from the amnesty bestowed on him by the republican regime headed by the then Prime Minister General Abdul Karim Qasim to return home again in 1958. He was quick to exploit the hostility of the Shah of Iran towards the new Iraqi republican regime[51] and, more than that the British hostility to the new regime, to regain his role as an influential political and belligerent leader in Iraq. Britain was instigated twice, first by Qasim's claim to Kuwait in June 1961, and second by the declaration of Law No. 80, December 1961, which deprived the oil companies of the right to explore anywhere they wanted in Iraq.[52] Thus, Mulla Mustafa Barzan enjoyed the support of many elements—Iran, Britain and later on Israel—when he staged his revolt in September 1961 against the new republican regime (in fact, his armed activities with other tribal feudalist leaders started in July 1961, and in September they were joined by the KDP rank and file). Because of Qasim's failure to deal wisely and peacefully with the problem, Mulla Mustafa Barzani became the undisputed leader of the Kurdish mountains. After their defeat in 1975, Mulla Mustafa and his sons took refuge in Iran with a few hundreds of their fighters, down from tens of thousands. An opportunity arose again for his sons when the Iraq-Iran war broke out. The new regime in Iran was quick to revive and extend big support to the Kurdish parties taking refuge in the country. Both Massoud Barzani, leader of the KDP, and Jalal Talabani, leader of the PUK, were summoned from Britain, where they were living, to lead the armed Kurdish activities against the Iraqi Army, together with other Iraqi Arab parties living in Iran and opposing the Baath regime. For eight years (1980–1988), both the KDP and PUK enjoyed the full backing of the Iranian regime, joined the Iranian armed attacks on Iraqi Kurdish areas and revived the hopes of the two Kurdish parties to regain control of the parts of Kurdistan they used to control before 1975. The Iraqi victory in this war (1988) led to the evaporation of the dreams of the Kurdish parties. This situation only lasted for two years. In 1990 the Iraqi regime took the catastrophic decision of militarily annexing Kuwait, only to give the United States and the West the excuse to do whatever they could to push the Iraqi troops out of Kuwait and at the same time to end the military might Iraq had acquired through its long war with Iran. One of the strategies to destabilize the Iraqi regime of Saddam Hussein was to encourage the two main Kurdish parties stationed in Iran to attack Iraqi territories. The successful war to oust Iraqi forces out of Kuwait was, in fact, a war that destroyed the infrastructure of Iraq and, most of its military forces. It also allowed the Kurdish parties to return victoriously to Iraqi Kurdistan. On top of that, the US-Western coalition provided the two parties with a new form of protection by declaring a no-fly zone over all Iraqi Kurdish provinces to prevent any aerial attacks by the Iraqi regime on the newly established Kurdish administration. But the two Kurdish parties, which failed to unite their efforts and generally remained at loggerhead, were hesitant during that period to show excessive optimism simply because they felt that the Iraqi regime at the time was still able to curb their influence and role. Finally, the golden opportunity came following the occupation of Iraq in 2003. This enabled the Kurdish parties, despite their dissonance and differences, to expand and escalate their demands to the maximum degree.

During all these circumstances, setbacks, temporary and illusionist victories, the two sides, the successive Iraqi governments and the leaders of the Kurdish parties, never thought that the only valid and lasting solution that can please and satisfy all sides lies in mutual coordination and understanding among themselves. They have failed to see that any concession given to a stable, strong, democratic and prosperous Iraq or made by each side to the other is better than any concession freely granted to foreign powers that aim only to achieve their own objectives and interests, which in turn, are incompatible with that of Iraqis, whether Arab or Kurdish. They also did not realize that taking advantage of the weakness of the other side to achieve unrealistic and short-lived gains cannot be a rational and permanent solution to the problem or a way to bridge the differences between the two sides. The experience of the post-occupation period and the vast form of federalism, which was, in fact, a complete and undeclared independence, had enticed Barzani to go into the referendum; the failure of this option and the success of the Iraqi government in wresting the disputed areas from the Kurdish Peshmerga must be seen from this perspective, the misguided approach of taking advantage of the other side's weakness to subdue it. Also, the idea of putting the other side in an awkward position to give more concessions never brought about a sustainable solution.

The Iraqi Arabs, in general, as well as the political parties, movements and national figures, have always proven that they were not against the Kurds enjoying their national, cultural and political rights. All these bodies or groups, and ordinary people, feel bad when they find that the Kurdish parties are ready to cooperate with foreign elements and countries that persecuted their fellow Kurdish brothers or even do not recognize the existence of their nationality; yet these parties are not ready to cooperate with the country that has granted them all their rights. Iraqis suffer when they notice that the Kurdish parties and their leaders have a strong relationship with governments hostile to Iraq, such as Israel, the side that occupies Arab and Islam's holy lands, kills the people of Palestine and confiscates their land on a daily basis, while the Kurds claim they are proud of being associated with the Kurdish Islamic leader Salah al-Din (Saladin) who defeated the Crusaders and regained Jerusalem. More than that, most Iraqis feel aggravated when they see that the celebration of the referendum or any other occasion in Iraqi Kurdistan is done by lifting and hoisting Israeli flags in the cities of Kurdistan or the hosting of Israeli representatives as guests in these celebrations. On their part, Iraqi Kurds sometimes have similar exasperations. A fair number of Kurds complained that, although the majority of the Kurds are loyal and committed to Iraq and always regard themselves as an integral part of the Iraqi national movement and the mass political parties, they were more than often marginalized and unjustly persecuted. They also complained that they were regularly and unfairly treated, condemned and persecuted because of the conduct of their leaders, who were mostly looking after their own parochial ambitions, and more than often were working for their own interests and that of their families. Some even say that successive Iraqi governments were also prone to giving concession to foreign powers to get their help to persecute the Kurdish people in Iraq. Yet, the political leaders of both sides have intentionally, consciously or sometimes naively deepened these feelings inside the minds of the two communities, Arab and Kurdish. Under such continued escalation and instigations, which by the way, is often sponsored and encouraged by outside elements, the two parts of the people of Iraq forget their common and mutual history. The two peoples overlook the main and fundamental fact that says they have lived together for decades or centuries, their blood and pedigrees are mixed, they have shared tragedies and joyful times, hard and prosperous periods and their common binding history is far more than the divisive memories. Finally, what they should both work together on is to build a democratic, secure and stable country (Iraq) governed by a constitution and laws that do not discriminate citizens on the basis of race, religion or language. Had there been a democratic, prosperous and stable Iraqi state, terrorism and terrorist militia organizations could not have infiltrated and destroyed it. Also, there would have been no chance for Turkey, Iran, Israel, or any other foreign power to penetrate it militarily, exert pressure on it and exploit it. On top of that, its vast wealth would not have been wasted and squandered through corruption. Due to the high level of corruption, Iraq has acquired some dubious distinctions among the nations of the world. It is a model of a country that is massively rich yet has about half of its children living below the poverty line, with one fifth of its inhabitants in internal refugee camps to escape terrorism, a country that has the largest number of orphans and widows, more than four million of its citizens living in exile against their wishes, with 40% of its population illiterate (three decades ago Iraq was commended by the UN for completely eradicating illiteracy and for its public health services). A final result is that Iraq is ranking high among the most corrupt countries and failing states. Of course, all of these shortcomings are to be blamed on the US occupation and on successive Iraqi governments that ruled since 2003, the Kurdish parties and representatives being an influential part of them all the while.

Perhaps the first and most important step to be taken in the right direction is to build mutual trust and confidence, as ill confidence and reciprocal mistrust have always characterized contemporary Arab–Kurdish relations in Iraq. Then there is a dire need to write a new constitution—by the Iraqis themselves and by purely Iraqi hands—that guarantees the interests and rights of all citizens without discrimination. But most importantly, is to draft it to render Iraq a more united, coherent and strong country. The third essential step is to put on trial all corrupt officials, Arabs, Kurds, and from other components of Iraqi society, letting the law and courts be the arbiter. Iraqis are longing to see the 'whales of corruption', from all the components of Iraqi society behind bars and what they have looted retrieved and returned to the Iraqi treasury. Fourth, there is a need to establish a state of law, in which the impartial judicial system prevails. These urgent and much-needed steps will not only be rejoiced over by the majority of Iraqis but will also make them more than enthusiastic and keen to serve their country.

Frankly speaking, the 'present Iraqi political elite', whether Arab or Kurdish, depending on what they have done for the last eighteen years, cannot be relied upon to repair what they have damaged through their corruption and sectarian ethnic, racial and repressive conduct. Neither do they have the desire and ability to reform or rehabilitate what the American occupation and the regional influences (Iranian, Turkish, Israeli and Gulf countries) have damaged in Iraq. In light of the incompetence to build mutual trust shown by these political cliques, other elements, such as popular and professional organizations (scientific and human societies, trade unions, etc.) can play such a role. For example, the different

Iraqi unions, Arab and Kurdish, can initiate periodic dialogues and meetings, constantly and continuously forming joint coordination committee among them to foster mutual cooperation. The universities and their staff, students or professors, can and should play a similar role through joint events, dialogues, workshops and conferences devoted to discussing the problems and crises suffered by all Iraqis, as well as future cooperation. Even the arts, theatre, cinema and media (electronic, print and online) should play a role by producing more programmes that encourage common understanding. At the same time, and in fact more importantly, people and entities from all sides trying to spread venom and hatred (through sectarian and chauvinistic racial talks) should be denied access to media platforms through which they have managed to generate discord and division among the people of the country in the past eighteen years. More than that, such people must be held legally accountable by the courts for stirring up strife and breaching the peace. The Arab and Kurdish tribes in Iraq can also be mobilized and encouraged to restore their historical relations and joint patriotic efforts. The restoration of unity and harmony between the different factions and components of the people is the best way to build collective trust and brotherhood between the two communities, something that was lost to political conflicts, differences and the activities of self-serving politicians.

All the evidence indicates that the powerful Kurdish parties, especially the two main ones, the KDP and PUK, have not yet made up their minds to find a permanent solution within one Iraqi state. One of the reasons for this thinking is the material and political gains made by the families that lead the Kurdish political parties, especially the two dominating ones. These families will still look for opportunities to regain the influence and dominance they enjoyed during the region's decades of chaos. Some new opposing Kurdish political parties—such as the Justice and Democracy Alliance, led by Barham Salih, now president of the republic; the New Generation Movement or Party, headed by the young journalist and media tycoon Shaswar Abdel Wahed—were recently established. There is also the older Change (Gorran) Party. But it remains too early to say how much influence they really enjoy or whether they can tilt the balance of power in the region. In the last elections (May 2018), the two traditional parties, the KDP and the PUK, won most of the seats allocated to the Kurds, with Gorran coming a far third, leaving only a very small number to the newer parties. The new parties registered serious objections, claiming that the two big parties had resorted to fraud and rigging to win. Their objections were supported by, at least, one member of the high commission supervising the elections, but nothing was done to amend the results. In addition, it is too early to judge the performance of these parties because their programmes are still not clear. There is also no proof whether they believe in one unified Iraq or will resort in the future to chauvinistic and separatist rhetoric to whip up sentiments and win support. The fact that these new parties have secured seats in the parliament does not mean they have the ability to make drastic or even minor changes in internal politics. This is simply because the internal security apparatus, as well as the Peshmerga forces, are fully and totally under the control and direction of the two main parties, the KDP and PUK. The best example is that although the success of the Gorran party in previous regional elections (2013) entitled it to the presidency of the Kurdish parliament together with some ministers in 2014, the party was a few months later expelled from the Kurdish parliament and cabinet by Massoud Barzani (October 2015). They were even barred from entering the regional capital Erbil at the time merely because they refused to grant Barzani another extension as president of the region. The party remained out of government until 2019 when it capitulated and agreed to most of Barzani's conditions.

On the other hand, most successive Iraqi governments have not adopted a means to speak directly to the Kurdish people—that does not go through the Kurdish parties—and convince the Kurdish masses that their interests are of paramount interest to the state. The situation worsened after 2003 when sectarian politics and quota system were adopted by the different ruling parties that came from abroad. The policies of the conservative-sectarian parties that dominated Iraqi politics since 2003 convinced the majority of the Iraqi people, the Kurds included, that their interests and wellbeing meant nothing to these parties who are only interested in looting the wealth of the country. None of these parties has put forward a plan to solve the outstanding Kurdish problem, together with other lingering issues. Nor has the Kurdish language been seriously taught all over Iraq to remove a major obstacle in the way of communication between the two communities. After 1991, the Kurdish regional administration had made a similar mistake by abolishing the teaching of Arabic in the region's schools and institutions. The result was the creation of Arab and Kurdish generations deprived of a common language.

Perhaps one of the very few positive results of the sadly oppressive and repressive campaigns against the Kurdish armed revolts was the policy of deportation, which previous governments followed to punish Kurdish activists by exiling them with their families to the southern cities of Iraq. This policy created a Kurdish generation that was educated in Arab cities, with strong ties to local Arab families in the southern regions. The same happened after 2003 when the religious parties implemented a policy of sectarian and area cleansing that forced a large number of Iraqi Arab families to migrate to Iraqi Kurdistan. These families sent their kids to Kurdish schools and educational institutions, which resulted in the creation of an Arab generation speaking Kurdish and having strong social ties with Kurdish families. These two generations must be recruited to build fraternal bridges between the two societies.

In conclusion, it seems that with the absence of mutual confidence between the two sides (the Kurdish political parties and the consecutive governments), in Baghdad and a strong powerful central government, as well as the existence of a constitution that encourage federal entities to go their own way, and federal Kurdish government that insists on acting independently without any consideration to the rest of the Iraqi state, it is very difficult to envisage a real end to the peculiar situation, where the federal entity control the central government. More dangerous is the fact the Iraqi Kurdish parties after almost three decades of enjoying de facto independence, grew unwilling to relinquish their privileges. Even the intermittent Turkish and Iranian intrusions did not make the Kurdish regional government accept the idea of cooperating with the central government and the Iraqi armed forces to draw a plan to safeguard the integrity of the Iraqi territories. The situation now, with the interference of so many foreign elements or actors, especially in Iraqi Kurdistan, necessitate at least nationwide consensus to solve the problem in the interest of Iraq. This consensus should revolve around the understanding that a Kurdish separatist solution cannot be viable, due to the strong objections of the states bordering, Turkey, Iran and Syria, who all have their Kurdish population and fear that they may ask for separation as well. Thus, irredentism which is still dominating the minds of the ideologies of the Kurdish political parties, and their desire to claim and expand into other mixed Iraqi provinces, will always be foiled by all the countries containing Kurdish population. In view of this complicated situation, the best way to solve the problem in Iraq remains the cooperation of all national element (Arabs, Kurds, Turkoman and other smaller minorities), to work together to create a democratic, prosperous Iraq in which human rights are respected, as well as the national and cultural differences of all the components of the Iraqi people.

NOTES

1. See the letter written by the then Iraqi Minister of Interior, Abdul Mohsin al-Sadoun, to King Faisal I, who dispatched him in 1924 to Sulaimaniya to prop the dithering attitude of its population towards the idea of crowning him as King for Iraq. The minister wrote that all the dignitaries and tribal leaders he met were enthusiastic to swear fealty to the new king and agreed to sign a memorandum to this effect next day. When they met again the next morning, they told the minister that since they cannot differentiate between what is right and what is wrong for them they would leave the matter to the British political officers to decide for them. See Saad N. Jawad, *Iraq and the Kurdish Question 1958-1970*, Ithaca, London, 1981, p. 30.
2. Turkey at that time was claiming the whole old Ottoman Mosul Vilayat, which included the five major Iraqi provinces: Mosul, Erbil, Sulaimaniya Kirkuk and Dahuk.
3. Saad N. Jawad, op. cit., p. 52.
4. This was said in Tehran on 12 March 1975, when Mulla Mustafa headed a delegation to meet the Shah of Iran who had few days ago signed an agreement with the Iraqi government in which he committed himself to stop any support of the Kurdish revolt and the KDP. See the booklet, al-hizb al-dimocrati al-Kurdistani (al-lajna al-tahthiriya), taqeem masirat al-thawra al-Kurdiya wa Inhiyaraha wa al-dorous wa al-Ibar al-mustakhlaza miha. (The KDR-preparatory committee: Assess the course of the Kurdish revolution and its collapse and the lessons learned from it.) December, 1977 (no publication place). First edition, p. 89.
5. Perhaps the only time an Iraqi government has done so was during the term of the Baath government in 1968–1970, prior to the signing of the March Manifesto, when the government, while conducting a military campaign against Mulla Mustafa's forces, took some important decisions to fulfil some of the Kurdish national demands and objectives, something that put Barzani in an awkward and embarrassing position. Ibid., pp. 239–245.
6. This was done between 1958 and 1961 by the KDP leader Mulla Mustafa during the first republican regime, and repeated by him between 1964 and 1968 during the regime of the two Aref brothers, and again between 1970 and 1974 during the Baath regime.
7. Saddam Husain, Ahadeeth fi al-Qadhaia al-Rahina (talks in current issues), al-Thawra Publishing Press, Baghdad, 1974.

8. Talks with Dr. Abdul Sattar T. Sharif, Kurdish political leader, head of a splinter political party and a minister in the central Iraqi government between 1975 and 1980 (April 1980), and Habib Mohammed Karim, Secretary-General of the KDP between 1964 and 1975 (Baghdad, July 1982).

9. It was said afterwards that the Iraqi government wanted the big exodus towards Iraqi Kurdistan to continue in order to burden the limited resources of the Kurdish revolt. And this is really what happened, as the KDP was soon to feel unable to feed and protect this huge number of new comers.

10. For the Israeli support to the Kurdish Peshmerga at the time, see the declaration of the former Israeli Prime Minister Menachem Begin in a public speech in September 1980 (Maarive and Yedioth Ahronoth, 30/09/1980). See also Shlomo Nickdemon, *The Mossad in Iraq* (Arabic), translated by Badr Aqeely, Dar al-Jalil, Palestinian Research Publication House, Amman-Jordan, 1997.

11. According to Colonel K. Shakir (head of the counter intelligence service in the Iraqi Mukhabarat who played a leading role in the talks with Talabani), the meeting was made possible through the mediation and endeavour of the late Abdul Rahman Qassimlou (Ghassemlou), (the secretary general of the Kurdistan Democratic Party—Iran, later assassinated by Iranian agents in Vienna in 1989). Shakir also said that Qassimlou relayed Talabani's wish to open a dialogue with the Iraqi government. The same source stated that the Iraqi government then took a decision to hold simultaneous dialogues with all Kurdish factions alike. Thus, at the time Shakir was negotiating with Talabani in Baghdad, another team, headed by Shakir;s deputy, Ihsan al-Dairi, was meeting with Massoud Barzani in a remote village in the Iraq-Turkey-Iran borders called 'Sadi Kan'. Massoud was persuaded to participate in these talks through the mediation of a Kurdish tribal leader called Izzat Dergalla, who was close to his late father Mulla Mustafa. The talks with the two factions were relayed regularly to the Kurdish officials participating in, or cooperating with the Baath Government.Correspondence with K. Shakir.

12. Interview with Jalal Talabani, al-Taliaa al-Arabia (Arabic) issue no. 65, 6 August 1984.

13. See Talabani's memoirs, part no. 49, https://xeber24.org/archives/159880.

14. Talks with Hamid Yousif Hummadi, personal secretary of the late president Saddam Hussein, minister of information in 1991, and member of the official negotiating team (October 1991).

15. Saddam Hussein talking to Kurdish representatives from Iraqi Kurdistan: https://m.youtube.com/watch?v=w-fxcaYp7So, http://www.bbc.com/arabic/middleeast/2014/04/140424_kurdistan_chronology.

16. During the negotiations with the Iraqi government (1983–1984), Jalal Talabani easily accepted to exempt the province of Kirkuk from the future deal. He even defended this idea publicly (Al-Taliaa, op. cit.).

17. For a concise, deep and brief history and armed struggle between the two Kurdish parties see: https://www.bbc.com/arabic/middleeast-41659670.

18. Figures of such debts varied hugely ($80–200 billion) because parts of these debts to Arab Gulf countries were not really financial debts. Due to the many obstacles Iraq faced in exporting its oil to finance the war, two Arab Gulf countries, Saudi Arabia and Kuwait, agreed to export certain amounts of oil on behalf of Iraq and that Iraq, once the war ended, should export the same amounts on behalf of the two countries. Following the invasion of Kuwait, both Saudi Arabia and Kuwait considered the value of oil exported in favour of Iraq as debts that should be paid in cash. Interview with Dr. Ramzi Salam (Head of the Oil Exporting Division, Iraqi Ministry of Oil) who signed these agreements with the two countries (June 2019).

19. Paul Bremer, *My Year in Iraq*, Simon and Schuster, New York, 2006.

20. http://www.bizturkmeniz.com/ar/index.php?page=article&id=275 27&w=.

21. Saad N. Jawad, *The Iraqi Constitution: Structural Flaws and Political Implications*, MEC, LSE, available online, http://eprints.lse.ac. uk/54927/1/SaadJawad_Iraqi_Constitution_LSE_Middle_East_Centre_ WP01_Nov2013.pdf.

22. http://www.asiannewslb.com/?page=article&id=27580,   http://www. masalah.com/ar/News/86546.

23. See Saad N. Jawad, An open letter to President Massoud Barzani (Arabic) (Rai al-Youm newspaper, 17/09/2017). http://www.raialyoum.com/?= 724787.

24. http://elaph.com/Web/News/2014/12/967073.html.

25. Michael Robin, Why have the Kurds supplied ISIS with weapons? (Newsweek, 26/04/2016). https://www.google.com/amp/s/www.new sweek.com/why-have-kurds-supplied-isis-weapons-452673%3famp=1.

26. https://www.non14.net/public/index.php/110099, https://ekurd.net/ category/kurdistan/corruption.

27. Saad N. Jawad, ibid.

28. http://www.alhayat.com/article/886334/-كردستان-استقلال-تؤيد-إسرائيل. العراق, https://alkhaleejonline.net/-عن-كردستان-إسرائيل-انفصال-تدعم-لماذاسياسة. العراق.

29. See the FT, 22/10/2017, https://www.google.com/amp/s/amp.ft. com/content/01e4c572-b5a2-11e7-a398-73d59db9e399.

30. http://iraqrawi.blogspot.com/2018/06/?m=1.

31. https://justiceforkurds.org/2017/09/06/the-kurds-are-not-children/ independence/?utm_source=Sailthru&utm_medium=email&utm_cam paign=Ed%20Pix%209-6&utm_term=%2AEditors%20Picks.

32. Peter Galbraith, *The End of Iraq*, Simon & Schusster, New York, 2006.
33. https://www.nytimes.com/2010/10/07/world/middleeast/07galb raith.html. It was also said that even former US president G. W. Bush and Vice President Cheney both had financial interests in Iraqi Kurdistan's oil investments. https://gpinvestigations.pri.org/the-curse-of-oil-in-iraqi-kurdistan-1c9a9a18efd1, http://www.greenmountaindaily.com/2009/11/13/will-the-real-peter-galbraith-please-stand-up/.
34. It was said that F. Zangana's fortune was made after 2003, and mainly through the services he rendered to the two main Kurdish parties. Qaradaghi, who was one of the staunch supporters of the invasion of Iraq, said that in public in a comment on a panel in Chatham House, Can Iraq Survive? 25 September 2014. https://www.chathamhouse.org/event/can-iraq-survive see also: http://www.alittihad.ae/wajhatdetails.php?id=81796. By the way, this is not the first time a Kurdish leader has claimed that Kurdish masses were demanding separation. In 2004, and before he became president of the Iraqi republic, Jalal Talabani claimed he had a petition signed by one million Kurds making the same demand. Funny enough, he forgot about this petition when he became president.
35. https://www.google.co.uk/amp/amp.dw.com/ar/.
36. http://www.alsumaria.tv/mobile/news/112991/.
37. https://www.google.co.uk/amp/www.aljazeera.net/amp/knowledge gate/opinions/2017/8/24/. Why Barzani insists on referendum, al-Jazeera centre for studies.
38. FT, op. cit.
39. See Chapter 4 about the illegal insertion of this article.
40. His press conference to all international media 20/09/2017.
41. http://m.thebaghdadpost.com/ar/Story/44166.
42. The Kurds have voted. Here's what Washington should do next (*The Washington Post*, 25 September 2017). http://www.google.co.uk/amps/s/www.washingtonpost.com/amphtml/nea/global.
43. Halabja, which was always used in Kurdish propaganda as the city that was subjected to chemical attack by the old regime in 1988, registered the lowest percentage of participation, 58%, and a high number of them voted "No" to independence (Al-Araby al-Jadid newspaper, 29/09/2017). https://www.google.co.uk/amp/s/www.alaraby.co.uk/amp//politics/2017/9/29/.
44. http://carnegieendowment.org/sada/73364?lang=ar.
45. The governor, Najimuldin Karim, a US citizen, and the co-chairman of the Israeli-Kurdish friendship society in the United States was recently arrested by the Interpol in Beirut based on a warrant issued by the Iraqi government for corruption. https://al-akhbar.com/Iraq/271028.

46. This was what a member of the Iraqi parliament said after meeting some Kurdish officials. https://www.google.co.uk/amp/s/www.radios awa.com/amp/397610.htm.

47. This was confirmed by the Iraqi (Kurdish) Finance Minister Fuad Husain in a live TV programme on al-Shraqia channel, https://www.alsharqiya. com/news/فؤاد-حسين. See also: https://www.azzaman.com/-الإقليم-يتسلّم الرواتب-وسط-إعتصام-الم.

48. Kamal Kirkukly, a leading figure in the apeshmerga https://www.google. co.uk/amp/s/www.radiosawa.com/amp/397610.htm.

49. http://www.nrttv.com/ar/Detal.aspx?Jimare=32936.

50. https://www.al-monitor.com/pulse/originals/2019/05/iraq-kurdistan-oil-kirkuk.html.

51. The Shah then feared that the change was a communist one that could threaten his regime.

52. Although the law was issued in December 1961, the tough negotiations started in 1960 with the British oil companies which failed to make Qasim abandon the idea. Before that law, oil companies had the right to explore wherever they wished in Iraq.

CHAPTER 6

National Reconciliation

HISTORICAL BACKGROUND

In the writings of researchers and scholars of Iraqi affairs, especially Westerners and foreigners, they normally refer to Iraq as a 'mosaic state', a clear indication of the country's ethnic, religious, and sectarian diverseness. Each ethnic or religious community in Iraq has its diversity that is subdivided into sects, denominations, factions, orders and other smaller entities. An Arab, for example, could be a Muslim or a Christian or even a Jew, who could come from any group or denomination within each of these religions. An Arab can also be a Sabian, Yazidi, or Baha'i. The same goes for the Kurds and Turkomans. Some of these religious and ethnic minorities are admittedly small in size. They nevertheless played effective roles in modern Iraq. Between the 1920s and 1940s, the Jews, for example, played a significant part especially in the financial and economic life of the nascent state. Their influence has undoubtedly diminished and faded away on account of the waves of mass emigration from Iraq after 1948.

In the history of Iraq, these multiple ethnic and religious differences in identity did not cause any major trouble or internal struggles. It was rather the pretext to protect the followers of a particular sect or religious faith by foreign powers that upset the Iraqi scene and caused regional wars. The wars between the Ottoman and Safawid states that took place on Iraqi soil between the fourteenth and nineteenth centuries were a case

© The Author(s), under exclusive license to Springer Nature Switzerland AG 2021
S. N. Jawad, *Iraq after the Invasion*, Middle East Today,
https://doi.org/10.1007/978-3-030-72106-0_6

in point. In other words, Iraq, the buffer zone became the battlefield for the two oriental empires. The historic rivalry between the two states however was ended by the British occupying Iraq during the First World War (1914). But the situation did not improve as the British, in keeping with their policy of 'Divide and Rule' endeavoured then to exploit the manifold religious and ethnic diversity of the Iraqi society.

It should be noted that despite all these racial, religious and sectarian variations, Iraq has not experienced any major civil or inter-communal war between the components of its diverse society, whether before or after the establishment of the modern Iraqi state in 1921. In 1932, Iraq was officially accepted as an independent state in the League of Nations. It was the first Arab state to receive such international recognition. One of the main reasons for the admission of Iraq as an independent state in the League was its modern, secular and equitable constitution, as well as its steady march towards modernization.

To be sure, all Iraqi governments and political parties from the inception of the new state proved that they place merit, efficiency, and patriotism above their ethnic or religious differences. Another testimony to the communal coexistence and tolerance in Iraq is afforded by the fact that the dominantly Shiite people of the South were quite enthusiastic and the first to welcome the installation of an Arab Sunni King, Faisal I in 1921. The Kurds shared this position and felt the same way, despite attempts by the Mandatory power, Britain, to dissuade them from supporting the King's inauguration until he and his government accepted to sign a long term and what is largely viewed as an inequitable treaty with the UK.[1]

King Faisal I and his seasoned entourage quickly and intelligently picked up the reality of the diversity of the Iraqi population. They were quite keen to deal with the complexities of the situation and put in place an ambitious programme that sought to melt the religious, sectarian and ethnic differences in the crucible of one Iraqi identity. King Faisal I, was perhaps among the first to get his feet wet, and in a fairly short time, he managed to understand the characteristics of and differences between his citizens who as pointed out earlier came from a wide range of different religious, ethnic and tribal communities.[2] More importantly is the fact that despite the myriads of obstacles faced by the new regime, Faisal did not waver or despair but diligently persisted in his worthy endeavour to create one unified Iraqi identity. Thus, he initiated a policy that would encourage all citizens to adhere to and believe in their (Iraqiness) and

Iraqi identity. He urged his ministers and officials to embolden all the country's components to be good Iraqis, and earnestly urged them to pursue state policies aimed at making their fellow citizens feel that they are all Iraqis of equal rights and responsibilities.[3]

The task however was difficult and involved an immense deal of continuous effort. During King Faisal I's rule and the years that ensued there were several crises and troubles that manifested themselves in disturbances, uprisings and rebellions by different Iraqi sects and ethnic groups. But most of those who led or participated in them were not usually objecting to their Iraqi identity. They were rather protesting against the central government's policies of spreading its influence and powers to all parts of the country. They felt that this extension of governmental presence would limit, if not deprive them of their authority, influence, and domination in the regions they used to control and rule without any state interference.

History has also recorded that, at that time, most of these disturbances and rebellions, especially the Kurdish ones, took place either when the treaty with Britain was about to expire, or when Britain wanted to amend it. Once the treaty was accepted and ratified by the Iraqi government, British air and ground forces were deployed to suppress and cut the Kurdish movements they had previously encouraged.

Significantly, despite all their religious, sectarian, and ethnic differences, the Iraqi people remained united, living in peace and harmony with growing intermarriage between them. This peaceful coexistence was reflected in the first Iraqi constitution, known as the Basic Law, and in other provisional constitutions before 2003. These charters never distinguished between the components of the people according to their religion, ethnicity, sect or language.

Successive Iraqi governments, starting with the royal regime until the US-led invasion of the country in 2003, including cabinet members, administrators, and high officials, were from all components of the Iraqi people. This could also be said about the political parties, whether licensed or clandestine. The leaderships of these parties were a mixture of different religions and ethnic or social backgrounds. In other words, the differences were political and not based on ethnic, sectarian or extreme religious beliefs.

An unmistakable testimony to the unity of the Iraqi society during the royal regime is manifested in the composition of the then outlawed but popular Iraqi parties, the Iraqi Communist Party (ICP), the National

Independence Party, the National Democratic Party and the Arab Socialist Baath party. This unity was culminated by the formation of the National Union Front (NUF) (1957) which included all these secret mass parties. Although, it was an exception, as it only included Kurds, the Kurdistan Democratic Party (KDP) also joined this Front after the success of the revolution that took place on the 14th of July 1958 which toppled the monarchy and established the republican regime.

THE ONSET OF DIVISION AND FRAGMENTATION

Signs of social and political division began to emerge after establishing the republican regime in 1958. The change was accompanied by a big migration from the countryside (rural areas) to the cities; this ended the role of certain social groups, such as the royal family, its entourage and the feudal class.

These events which impaired and shook the social structure of the country were significant precursors of deep divisions between the different political parties. At the outset, the ICP, due to its influence showed early and hasty intentions to dominate the political scene. Together with the KDP, they distanced themselves from the NUF. The two parties preferred to strengthen their relationship with the new regime than to stay in a united front that could check and observe the work of the new government.

The last division on the political level came over the issue of unity with the now-defunct United Arab Republic (UAR, Egypt and Syria). The division was manifested by the divergence between the Arab nationalists represented by the Baath Party and the Nasserites (supporters of President Nasser of Egypt) on the one hand, and the leftists, represented by ICP and to a certain extent the KDP on the other.

Although the split was very deep and indeed harmful to national unity, it was nevertheless based on purely political issues than religious or ethnic differences. Sooner than expected the two sides then moved from coercion and intimidation to violent confrontation and physical liquidation, initiated first by the ICP and the KDP against the followers and supporters of Baath Party and the Arab nationalists' bloc (1959–1962). This was later followed by a brutal and sanguinary campaign waged by the Baath party against the Communists and the KDP after the overthrow of the first republic in February 1963.

The division deepened and took a critical course when an armed Kurdish revolt erupted in 1961 in the north of the country against the republican regime. Note that this revolt was first initiated by Kurdish feudalists, who felt that the new Agrarian Reform Law, declared by the new regime (September 1958), would strip them of their large and extensive feudal fiefdoms.[4] This rebellion developed and spread to several Kurdish areas, giving different foreign powers hostile to Iraq an open opportunity to exploit it. Eventually and quickly the insurgency escalated and spread ending up a large-scale confrontation and hostilities between the Iraqi armed forces on the one hand, the KDP, and some Kurdish tribes on the other. Because of the continuous failure to solve this problem peacefully and wisely by the central government, these armed activities evolved to become almost a never-ending revolt and confrontation between the central government and the KDP.

The most threatening aspect of this revolt was when it turned into an ethnic and sometimes chauvinistic struggle. The KDP, which denounced the tribal rebellion as a feudalist and regressive one at its outset, adopted it later and hailed it as a national revolution against the (Arab domination) in spite of the fact that the new Republican regime hastened to recognize the Kurdish aspirations, widen their social, cultural and civil liberties and legalize the Kurdish political party (the KDP), professional associations and newspapers. On the other hand, the Arab nationalists denounced the revolt as an attempt to create 'another Israel' in the north of Iraq, in spite of the fact that Kurds being indigenous people of the land. Huge foreign intervention in the Kurdish movement, not only enabled the revolt to continue, but also etched even deeper the rift in the Arab-Kurdish relations in Iraq.

It is pointed out that there were other significant factors that had come to aggravate the situation and create a serious crack in the social structure and political relationships in Iraq. Chief among these were three major events or developments which took place during the 1940s and 1950s. The first was the establishment of an exclusively Kurdish party in 1946, the Kurdish Democratic Party (KDP). (Other Kurdish parties had earlier been formed but those were not as influential or popular.)

The KDP succeeded in attracting most of the Kurdish political figures, who were members and even leaders and prominent cadres in other large Iraqi parties, such as the Communist Party (ICP). More deleterious were the policies of this party which, intentionally or unintentionally, managed to drive an ethnic wedge between the Arabs and the Kurds. This was not because it was founded on a purely nationalist basis (in a country normally ruled by constitutions that guaranteed the equality of all rights and freedoms of all Iraqi citizens) rather, it was because first, some of its leaders adopted national chauvinistic attitudes[5]; second, the KDP resorted to incitement against Iraq and its national unity, and finally because it refused to unite its struggle with that of the rest of the Arab opposition parties in Iraq. Ironically, in its original mission statement and articles of association, the party had initially adopted the slogan of 'voluntary unity between the Arab and Kurdish people in Iraq'.[6] It became increasingly clear among most leaders of the KDP that the drive to separate Iraqi Kurdistan from Iraq was stronger than the urge to meet national unity. The aims and desires of the other Kurdish parties established after the KDP were not different.

The second important development was the emergence, for the first time in Iraq's history, of ultraconservative Islamist parties. The first party that was formed during the late 1940s was 'Al-Ukhuwa Al-Islamiya', a branch of the Muslim Brotherhood, which was formed secretly at first then overtly albeit unofficially later. This development resulted, not only in the emergence of religious parties but also in the implementation of one-colour sectarian Islamist parties. The ideology and practices of this party have been and is still devoted to the propagation and dissemination of Sunni sectarianism.[7] Another harmful effect of establishing this party was the threat it represented to the sentiments and beliefs of the followers of the Shiite sect, who represent a majority in Iraq.

The third harmful event was the creation, by extremist Shiite religious men a few years later, of another sectarian party under the name of the 'Islamic Dawa' Party. The political aims of this party did not pose any real threat to national unity however, the habitual recourse of its extremist leaders to attack the Companions of Prophet Mohammad (peace be upon him) was particularly damaging to the Sunni-Shiite accord. Chief among those targeted were the three caliphs who succeeded the Prophet (Abu Bakr, Omar, and Othman) as well as lady Aisha (mother of all believers), the wife of the prophet. These figures were venerated and held in high esteem by all Muslims, especially by the Sunnis. The verbal attacks by the Dawa leaders on these prominent figures never ceased even though most high religious scholars of the Shiite sect spurned and rejected this toxic trend.[8] What was really alarming was the fact that these events started to have political repercussions.

Although in the beginning, these developments had little impact on Iraqi society, their effects have nevertheless been felt in the political scene in the sense that people were for the first time presented with divisive religious dialogues disguised and clad in political attire. Sowing the seeds of division and discord among the components of the Iraqi people was a more serious effect on these developments.

In the meantime, the growing conflict between the Arab nationalist and their adversaries' leftist movements, and their mutual failure to fulfil the hopes and aims of the Iraqi masses, helped to give rise to, and increase the influence of the religious and sectarian movements and dogmas. To make matters worse, the political conflict between the different secular parties heightened the growth of religious trends in general and deepened the division of sectarian and ethnic groups. But the conflict did not shake the national unity or impact the Iraqi social fabric as its essence generally speaking remained political. In other words, the political influence of the conservative religious parties remained quite limited mostly because of the overwhelming secular and progressive inclinations which had taken root in the consciousness of the Iraqi society.

This modern progressive trend reflected in all the Iraqi constitutions which continued to emphasize and highlight the Iraqi identity, freedom of thought, conscience and religion. A special mention was made of respect for Kurdish rights. State positions and high offices were generally awarded based on merit, competence, integrity and patriotism, regardless of religious or ethnic differences.

The first sectarian overtones in modern Iraq surfaced on the political scene during the rule of former president Abdul Salam Aref (1963–1966). Although the man did not in general base his decisions or high office appointments on sectarian foundations, his affiliation with sectarian partisans had come to cast a sectarian shadow over the way he conducted official business. Also, his practice of performing the Friday prayer in public and transmitting this event by the state-owned television tinged his action with sectarian motives, as no Shiite Friday prayers had the same privilege. As a result, many of his actions and practices were interpreted by large swathes of people as sectarian.

This public perception was reinforced after the return of the Arab Baath Socialist Party to power in July 1968 (its first short-term was in 1963). Perhaps this notion was intensified by the fact that an overwhelming majority of the party and state leadership came from not only one component, but also from certain Sunni dominated areas in western Iraq, stretching between Tikrit, al-Dawr, Ana, and Haditha. The fact that the Baath party was secular, and that a large number of its cadres were from the different components of the Iraqi people, Shiites, Christians, and even some Kurds, did not absolve the party of this imputation.

The event which aggravated the situation and had the most impact on agitating sectarian sentiments was the eruption of the Islamic Revolution in Iran. The revolution, led by extremist religious fanatics, had from the beginning founded itself on and advanced religious slogans. Its meteoric success intensified the sectarian conflict throughout the Muslim world especially in neighbouring Iraq to an unprecedented level. The new Islamist regime in Tehran soon embarked on an intensive propaganda campaign that targeted the Shiites in Iraq, who constitute a majority in the country. The new rulers made much of the injustices inflicted on them, deploring their marginalization and manipulation by the minority Sunnis. Then the war of words escalated hitting a fever pitch and turned into an open call upon Shiites of Iraq to revolt against the (Sunni Baath regime), which was profusely vilified and denigrated as an (atheist regime).[9] The intense propaganda campaign was a political attempt to embarrass and destabilize the Baath regime in Iraq, and not to uphold or defend the rights of the so-called (oppressed Shiites).

In the meantime, Israel and the West promoted the idea that they must "defend the Iraqi Kurdish people who the Arabs suppressed". These allegations were to incite the Kurdish people in Iraq against the anti-western and anti-Israel Baath authority which began to emerge as a growing regional power. In both cases (the Iranian and Israeli propaganda), the premise was wrong and intended to instigate sectarian and ethnic strife in Iraq. The fact was that the Iraqi Baath government was neither entirely Sunni, nor was it persecuting Shiites because of their religious beliefs or the Kurds because of their ethnicity. It was rather a totalitarian government made up of all different components of the Iraqi people but used excessive power against all those who opposed it, being Arabs or Kurds, Sunnis or Shiites, Muslims, Christians, or any other sects.

The situation worsened when the Baath government decided to forcefully expel tens of thousands of Shiite families over the borders into Iran because they were of Iranian origin, even though the majority of them were naturalized Iraqi citizens or citizens by birth, descendants of parents born in Iraq. The notorious and widely criticized move was based on the allegation that some members of these families carried out terrorist acts, bombings, and assassination attempts against Baath leaders as instigated by Iran.[10]

Besides the unrelenting Baath policy of displacing families of Iranian origin, the failure to reach a fair and peaceful solution to the Kurdish problem exacerbated the situation even further. The deteriorating relations with the Kurdish political parties meant that a fair number of displaced Iraqis of Iranian origin, as well as armed Kurdish fighters (from the two main Kurdish parties, the KDP and the Kurdistan Patriotic Union PUK) who had sought refuge in Iran were left in Iran to be used against Iraq at any time. Furthermore, the regime's unwillingness to engage in dialogue with its opposition parties created other bases for fractures and rifts (both doctrinal and ethnical) within the Iraqi political community.

It was against this background that the Iraq–Iran war erupted. This pointless, needless and protracted war (1980–1988) fuelled and intensified the sectarian discourse which gave the new regime in Tehran a card they attempted to exploit during its conflict with Baghdad. During the war that lasted eight years, the Iranian Islamic regime extended and intensified its support to the two main Kurdish parties (the KDP and PUK), the Shiite al-Dawa party, and many Iraqis expelled for the purpose of having Iranian origin. It provided financial assistance, training as well as arms and encouraged these groups to launch attacks inside Iraqi territories.

It should be remembered that the majority of the Iraqi army's rank and file and middle-rank officer corps, who succeeded in foiling all Iran's attempts to occupy Iraqi territories, were predominantly Arab Shiites. This however did not quash or dispel Iranian accusations and charges against the Baath regime which was vehemently attacked and labelled as sectarian and hostile to both Shiites and Kurds. Neither did many Iraqi tribes, Arab Shiite from the south and Kurdish in the north, were fighting alongside the Iraqi army against the Iranian army and its allies from Iraqi Kurdish and Shiite militias.

The fact that Iraq had won the war against Iran (militarily) did nothing to alleviate the ethnic strife or sectarian discourse. The Baath regime's 'victory' failed to silence or even placates the different opposition parties especially the ones operating outside Iraq which intensified its work against the Baghdad regime which they now viewed as posing an even greater threat.

Thus the so-called 'external' opposition, composed mainly of Iraqi expatriates, continued to wage smearing campaigns against the Baath regime, assisted by some regional and international powers that felt uneasy about the outcome of the war. Against the strong grip of the Baath regime over all aspects of daily life and human activities in Iraq, the external opposition could not present any real challenge to the Iraqi regime. Furthermore, being a society mostly rose on secular heritage, narrow sectarian ideas did not appeal to most Iraqis. Fear of brutal reprisals on the other hand was another reason the religious and sectarian ideas did not flourish under the Baath regime. (The Baath party in Iraq boasted that it had around 1.2 million members before 2003, not to mention the huge number of its sympathizers and supporters. With the possible exception of al-Sadr's faction who was operating clandestinely in Iraq. Members and supporters of the opposition parties, Kurdish or Arab, did not exceed a few thousand at best).[11]

Finally, a confluence of tragic and disastrous circumstances conspired to arouse and invigorate sectarianism and led to the creation of ultranationalist and sectarian parties in Iraq. Chief among these are the catastrophic invasion of Kuwait (August 1990) and the utterly callous and irresponsible rejection of all Arab and international calls to withdraw from it, the destructive war led by the United States against the forces of Saddam Hussein, and of course, the crippling and most hurtful sanctions imposed on the country which continued for 13 years (1990–2003).

The impact of these fast and dramatic developments meted out an immense blow not only to the stability and indeed the existence of the Iraqi state but also to the social fabric of the fledgling nation. The devastating war to drive Saddam Hussein's forces out of Kuwait wreaked havoc on the country's infrastructure and its military capabilities, not to mention the dismantling and destruction of the prestige of the state and its standing in the Arab world, the region as well as the world at large.

It was inevitable that the situation obtained after the eviction from Kuwait should create an increase in the contentions and differences inside the Iraqi society. Of course, this situation played in the hands of external powers, especially the USA, Britain, Israel and Iran, which were more than enthusiastic to remove the Baath regime from power. Yet Saddam Hussein's decision to fire 39 long-range missiles at Israel during the Gulf war (1991), for the first time in the history of the Arab-Israeli conflict, made Israel, the USA, and the Western powers in general, more determined to remove the regime and replace it with the 'external' Iraqi opposition. Israel on its part revived a plan it had introduced during the Iran-Iraq war, based on dividing Iraq into three entities: Shiite, Sunni and Kurdish. Furthermore, the situation in Iraq was shown in the US-Western media as a regime specifically targeting Shiites and Kurds, rather than a totalitarian regime ruling the country with a Stalinist iron fist demanding submission through coercion and brutal security means.

Despite the fact that the parties of the Iraqi opposition abroad were disjointed, divided along sectarian and racial lines, most of its leaders' reputations were tarnished and had little support inside Iraq, Israel, the US, Britain and the west chose to support it, especially the Shiite and Kurdish part of it. The latter two parties were further promised to be the new rulers of Iraq after toppling the regime of Saddam Hussein. The tragic events of 9/11 were in a way a Godsend gift to the Iraqi opposition. The United States arbitrarily and without any basis or evidence pointed the finger at Iraq, accusing it of being an accomplice with the perpetrators of that atrocity. It is against this background that the tripartite (US, UK, and Israeli) secret plans to invade Iraq gathered momentum. Much was made in the media and diplomatic circles of the false and fabricated allegations (as subsequent events showed) Iraq's WMD and other falsehoods to give some sort of legitimacy to their secret design. Perhaps even more harmful than the plan to invade Iraq were the ceaseless and intensive efforts to sow the seeds of ethnic and sectarian strife and even deeper ethnic and religious rifts and fault lines within the Iraqi society.

THE OCCUPATION AND ITS CONSEQUENCES

Just as occupying Iraq in 2003 represented a regional and international disaster by any standard, and opened the door for regional instability and terrorism; it also dealt a devastating blow to national unity, the social fabric of the people and to the status of the Iraqi state itself both on the regional and international scenes. It also became clear that the ultimate aim of the Israeli and US administrations was to dismantle Iraq and end its existence as a regional power and as an independent entity. To that end, the occupying powers followed well-planned strategies that can be seen in:

First, the occupying powers, especially the United States, kept reiterating that: (a) Iraq is an artificial state, created by the British in 1921; (b) it is a state made up of Shiites, Sunnis, Kurds and other smaller components, and that these different ethnic and religious communities failed to coexist peacefully or integrate into one identity. In so doing, the United States was simply trying to erase the national characteristics of the Iraqi society and deny the fact that most of the Iraqis were Arabs. It is significant to classify the Arabs as Sunnis, Shiites or Christians, etc., while treating the Kurds who were also divided into Sunnis, Shiites and Christians as one homogeneous nationality and unified entity. In other words, ignoring the religious and denominational divisions by which the United States defined Iraqi Arabs when it came to the Kurds. This insistence on applying labels to Iraqis was soon to become a normal practice when Paul Bremer, the absolute US civil administrator of Iraq, formed the (Governing Council).[12]

Bremer was quite determined to compose the Governing Council of representatives of the racial and sectarian parties which had collaborated with the United States. The new governing body was thus made up not of political figures representing movements and ideologies but ethnic or religious, mainly Shiites and Kurds, with few members of Sunni, Turkoman, and representatives of the other communities. Furthermore, Bremer insisted on citing the sectarian and ethnic affiliation of each member of the Council before his name: This member is a Shiite and the other is a Sunni but this is a Kurd and that is a Christian, and so on, ironically, referring to the appointed Secretary General of the Iraqi Communist Party in the council as a Shiite and not the leader of a secular and cosmopolitan party.

Second: The administration of Iraq during the occupation, as well as the US and British high officials, reiterating, loudly enough, that the Shiites and the Kurds had been oppressed, maltreated in the past, previously barred from governing Iraq, and that the time has come for them to have this privilege. Not only did the Shiite and Kurdish religious parties prevail and hold sway over the government, but they also laid the foundation for a quota system that is being adhered to till this day. According to this apportionment scheme, the president of the republic is required to be a Kurd, the prime minister a Shiite, while the speaker of the parliament a Sunni. The Cabinet members and the positions of deputy ministers were also divided in the same way. Today each party speaks about this or that position or ministry as it were their own freehold property or share acquired as it were by divine right that nobody can tamper with or waive. More pernicious was the fact that those chosen for public offices were not chosen according to their merit, experience or high qualifications, they were simply appointed because they happened to belong to a certain party, sect or ethnic group. Moreover, the minister or any high-ranking official would not be questioned, or judged by how they served the people in general, they were rather expected to consecrate the budget allocated to their department to the party or group that nominated them for the office.[13]

Third: The Sunni component was not only marginalized but was repeatedly accused, incriminated, and eventually persecuted because (it was loyal to the former regime). This practice was soon codified through legislation of the de-Baathification Law and the order to disband the Iraqi armed forces. The two laws were used arbitrarily, especially the law of de-Baathification, which focused on the Sunnis and not on other components (By the way, the harsh Arabic word used to name this law was (ijtithath) which means uprooting). To make matters worse, different militias and 'unknown' armed gangs waged a large-scale campaign to assassinate, kidnap and terrorize prominent Sunni figures and members of the dissolved Iraqi armed forces. Regions with Sunni majority furthermore faced what amounted to sectarian cleansing and continuous harassment. The occupation forces did nothing to protect those targeted, something that international law regarded. The failure to protect the weak, vulnerable and powerless is a flagrant betrayal of the obligations and responsibilities of an occupying power.

Fourth: A constitution was prepared for Iraq, mainly by American experts, which supported division among the people of the same country and laid the foundation for its permanent schism. It is enough to mention that it stressed that Iraq is a federal state and not a unified state, and did not mention maintaining the territorial integrity of Iraq as a fundamental goal, as is the case with all the constitutions of the world. Even the oath of the President of the Republic did not contain the words preserving and maintaining the territorial integrity and unity of Iraq.[14]

Fifth: Trained sectarian and religious militias abroad, especially in Iran, came back with the invading forces and were allowed to enter Iraq with their weapons, only to take the law into their own hands. Dissolving the Iraqi army, the police, and all other security services made these militias the only power on the ground. When these armed groups started to commit sectarian crimes and sectarian cleansing, especially in Baghdad, nobody stepped in to stop them from doing so. To make matters worse, the occupying administration established a new army (indicatively it was named the National Guards), mainly by combining different sectarian militias. This new so-called army also pursued a policy of liquidation and area cleansing (on a sectarian basis), while the Kurdish Peshmerga forces did the same in the areas surrounding the Kurdish provinces in Iraq.[15]

Sixth: The clergymen, loyal to the ruling and influential religious parties, were granted the freedom to act on dominating and controlling the society. This was done even though the teachings of the two main and dominating religious sects in Iraq, the Jaafari Shiites and the Hanafi Sunnis, have for centuries been known for their moderation, keenness on Islamic tolerance and brotherhood. The history of the (imams/religious leaders) of both sects demonstrated how they actively advocated and called for harmony and peaceful coexistence between the two sects. However, a fair amount of clergymen, from both sects who were involved in politics and public affairs, began to sow the seeds of discord and hatred (either deliberately, unwittingly, or naïvely), inciting sedition and hatred between Muslims of different denominations. More harmful and serious was the fact that a good number of these religious figures had assumed high and influential posts in the new government, thus were able to tender their sectarian leanings and declarations as official policy. In fact, their fanatical, extremist and sectarian discourse was interpreted as representing all of those who belonged to the same sect and ethnic group, which is of course a fallacy. Needless to say, the behaviour and discourse of one component aroused resentment and hatred among followers of other components. When some of the Kurdish leaders sounded too partisan and chauvinistic in tone, they were, in turn, met with chauvinistic statements from those who claimed to defend the Arab identity of Iraq.[16]

Seventh: The neighbouring countries were allowed to expand their influence inside Iraq either by sending elements to sow the differences between different communities or through supporting local militias to do so. All this was happening while successive governments were turning a blind eye to the influx of terrorist organizations. The fact that the occupation had left the Iraqi borders undefended and unguarded did of course help these elements to easily enter Iraq with their arms. Each foreign element claimed that it was extending support and protection to a certain side, sect or ethnic group, against the encroachment of the other. This support included large funds, armaments, and training. In the end, each neighbouring country had a militia following its orders. Iran had supported the Shiite parties loyal to it under the pretext of preventing the Sunnis from regaining power; Turkey did the same on the pretext of supporting the Iraqi Turkoman and some Sunni parties to counter the encroachment of Shiite and Kurdish parties (It also claimed that it was in hot pursuit of the followers of the outlawed Kurdish party the PKK). Israel on its part has intensified its military cooperation and support for the Kurdish Peshmerga forces on the pretext of strengthening the Kurdish regional government against any attempts by any Arab government to restore its influence in their region, while the Gulf States supported the Sunni parties and figures claiming that they were trying to protect them from the transgressions of the Shiite militias, and so on. One does not need to explain the real goals behind the support of each party, which was never for 'the love of their blue eyes' i.e. the interest of these components. The result of this external 'help' was deepening the divisions inside Iraq, with incitement and counter incitement. In other words, sectarian division has become the main feature of Iraq after the occupation. Of course, these divisions were encouraged by the local elements that ruled Iraq with the covert and sometimes overt support of the occupation forces since 2003.[17]

As a result fragmentation, division, political hostility, and sectarian violence that characterized the conduct of political parties were transferred in the form of sectarian and ethnic hatred into the body politic of the Iraqi society. The effects or the dangers of these policies were soon to build up and mount. The sectarian religious and nationalist parties, involved in the political process started promoting these concepts for political ends. Simultaneously each of these parties spread the lie that it was becoming intransigent and violent only because the adversaries, i.e., the other component threatens it's very existence and wants to liquidate them. Thus, the division became horizontal and vertical at all levels. Most of the media that emerged after the occupation concentrated on and used a highly divisive discourse. The newspapers and other organs of these parties especially their highly partisan satellite stations mainly engaged in inflammable hate speech fuelling and etching stronger hatred and suspicion between the different components of the same people.

The discourse of most parties participating in the political process soon became characterized by narrow sectarian and highly nationalistic and bigoted tone. Each component now threatened either to secede or divide Iraq if its demands were not met. As these parties found that their participation in the government has opened the door for them to loot Iraq and accumulate wealth with impunity, through corruption, without any oversight or accounting, they no longer considered waiving these policies that earned them wealth in millions or billions of dollars, which they are now using to entrench their positions and stay in power.

Regrettably, a substantial percentage of Iraqis, either because of their ignorance or hatred of the former regime, or because of some sorts of material benefit, or because of sectarian or chauvinistic affiliations, were initially swayed by such policies and came to endorse them. However, after more than 18 years of occupation, an increasing proportion of Iraqis began to discover the falsehood of the politicians' claims and allegations; they started to notice how the politicians and their families took advantage of this fiery discourse. They felt how the majority of Iraqis, Arabs, Kurds and Turkoman, Christians, Sunni and Shiite Muslims, lived in extreme poverty and in dire need, while the politicians who pay lip service to the poor were, living in an extravagant and lavish style.

If one is to add to this widespread corruption, the other daily tragedies such as assassinations, bombings and the dominance of illegally armed militias, one could understand the changing mood of the Iraqis. The last straw was the occupation in 2014 of three major provinces west and north-west of Iraq: Mosul (Nineveh), Tikrit (Salah al-Din) and Ramadi (Anbar), by the terrorist organization the Islamic State of Syria and Iraq (ISIS, ISIL also known Daesh). The new Iraqi army abandoned these provinces they were supposed to defend and simply ran away. In the end, this occupation ended more than three years later, with huge sacrifices and shedding of Iraqi blood from all the component of the Iraqi society. On top of that, the liberation process (2016–2018) resulted in destroying the provinces occupied by Daesh. Regrettably, some fanatic Shiite politicians used the acts and crimes of the Daesh terrorist organization as a way of winning and inciting their component by claiming that (this Sunni organization) intended to (liquidate the Shiite community), even though Daesh terrorist organization was killing more Sunnis, Christians, Turkoman and Kurds than Shiites in the provinces they overran.

It has now become clear that among the main reasons behind the emergence and spread of this terrorist organization were the corruption, mismanagement and failures of those that wielded power since the 2003 invasion who were mostly expatriates who had practically lost touch with Iraq which they re-entered with the occupation forces. It also became clear that some influential political parties and leaders from all religious and ethnic groups (Kurds, Turks and Arabs), often clandestinely collaborated with ISIS in two fields: first in facilitating occupying Mosul, and second in helping ISIS smuggle and sell the oil which the terrorist organization extracted from the territories it controlled.

There are now widely circulating reports that some Kurdish and Arab Islamist parties were involved in protecting leading members and some fighters from ISIS. They furthermore secretly incorporated some of the

ISIS members and affiliated them in their militias.[18] There are also reports that even the US forces in the area provided safe havens to some Daesh fighters.

It is these facts that have made a majority of Iraqis reconsider their attitudes, reject sectarian policies and started focusing on the common bonds and features of the Iraqi society, as a step in the right direction, i.e., promoting national unity again. This was manifested first by concentrating on the fact that their society was not familiar with these divisive policies and sectarian discourse; secondly, and most importantly, their reluctance to take part in the general elections of 2018, especially after realizing that the majority of nominees, people or coalitions, were the same people who had since 2003 ruled and miserably failed. Statistics showed that only less than 20% voted in the last elections (2018), with some sources saying that those who went to the polling stations did not exceed 17%.[19] The third manifestation of the Iraqis' rejection of the policies pursued since 2003 was the huge demonstrations of 2015, 2018 and 2019 which engulfed Iraq from the north to the south. The most significant ones were the protests which overwhelmed Baghdad and the southern provinces, dominantly populated by Shiites, which erupted in October 2019. They were significant because the sectarian parties kept on claiming that they enjoyed the support and trust of the communities of these provinces. But these communities took to the streets and angrily protested against these rulers' corruption and dismal failures. The same happened in the Kurdish provinces. All protests through oppression and the use of force including live ammunitions were silenced.

Attempts at Promoting National Reconciliation in Iraq and the Requirements to Achieve It

It is ironic that after the chaos caused by the disastrous occupation, the first call for national reconciliation in Iraq came not from the Iraqis themselves but externally. Iraq's immediate neighbours and other countries in the region felt an urgent need to intervene. They were either driven by fear that the Iraqi whirlwind might in one way or another sweep their lands, or the desire to play a bigger role and gain greater influence in Iraqi politics. It was not surprising to see conferences held for this purpose first in Cairo under the auspices of the Arab League, then in Turkey and Qatar, under the auspices of the governments of the two countries, with other meetings in Jordan, Saudi Arabia, Kuwait, and the UAE. It could be said that these countries, especially the immediate neighbours, were mainly apprehensive that things might get out of hand, and violence could spread to their countries or to the region. Later on, more specifically since 2007, successive Iraqi governments, paid lip service to this process. It could be said that they felt compelled to do so for the simple reason that they did not want to be forced, through these external meetings, to reconcile or even sit with representatives of the Baath Party or its supporters, or engage in any dialogue with those who were representing the Iraqi resistance.

In general, however, all these governmental activities and attempts were meant to achieve reconciliation between the political parties already participating in the political process and those parties which had been excluded from this process. In other words, these attempts were not meant to achieve a general communal reconciliation or to bridge the rifts and mend the fractures which had undermined national unity. Neither were they initiated to address the sharp divisions between all components of the Iraqi people, caused by the policies of the ruling sectarian, religious-conservative and racial parties.

For several reasons, these calls did not appeal to most of the Iraqis and failed to achieve the required (declared) goals. First, the public realized from its own experience with the governing parties, that the calls for national reconciliation were not sincere but merely uttered for public consumption. The Iraqis also felt that these calls were empty and would not produce the desired results, ease their suffering, or show positively on their lives. At best, all that it will result in is appeasement and reconciliation between sectarian, racial and corrupt parties already participating in the government. These calls that external powers pressed were further feared to allow other corrupt, sectarian, or failing parties and personalities to join the government.

Secondly, most of the people the successive Iraqi governments assigned to lead the preparations for a general reconciliation dialogue were notorious for their corruption and their sectarian and racist bent of mind as well. In addition, there were huge doubts about, and little faith in their convictions, loyalty, or commitment to reconciliation. Finally, critics observed that all those asked to incentivize the reconciliation process were already part of the government that was rightfully accused of abetting sectarianism and marginalizing huge parts of the Iraqi society since their arrival with US forces in 2003.

As for the foreign and external efforts in this field, the processes did not go beyond the call for much-publicized meetings, elaborate ceremonies, and fanfare with too many promises and pledges and then everything ends after these gatherings. No permanent or follow-up committees were established to supervise the process and make sure the resolutions are implemented. In other words, everything ends with the end of each conference or meeting with nothing achieved at all.

For any genuine, real, and effective attempts at national reconciliation, some basic issues should be addressed: <u>First</u>: If the government wants to adopt such a worthy process or play such a role, it must first show an earnest desire to work out a general and comprehensive reconciliation arrangement that does not exclude anyone. This should be accompanied by a sincere sense of responsibility to keep the unity and integrity of Iraq. To develop an integrated strategy to do this, it is important that implementing this strategy be preceded and accompanied by real steps that leads to combating some of the negative phenomena which have plagued the country such as corruption, bribery, nepotism and appointments based on ethnic or sectarian allegiance. Only through these steps can the earnestness and credibility of any government in supporting reconciliation efforts be tested or ascertained. The rule of law should furthermore be allowed to play its role by allowing courts to fight any illegal phenomenon. These essential prerequisites if carried out would most certainly elicit the approval and support of the majority of the people. They would also restore some confidence in the political process, make the society as a whole feel the seriousness of the government, and put reconciliation on the right track.

<u>Second</u>: if on the other hand, successive Iraqi governments fail to achieve this noble goal and continue to prove their inability to bring about peace and tranquillity, the task should then be entrusted with other elements in the society who are truly dedicated to the process of reconciliation, and more importantly, who believe in its necessity. Prominent, distinguished and generally respected people (such as community leaders, dignitaries of all components, heads of professional unions, university professors, etc.) should lead the way. It is equally important not to allow parties engaged in the political process have control, or even be involved in it unless they rise above their prejudices and expurgate their organizations of all ills and bigotries and silence all voices inciting sectarianism and ethnic chauvinism.

Third: Conduct a massive and well-publicized campaign to explain and define the meaning of reconciliation and what it wants to achieve. Social and political reconciliation should be differentiated. It is also essential to clarify that the aim is not to reconcile the parties and political forces that have been involved in the political process since 2003. It should also be made clear that reconciliation is not meant to be between the governing coalitions and those who are competing with them. If the aim is to achieve the latter, then this is not national reconciliation. If the objective is to achieve communal and societal reconciliation, which is hopelessly needed, then it must be entrusted to some other bodies and elements that are known for their objectivity and are far removed from political ambitions that can draw up a plan of action and focus of following a clear and comprehensive strategy.

Fourth: All civil society organizations and international organizations operating in Iraq must be involved in this process to create interaction and a sense of wide range of popular support.

Steps and Strategies to Ensure the Success of National Reconciliation

The first step towards achieving genuine and serious national reconciliation is to amend the current Iraqi constitution through the expurgation of all references and clauses that instigate or encourage sectarianism, favouritism and prefer one component over the others.[20] It should also be refined from any notion that may encourage fragmenting Iraq. Sectarian and divisive references such as the Husseini processions, the Shiite (Marja'iya), the (Disputed Areas) as well as other negative allusions contained in the preamble should also be removed or edited.[21] Care should be given when redrafting this document to avoid the use of clauses that might carry more than one meaning and purpose.

Such a step however can be challenging. To start with, the constitution stipulated that certain articles (regarded as very controversial and harmful for national unity by many analysts), cannot be amended, changed or deleted. Moreover, judging by lots of experts, how the constitution was drafted, show that those who wrote it had intentionally wanted it to be sacrosanct, not to be touched, amended or altered to keep Iraq weak and divided. More important is the drafters have practically made the issue of amending it very difficult, if not impossible. The constitution for example stipulated that any amendment would not be adopted if refused by at least three governorates.[22] As the Kurdish parties, the main beneficiary of the new constitution, already control three provinces, Dahuk, Erbil, and Sulaimaniya, and were given the right to expand their region to include other 'mixed areas', termed in the constitution as 'disputed areas', one could understand why it is difficult to amend this document. It could be said that the Kurdish parties have cleverly tailored most of the paragraphs of the constitution to suit their ambitions and desires. Therefore it is almost impossible to see these parties relinquish any of the powers and advantages bestowed on them by the new constitution. In fact, on many occasions, some Kurdish leaders announced that they had intentionally put certain phrases and articles in the document to resort to them when they find it convenient to secede from Iraq.[23] More important, and indeed more harmful, is the deliberate omission of any reference to the unity and integrity of the Iraqi territory. Bearing all these citations and implications in mind, how can anyone imagine that the Kurdish parties will accept any amendment? They have consistently regarded any call for amendment as attempts to curtail their powers, or as a move for depriving them of the de facto independence they have enjoyed for decades. They also view any such effort as trying to deny them their 'right' to expand beyond the area of the 'Kurdish region' to the so-called (disputed areas).

On the other hand, how could anyone expect the leaders of the sectarian Shiite parties to accept any amendment which might alter, change or even touch the articles about the preamble or the references to some sectarian rituals and ceremonies, especially after the benefits and advantages this document has given them. It is now common knowledge that these bigoted religious parties used the constitution to exploit the ignorance of a fair majority of their fellow Shiites and, by promoting sectarianism, managed to gain their votes in the general elections.

Finally, any amendment to the constitution would give the impression that it would be a step to restore Iraq as a strong and influential country in the region. Such a thing would upset Israel, the United States as well as the West, not to mention Iran and some Arab Gulf states, who would like to keep Iraq weak, divided, and embroiled in its internal problems, so as not to pose any threat to them. In other words, there will be an internal, regional, and international rejection of such a step, whether explicitly or implicitly.

The second step should be to restrict the right to keep and bear arms to state forces only (the army and the police). This should be accompanied by a legislation aimed at dissolving all illegal or unofficial armed militias belonging to sectarian and nationalist (ethnical) political parties, or those controlled by outside powers.[24] The unconstrained and undisciplined activities of the widespread illegal militias have and are still associated with a number of heinous crimes which have deepened the divisions inside the Iraqi society and have driven wedges between all of its components, Arabs, Kurds, Turkoman, and the rest of other sects and minorities.

It has become a daily phenomenon for militia factions, to whichever component of the Iraqi society they belong, to target and liquidate whoever differs with them. Certain components of the Iraqi population, as well as each political party participating in the political process, have their militia, over which government has no control. These militias have mushroomed over the years. Although Shiite and Kurdish ones are more in number and brutal in tactics and practices, Sunni and Christian militias who claim they are only defending fellow citizens of their components, have, however, committed similar crimes. These infringements of the law caused chaos and cracks in the fabric of the Iraqi society. Iraq needs decades of national campaigns, and mammoth, sincere efforts to heal this deepening rift. In most Third World countries, the armed forces are in general regarded as the melting pot of all differences and divisions. In other words, military discipline was always regarded as the crucible in which ethnic, religious, and sectarian differences melt. Attempts to weaken this national institution, the army while elevating instead the role of militias will only lead to enfeeble and harm to national unity. There are indications that some external and internal elements wanted to strengthen sectarian and ethnic militias at the cost of the Iraqi army. Such intentions and designs, if successful, will only lead to dominating armed militias and the total demise of Iraq as a nation. All efforts should be focused on rehabilitating the official armed forces institutions, because they are, as it were, the best crucible to lay the ground for Iraqi national unity.

The third step is to withdraw all TV broadcast licenses and stop (totally end) transmitting all satellite channels and radio stations which incite the populace and propagate sectarian sedition, extremism, and chauvinistic ideologies. Similar measures should be taken to tackle local and foreign newspapers, which cultivate poisonous and divisive creeds and dogmas among Iraqis or encourage them to engage in outdated and backward religious practices.[25] Instead, focus should be made on enlightening programmes, discussions, lectures and historical experiences that promote patriotism, solidarity, and unity inside the Iraqi society, and advocate tolerance and peaceful coexistence.

The fourth essential step, which is related to the previous point, is to activate all the laws that impose the harshest penalties on anyone who proves that they were involved in, made statements, wrote or published anything that provoked sectarian, ethnic or religious division. Moreover, new legislations and regulations should also be issued to combat whatever causes division inside the society.

The fifth action should be taken to intensify popular participation in the campaigns to combat whatever causes, or leads to rifts and divisions. The fact that the occupation traumatized Iraq, dominating failing and corrupt politicians and governments, has and continues to prove, that the post-occupation governments and politicians are not only a major cause of the problems that engulf Iraq but also that they are incapable of solving the problems they have created. They cannot start such a process properly. The biggest evidence of this is the failure for more than a decade of successive governments to launch an inclusive round table dialogue involving all political parties. Their pretext is that they are not ready to start dialogue with certain parties or with representatives of foreign parties or elements.[26]

It is a sad reflection on the state of affairs in Iraq when the ruling politicians still insist on stirring up sectarianism and division among simple and naïve people. It is, therefore naïve to entrust those who have caused most of the problems since 2003, through corruption, intimidation, and rigged elections, with the heavy burden of putting an end to this gigantic problem. This unscrupulous and untrustworthy clique should not be allowed to take part in this process let alone lead it.

It defies belief that more than eighteen years, since the invasion of Iraq in 2003, not a single corrupt senior official has been held accountable, brought to justice or imprisoned despite the huge amount of evidence condemning them of mismanagement, obstruction of justice, and corruption. Even in the very few cases of some being sentenced to jail; those convicted have either been smuggled out of the country by some ruling Iraqi officials or by coalition forces.[27] The other reason why these politicians are neither capable nor qualified to lead any reform is that most of them are more ready and willing to defend the interests of outside powers (such as the United States, Iran, Turkey, Gulf States and even Israel), than to defend Iraq's interests. For these reasons, the main responsibility must be shouldered by the Iraqi people (professional organizations, trade unions, civil society organizations, cultural associations, universities, social clubs, artists etc.). All these bodies must rise to the challenge and work actively to spread the culture of social reconciliation and suggest ways of bringing all components of the Iraqi people closer to each other.

The sixth prerequisite measure is to work out plans or programmes for ensuring the restoration of essential services to most of Iraqis. Plans for employment and skill acquisitions should also be carefully implemented to give training and work for the huge number of unemployed. The spread of unemployment, lack of vital services, and the widespread feeling of injustice and marginalization which engulf some provinces are issues that need to be urgently addressed. It is to be borne in mind that there are some provinces in Iraq that have received more than their fair share of care from the government. Other provinces by contrast are neglected on a sectarian basis. This state of affairs increases division and impedes any attempt at national reconciliation.

The Seventh important measure should be to combat the harmful practice of imbibing backward ideologies and sectarian religious notions in the minds of children and adolescents to influence their belief systems, worldviews, and thinking process.[28]

This requires a careful revision of the educational system and curricula aimed at removing all elements capable of inciting social, ethnic or sectarian clashes between the different components of the society. Children, juveniles and young students should from an early stage, be taught to exercise tolerance and accept differences. More importantly, they should not be forced to attend courses that teach, train, or show outdated sectarian practices or notions. It is a matter of great importance and urgenc that educational institutions and centres of learning should be immunized against political or religious parties influence from whichever quarter they may come.

Lastly, any attempt or trend at promoting the role of religious institutions (Sunnis and Shiites alike) that presents them as defenders of national unity must be curtailed. From the beginning of the occupation, these religious authorities and their leaders have shown no genuine interest or seriousness to fight corruption or combat attempts to tear down national unity. Furthermore, they have failed to provide any example or role model for religious unity and integrity. Their roles in society should therefore be limited to organizing and participating in joint religious celebrations or events in which Muslims, in general, agree (For example, celebrating the birth of the Prophet Muhammad, the battle of Badr, etc.). They should also encourage joint celebrations and religious prayers by Sunnis and Shiites and instigate good relations between non-Muslim leaders and the communities of Iraq.

INFLUENTIAL PARTIES AND GROUPS WHICH SHOULD SHOULDER THE RESPONSIBILITY OF INITIATING THE PROCESS OF GENUINE NATIONAL RECONCILIATION

Official government interest in achieving national reconciliation has never been serious or perceptible, to say the least. Apart from some occasional statements and remarks uttered every now and then for local or regional consumption, no government has expended any real effort towards national reconciliation since 2003. In a quest to display their total outrage at the sectarian and divisive policies of many government regimes and the widespread corruption, the Iraqi people have staged several massive demonstrations, rallies and sit-ins which have resulted in several violent rioting. In a few cases of such violent protests, headquarters and central offices of the ruling parties, especially the religious ones, have been attacked and burnt down.[29]

Without any doubt, this reaction has confirmed that the majority of the people rejected the corruption, exclusionist policies and the whole system of governance since 2003. Popular support for these demonstrations was overwhelming and nationwide from north to south and regardless of all ethnic, religious or sectarian differences. The same supportive attitude was widely demonstrated in providing humanitarian aid and shelter to the millions that were displaced after the terrorist Daesh fighters had overrun and ransacked towns and villages. This act of solidarity was soon to be repeated during the vigorous campaigns that defeated and expelled the Daesh terrorists. These events, including the uprising of Baghdad, the southern provinces and the Kurdish northern governorates, afforded unmistakable evidence of the communal solidarity and sense of brotherhood among all components of the Iraqi people regardless of their religious or ethnic affiliation.

In contrast to the popular prompt and wilful support provided by the private citizen's rich and poor, the government grants that were earmarked for reconstruction purposes with particular reference to allotted funds for the rebuilding of the Western areas were all but plundered and looted by the very same people entrusted with disbursing these disaster relief funds.[30]

There is a growing popular awareness for the need to fight all that seek to perpetuate rift and division within Iraqi society, punctuated by the insistence of these popular protests to fight corruption, hold to account any corrupt official regardless of their religious or ethnic affiliation, those who participated in the killing of demonstrators as well as those with links to foreign powers that are responsible for the misery suffered by the people. The leaders of the ruling Shiite parties have tried to promote the idea that their main objective is to improve the status of the Shiite component and (remove decade long historical injustices) it has suffered. This claim proved to be false because the southern provinces, which comprise the majority of this component, were the first to rise up against these parties. In the same vein, the Kurdish parties who claimed that they were endeavouring to provide the Kurds with peace and prosperity also proved to be no less false and hypocritical than their Arab counterparts. The massive anti-corruption demonstrations that covered the entire Kurdish region (2018 and in 2020) were clear examples of the failure of these parties to fulfil their promises. Other Kurdish complaints and grievances are the high rate of unemployment, the domination of Kurdish security forces, the corrupt policies of the two major Kurdish parties (KDP and PUK) which is characterized by embezzling the revenues of oil smuggled out of Kurdish oil fields and that of the border checkpoints accompanied with the failure of the Kurdish regional administration to pay employees their salaries.

The same goes for the inhabitants of the western provinces, which include most of the Sunni component. For years the Sunni parties claimed to defend this component but events have proven that the majority of the leading members of these parties are devious and corrupt. They pay little or no attention to the suffering of the people of this component. Consequently, these leaders have lost their credibility and support among the Sunni community. The mistrust for some of these leaders was further deepened when they chose to propitiate Iran to win their parliamentary seats or a place in one of the cabinets. Presently, these leaders find it very difficult to meet with members of their own angered community.

Therefore, the only constituent with a genuine interest in bringing about sincere, forthright and capable societal reconciliation is the Iraqi people themselves.

The ways and means to achieve reconciliation can be worked out with leaders of the popular protest movements, demonstrations civil society organizations, trade and professional unions, university academics, tribal and community leaders. These constituents, individually and collectively, are capable of initiating and achieving a comprehensive national reconciliation programme through mass gathering, rallies, cultural festivals and other activities.

Leaders of the popular demonstrations and movement should therefore not limit their activities to their own province but instead, should coordinate and collaborate with their counterparts from other provinces. Likewise, trade unions and confederations that are branched throughout Iraq can also take part in this national effort. They can do so by sponsoring mutual and diversified national events, public lectures and TV programmes, to heighten national unity awareness. They should also defend the rights of all Iraqis, not just their members but also men and women, without distinction on the basis of gender, religion, language or ethnicity. Civil society organizations (not those funded by the occupation and external powers) can of course take part in this effort and do the same. As for the universities and research centres, they can run scientific conferences and seminars, conduct studies, publish articles and encourage graduate students to write specialized researches and studies on patriotism, good citizenship and national unity. Furthermore, they can sponsor seminars and symposia that commemorate recent or historical events that portray a sense of solidarity and unity among Iraqis in the face of foreign enemies. Iraq's modern history abounds in such cases typical examples. These include the 1920 popular revolution that forced Britain to abandon the idea of colonial direct rule; the revolution of 1941 which defied British domination, the participation of the Iraqi armed forces in the 1948 war in Palestine, the heroic participation of the Iraqi armed forces in the 1973 war against the Israeli army, the epic defence of all the components of the Iraqi people of their homeland against Iran's attempt to occupy it during the Iran–Iraq war and the national resistance that foiled the occupation's plans, to name but a few. Such topics and themes that encourage love of one's homeland are definitely more beneficial to students and society than encouraging them to write researches about controversial denominational issues, sectarian, religious parties or ethnic chauvinism. These events can in other words intensify public awareness of the necessity for solidarity and national unity and significantly contribute to the process of establishing the foundations for national reconciliation.

The Possible Impact of Reconciliation on Iraq's Position Internally, Regionally and Internationally

Since 2003 Iraq has become one of the most corrupt countries in the world and one of the most dangerous places to live in. It has further become one of the most fragile and failed states with more than four million of its people internally displaced, living in camps and temporary shelters, and a similar number who have emigrated outside Iraq. The political, social and security upheaval caused by the US invasion has left more than 3 million widows and more than 2 million orphans. Sectarian violence, religious and ethnic encroachments as well as the insistence on following vindictive policies which seek revenge rather than appeasement has exacerbated the situation.

The countless failures of the parties participating in the political process have gradually and significantly eroded what popular support they may have enjoyed. This dramatic development however did not prompt them to devise or think of ways to bolster their positions. As a result of their determination to remain in power by any cost and means, they have resorted to three devious methods: Firstly, to continue fanning sectarian flames to gain support of the ignorant and naïve or those who are benefiting from this policy. Secondly, to plunder Iraq's wealth and resources as well as embezzle huge sums estimated at hundreds of billions of US dollars. This ill-gotten wealth has enabled them to buy cheap support and influence and also to establish or buy up a variety of media outlets such as satellite TV channels, radio stations, newspapers, magazines as well as social media blogs. They also organize special mass celebrations and meetings to lavish costly gifts on supporters and prospective followers. Consequently, each party now wields immense power to influence its own communities and no doubt some parts of the public at large. The third method is to form armed militias aimed at providing personal protection defending their headquarters and institutions. So far they have succeeded in silencing any opposition, but seemingly, their methods are beginning to backfire as they have created many conflicting centres of power, militias and propaganda organs. The 2018 elections proved that their methods were negative and ineffective. Failing to secure popular support among its people, almost all the ruling parties have resorted to seeking support from external regional or international powers by being subservient to them and their interests which has been placed over and above those of the Iraqis. This made some sarcastic Iraqis say that when some of today's politicians talk, one cannot judge whether they are truly Iraqis or representatives of foreign powers in Iraq. This applies to parties and politicians of all sects, ethnic groups and religions. It has now become quite customary to see politicians rushing to neighbouring countries or to the United States and the West to seek support when they find themselves in trouble, or when they want to maintain or get a certain position. By so doing, they compromise and jeopardize national political and economic interests. This shameful conduct has weakened Iraq internally, regionally and internationally. After it was a regionally and internationally recognized power, Iraq has become a country governed from abroad, where the influence of neighbouring countries and regional powers has become much greater than that of the official Iraqi state itself.

Real reconciliation will certainly ease the sectarian tension and bring peace, security and stability to the country. This will in turn revitalize society and strengthen the state. It will also restore Iraq to its normal and influential position regionally and internationally. A real and genuine social reconciliation will surely remove the corrupt and failed leaders, replacing them with patriotic, meritable, efficient and capable Iraqis who have the ability to maintain the sovereignty of their country, and restore Iraq's lost dignity and stature.

NOTES

1. See the letter written by the then Iraqi Minister of Interior, Abdul Mohsin al-Sadoun, to King Faisal I, who dispatched him in 1924 to Sulaimaniya to prop the dithering attitude of its population towards the idea of crowning him as King for Iraq. The minister wrote that all the dignitaries and tribal leaders he met were enthusiastic to swear fealty to the new king, and agreed to sign a memorandum to this effect the next day. When they met again the next morning they told the minister that since they cannot differentiate between what is right and what is wrong to them they leave the matter to the British political officers to decide for them. See Saad N. Jawad, Iraq and the Kurdish Question 1958–1970, Ithaca, London, 1981, p. 30.
2. See the King's memorandum to his ministers, Majid Abdul Hamid, algardinia, 14.09.2018. https://www.algardenia.com/maqalat/36983-2018-09-14-07-05-48.html.
3. Abdul Razzaq al-Hassani, Tarikh al-Wizarat al-Iraqia (History of Iraqi Cabinets), Vol. 2, p. 47.

4. Saad N. Jawad, op. cit., p. 52.
5. See for example the booklet issued by the then SG of the KDP, Ibrahim Ahmed, al-Akrad wa al-Arab (The Kurds and Arabs), Baghdad 1960 (2nd edition).
6. See the KDP programme of 1966 in Saad N. Jawad, op. cit., pp. 338–348. Saad N. Jawad, Ibid., p. 337, article 7.
7. When General Qasim legalised some political parties in 1961 the Islamic Party (Muslim Brotherhoods) applied for a licence, but it's request was rejected.
8. See some of the Fatwas of the high ranking Shiites Imams in: http://www.wata.cc/forums/showthread.php?25830 and https://www.alsumaria.tv/mobile/news/84240/iraq-news.
9. See the review of Dr. Abdul Sattar al-Rawi, the last Iraqi ambassador to Iran before 2003, of Dr. Ali Sabti's book al-Harb al-Iraqia al-Irania 1980–1988 (The Iraq Iran war 1980–1988) in: http://wijhatnadhar.org/article.php?id=11947.
10. Among those targeted were Tariq Azizi, a member of the Revolutionary Command Council, and the regional command of the Baath Party, and Latif Nusaif Jassim then minister of Information, both in 1980.
11. These parties only success before 2003 was abroad among Iraqi immigrants.
12. Ironically the SG of the ICP was appointed in this council not because he was leading a popular party, but because he was a Shiite, and that was what was written in the order after his name.
13. All the parties that participated in the political process after 2003 established (economic offices) to direct and manage the ministries that were allocated to them. These committees were literally to (loot) as much as possible from the budgets of these ministries.
14. See the text of the oath in the Iraqi Constitution, 2005, article 50.
15. Some confessions by those who carried these acts in different Arab areas could be found in: https://carnegie-mec.org/2014/09/23/ar-pub-56779.

As for examples of the same acts carried out by the Kurdish militias in Kirkuk, Mosul, Diyala and Takrit see: http://www.bbc.com/arabic/middleeast/2016/01/160119_iraq_kurdish_force_aminsty. https://www.raialyoum.com/index.php/كبيرة-اعداد-دمرت-كة-البيشمركة-ووتش-رايتس/.
16. See some of the declarations of some of the leading members of the KDP, especially Masrour al-Barzani, son of Massoud Barzani, in World Street Journal, 4/12/2015, and the threats of some sectarian militias to the Kurdish inhabitants of Baghdad, al-Arabi al-Jadeed newspaper 26/6/2017. See also Saad N. Jawad (Resala maftouha ila ra'yis iqleem Kurdistan), an open letter to the president of Kurdistan region, Rai al-Youm, London, 11/8/2017.

17. It is difficult to count the TV satellite channels that inseminate sectarian and racial poisons. It was said that it reached more than 50 TV stations in the first years of the occupation. The number of newspapers has exceeded 200, most of them funded by the political parties of the political process; many of them have been stopped due to financial difficulties. Now some sources estimate the number of newspapers published in Iraq is 35 newspapers, 29 Arabic, 2 English, and 2 Kurdish, with a big number of electronic ones and blogs, most of these newspapers are known for spreading divisions and hatred among the Iraqis.
18. https://www.newsweek.com/why-have-kurds-supplied-isis-weapons-452673.
19. Iraqi official sources claimed that the participation percentage was around 40%, other sources said that the percentage was not more than 20%. See: http://aliraqnews.com/مصادر-سياسية-بريطانية-٢٠-نسبة-المشاركة/.
20. Saad N. Jawad, The Iraqi Constitution: structural flaws and political implications, LSE, MEC, issue no. 1. 2013.
21. See for example the Preamble of the constitution, and articles 10 and 43 a.
22. Article 143.
23. See Chapter 5.
24. Officially the Iraqi Parliament named 62 militia groups as members of the Popular Mobilization Forces, all regarded as part of the Iraqi armed forces, but they are not affiliated to the Ministry of Defence. They were under the command of the prime minister, who is the commander in chief of the Iraqi armed forces. But many of these militias declared their loyalty to Iran and not to Iraq. Al-Arabi al-Jadeed newspaper, 9/2/2017.
25. Like the practices of hurting the body to show allegiances to the descendants of Prophet Mohammad, Instead of concentrating on the daily sufferings of the Iraqis.
26. The successive governments foiled many attempts to open dialogue with other parties or coalition outside the political process on the pretext that they do not want to sit down with representatives of the old regime. See: https://www.alsumaria.tv/mobile/news/51686/iraq-news.
27. A former minister of electricity, who was sentenced for corruption and jailed, was smuggled out of his prison in Baghdad and out of the country by a private security company working with the US army. Another former Iraqi minister of trade was freed from his imprisonment for corruption twice by orders from a prime minister, and sent to Britain, as he holds also a British passport. There are now more than a dozen of former ministers living abroad enjoying what they have looted from the Iraqi treasury, despite the many legal decisions taken against them by Iraqi courts.

28. Some primary schools in the south of Iraq give early morning lessons to the kids teaching them how to hurt themselves to show their (allegiances to the descendants of Prophet Mohammad). See: http://www.m.ahewar.org/s.asp?aid=534980&r=0&cid=0&u=&i=448&q=.

29. The best example is what happened in Basra in September 2018–2019 and after, when the headquarters of the religious parties were attacked and burned down, together with the Iranian and US consulates.

30. https://albaghdadiatv.com/alhgrt-alneabet-alfasdon-oalmtnfzon-srqoa-90-mn-alamoal-almkhsst-llnazhen/.

CHAPTER 7

Conclusion

Most analysts, or those capable of writing fictional stories in their wildest dreams could not have contemplated what had befallen Iraq since 2003. No one would have thought a new occupation will subject Iraq in the twenty-first century, at a time when the world considered the sixties of the last century as the end of the colonial era. It should also be remembered that the Iraqis have staged out a popular revolution in 1920 that succeeded in forcing the biggest colonial power at that time (Britain) to install an Iraqi government and drop the idea of direct colonialism. The regime that resulted from this revolution was dominated by Britain and bounded by unequal treaties, but it is also true that the then Iraqi ruling elite could have their say. Their fruitful efforts culminated in 1932 when Iraq achieved its independence and was the first Arab state to be a member of the League of Nations. Later on, Iraq became one of the founders of the United Nations, and played a role in helping other Arab countries to get their independence.

Most importantly the early rulers of Iraq (especially King Faisal I and Nouri al-Said, the man who formed 14 cabinets under the monarchy) realized that the country, after years of Ottoman domination, was in dire need for a sense of affiliation to, or consociation under the Iraqi identity. Despite all that was said and written about the monarchical period (1921–1958), one cannot deny that the regime endeavoured, and succeeded in

© The Author(s), under exclusive license to Springer Nature Switzerland AG 2021
S. N. Jawad, *Iraq after the Invasion*, Middle East Today,
https://doi.org/10.1007/978-3-030-72106-0_7

developing a sense of Iraqi citizenship. Yet this feeling was not an innovation. Such a spirit or feeling already had its roots among the Iraqis. It existed among Iraqis in general due to the common features that tied them together (language, religion, common social ties), and most importantly the close economic connection between the three Willayat (Baghdad, Mosul, and Basra). What Mosul harvests is sold to Baghdad and the southern regions, and vice versa. What Iraq needed in terms of essential commodities and foreign trade, reached all of Iraq through the port of Basra, linking a well-established sea-line with India, and then distributed to the rest of Iraq through two major rivers, Tigris and Euphrates.

When Britain announced its intention to nominate a new king for Iraq, candidates came from all walks of life in the Iraqi three Willayats, as well as from Arabistan (later annexed by Iran) which was then affiliated to the Greater Basra Wilayat. In other words, the citizens of all of what is known as Iraq felt that they had the right race for the throne. More indicative was that members of the three Willayats considered Baghdad as their capital, and indeed it was the administrative centre of all the three Willayats. In the end and as a final proof of the Iraqis consensus, most Iraqis accepted King Faisal I as king of Iraq.

The overthrow of the monarchy to a republican regime in 1958, which was received with overwhelming popular support, did not affect the spirit of Iraqi national unity, nor the feeling of citizenship or belonging to Iraq, it rather strengthened it. This was manifested by the staged massive demonstrations in favour of the change. However, the officers who assumed power after that date were unable to lay the foundations for an institutional democracy. Individualism and militarism were what characterized the new regime, and all the regimes that followed. The result was different types of dictatorships, whose hegemony and power increased and decreased according to the ruler's ability and desire. Gradually the deep differences between the various political parties or coalitions led Iraq to years of instability and internal sanguinary confrontations. Later on the Iraqi national figure, Hussein Jamil, who was a staunch opponent of the monarchy and a member of the National Union Front that supported the revolution, admitted the mistake of supporting the military coup against the monarchical regime by saying (unfortunately we sacrificed a bit of democracy for the sake of no democracy).[1] However, despite all the internal turmoil, tragedies and massacres that occurred, the differences remained political and not sectarian, religious, tribal or racial.

The most important thing is that these struggles did not affect the spirit of citizenship and the feeling of belonging to Iraq. Even the Kurdish parties (which were struggling for autonomy) always reiterated that they were not aiming at separation. This regrettable feeling or desire to separate and divide Iraq was not demonstrated until after the occupation in 2003.

Some analysts argue that the main reason for what happened to Iraq was the coup that toppled the royal regime. They insist that the monarchical regime had then initiated ambitious plans to develop Iraq and turn it into a model for the Arab nation, especially the eastern part of it, not to mention the fact that it already made Baghdad the second Arab centre of power similar to Cairo. In contrast, other analysts attributed all the tragedies that befell Iraq on the arrival to power of the Arab Baath Socialist Party for the second time (1968–2003, the first period being February to November 1963). Holders of this opinion believed that the Baath regime only succeeded in establishing a totalitarian regime that led Iraq to many internal and external crises. While supporters of the Baath party insisted that the regime succeeded in initiating and carrying out development plans that were described as (explosive) and very ambitious (especially after the nationalization of the oil industry in 1972 and the significant increase in its prices after the Ramadan War in October of 1973). Some economists thought that if Iraq continued to carry out these ambitious development plans at the pace it did; it would have made the country a regional economic power to be reckoned with. According to those holding this opinion, international powers (mainly the United States and Britain) and regional powers (Israel, Iran, and some Arab states, especially the neighbouring Gulf countries), were alarmed at the speed and size of the development, as well as the growing power of Iraq. Hence they endeavoured to foil these plans. Those who supported this opinion cited the many plots and intrigues manipulated by the late Shah of Iran, Israel and the USA, to weaken the Iraqi regime; the most obvious of them was the continuous incitement of the war in Iraqi Kurdistan. The Shah of Iran followed this policy since the beginning of the republican system in 1958 and was assisted by Israel at the beginning of the 1960s. The main Kurdish leader Mulla Mustafa al-Barzani, on his part, played in the hands of the Shah and refused to stop his armed revolt. Even when the Iraqi government agreed in 1970 to award the Kurdish region autonomy, after years of refusal, Mulla Mustafa refused the autonomy law upon the orders of the late Shah and resorted to war again in 1974 after four years of peace. All the efforts to convince Mulla Mustafa to accept the autonomy plan and try to develop it through practice were in vain. The damaging results of the continuous war in Iraqi Kurdistan (1961–1991) were huge in terms of human casualties (Arabs and Kurds), destruction and waste of financial resources. The most harmful effect was the damage and rift it caused to Arab-Kurdish relations in Iraq. It also left the door wide open for foreign interference. Through Iran, all the countries that were interested in weakening Iraq (mainly Israel, the Gulf countries, Syria and Libya) extended military and financial support to the Kurdish revolt. Needless to say that the Shah of Iran, and later on the Islamic regime, were not doing this for the blue eyes of the Kurds, as they were, and still are persecuting their Kurdish population. The Shah's main aim was to use the continuous war in Kurdistan as a pressure tool to force Iraq to accept the principle of sharing the Shatt al-Arab river, the only water outlet Iraq had to the Arabian (Persian) Gulf.[2] While Israel's main ambition was to keep Iraq embroiled in an internal war to weaken the Iraqi army and prevent it from participating in any war against the Jewish state.

When the war in Kurdistan erupted again in 1974, and despite the initial successes for the Iraqi armed forces, it became obvious that the armed Kurdish militias, the Peshmarga, were holding out only because of the Iranian armed support. At that stage, the Baath leadership opted for the idea of conceding to the Shah's demand rather than giving concessions to the Kurdish people.

What was unfortunate at that time was that Mulla Mustafa, despite all the remarks on his intentions and disbelieve in democracy, overlooked or was ignorant of the important fact that he and his party were a significant factor or barrier standing against the Baath Party's attempts to monopolize power. Also, the KDP's influence was so big that it was able to limit the excessive power and authority of the Baath government and defended the views that differed with the Baath policies in Iraq. This situation could have developed into a sort of a balanced situation between the authority and the opposition; unfortunately, it was thwarted by the submission of the leader of the KDP to the interests of external parties.

The Iraqi leadership, in turn, made the mistake of opting to make concessions to Iran, which resulted in the signing of the 1975 Algiers Agreement. In the end, and after the total collapse of the Kurdish revolt, the signature of that unjust agreement was what made the Iraqi Baath regime fish for any opportunity to abrogate it; hence was the decision to go to war against the new Islamic regime in Iran in 1980. This war and because of the economic burden it caused to Iraq, led to invading Kuwait in 1990, which in turn caused the imposition of the strict UN sanctions in the same year, then the 1991 war to oust Iraq from Kuwait, and finally the occupation of Iraq in 2003. Thus what the Iraqi Baath regime saw as an agreement that would end the continuous war in Iraqi Kurdistan, as a major threat to it, ended up being the first step, or cause for the fall of the regime itself later on. On the Kurdish dilemma in Iraq one could conclude that its persistence up till the present time was mainly due to two major issues: First, the reciprocal mistrust and ill-confidence that dominated the relations between the two sides: the successive Iraqi governments and the leaders of the Kurdish parties; Second was, and still is, the exaggerated demands, or over ambitions, of the Kurdish parties, as compared to an obsessing and dominating belief of all successive Iraqi government that the only way to solve the problem was by totally subduing the Kurdish region to the central authority.

Some other researchers argued that the success of the Iranian Islamic Revolution, its adoption of the principle of (exporting the revolution), and its attempts to encourage some components of the Iraqi people to destabilize Iraq and overthrow the Baath regime, were the causes and the basis for the initiation of hostilities which led to total war between the two neighbouring countries.

On his part, the Iraqi president, noticing the chaos Iran plunged in after the downfall of the Shah, thought that it was a golden opportunity to abrogate the Algiers agreement. Some subversive activities carried out by Iranian agents inside Iraq encouraged him, as well as assassination attempts against members of the Iraqi Baath leadership. Also, Iranian attacks initiated on Iraqi border towns and posts.

Thus the leadership of the two countries (Iraq and Iran), rushed to a war that was needless, useless and could have been easily avoided with little wisdom and prudence. The disastrous effects of the war were countless. Suffice it to say that it emptied the treasuries of the two countries and caused huge foreign debts, especially in the case of Iraq.

Perhaps the only positive result of this war for Iraq was that it showed the real tenacity of the character of most Iraqis. Through their surge to defend their homeland, the Iraqis proved their adherence to their Arab-Iraqi identity and their refusal to be conquered by non-Arab Iran. On his part, Ayatollah Khomeini, who thought that he could topple the Baath regime and rule Iraq with the help of the Shiites of Iraq, had to drink the cup of poison and accept a permanent ceasefire, as a sign that his strategy failed. The Iraqis love for their homeland proved to be deeper than their sectarian affiliation. However, Khomeini explained the issue in a sectarian and racist way.[3]

Of grave concern was the unprecedented boost of the new Islamic regime in Iran, and later on, the Iraq–Iran war gave to sectarianism and sectarian ideas, parlance and notions. The new Iranian Islamic regime tried very hard to fuel sectarian sentiments among the Arab-Iraqi Shiites, calling upon them to get rid of the Sunni-dominated rule. Whereas the Baath regime also pursued a sectarian policy by deporting a huge number of Iraqi Shiite families to Iran, on the pretext that they were of Iranian origin, even though many of them were born in Iraq or have inhabited it for tens of years, or even more than a century for some. Some members of this category were among the leaders of the national movement in Iraq, and a fair number of their sons were qualified and efficient employees and even members of the armed forces. The Baath regime at that time was or has invoked some of the demonstrations that occurred in Iraq before 1979, and later on, some terrorist acts encouraged by Iran and carried out in Baghdad by a small number of people of Iranian origin. This violent approach by the regime was not detracted because the Baath Party was secular and the founders of its branch in Iraq, together with its first leaders there, and a majority of its followers were Shiite Arab youths. On top of that, these terrorist acts did not pose a real threat to the Baath regime, as its efficient security apparatus was able to thwart these acts, arrest the perpetrators, and quickly dismantle the cells that carried them out. The essence of these policies caused a deep crack in the Shiite–Sunni relations in Iraq, which was only muted by Iranians' continued wish to invade Iraq during the war and the ruthless way the security institutions in Iraq dealt with any opposition.

With the increasing sectarian tension, together with the escalated war with Iran, the idea of dividing Iraq into three entities emerged. Not surprisingly it was Israel that promoted, adopted and encouraged that idea in 1982. This idea indeed failed because Iraq was able to end the war in its favour, and it was considered at that time a funny and unrealistic idea, but the mere presence of it made many parties revive and adopt it (especially the United States), to end any future Iraqi attempts to play a leading role in the region. After the occupation of Iraq, the then vice president Joe Biden advocated this idea for a while.

The massive military power Iraq acquired during the war, accompanied by the large debts caused by it, pushed the late president Saddam Hussein to take the catastrophic decision to invade Kuwait in August 1990, in the hope that this measure will rid Iraq of its economic problems. Apart from claiming that historically Kuwait was part of Iraq, he tried to prove his action by claiming that it was the only way to stop an economic war being waged against his regime by some Arab Gulf countries under the orders of the United States and Britain. While it was true that Kuwait and the United Arab Emirates were flooding the oil markets, a policy that caused a huge drop in oil prices and so increased the economic suffering of Iraq, and Kuwait seized the opportunity of Iraq's embroilment in the war with Iran to explore and extract oil from Iraqi oilfields on their mutual borders, but the real reason to annex Kuwait was the serious economic difficulties and debts on Iraq due to the long war with Iran. The Iraqi leadership after the end of the war thought that the creditor countries, especially the Arab Gulf states, would waive the debts that they provided to Iraq during the war, or at least significantly cut them because Iraq's sacrifices saved these states from a possible Iranian infiltration, domination or even occupation.

It escaped the mind of the head of the Iraqi regime then that the major powers, especially the United States and Britain, and the regional countries headed by Israel, were alarmed by the large military power Iraq possessed. Thus they were not ready to turn a blind eye to the decision to annex Kuwait which would certainly add great economic power to the Iraqi regime. At the end, invading Kuwait provided the instigation of United States and Britain, by Israel; with the pretext of launching an attack that would drive the Iraqi forces out of Kuwait, destroy its military strength, its infrastructure, and tighten the strict sanctions on it. One could also argue that the end of the 1991 war saw the first steps to disintegrate Iraq, as the United States and the European countries declared the northern and southern no-fly zones in Iraq, a decision that resulted in curbing any presence of the Iraqi authority in the north, and greatly limited it in the south.

Perhaps the most eager party to topple the regime of Saddam Hussein at that time was Israel. This was because of the decision of the late Iraqi president to fire 39 long-range missiles at Tel Aviv during the 1991 war. In fact, this decision inaugurated a new Arab strategy (which all resistance factions later pursued), to end the Israeli military superiority that prevailed until that moment. Israel considered that the daring decision represented a great challenge to its existence and that Saddam Hussein if allowed to stay in power could do the same at any moment.[4]

Although the goals of liberating Kuwait and destroying the biggest part of the Iraqi military forces were successful, together with the measure taken to restrict Iraq's attempts to return as a regional power, such as maintaining the strict sanctions, neither Israel nor the Iraqi external opposition was satisfied with. It also seemed that some parts of the US administration were also not happy to see defiant Saddam Hussein remaining in power. The effort of all these parties prompted President Clinton's administration to issue (the Iraq Liberation Act 1998), as well as carrying several destructive air attacks on the capital (Baghdad).

Following the 9/11 terrorist attacks, and because of the US failure to avoid them, the neo-conservative administration decided to take action to show the world that it was still the supreme international power. Al-Qaeda terrorist organization was signalled out as the group declared responsibility for planning and carrying out the attacks. Iraq was also accused of being an accomplice, although the United States could not produce any proof to support this claim. Lately evidence emerged categorically confirming that few days after these attacks the US administration decided to topple the Baath regime in Iraq, accusing it of conniving with the Al-Qaeda terrorist organization. This false accusation was similar to the one that was widely publicized by the USA, Britain, Israel and western media networks, after the 1991 Gulf war, that Iraq was either hiding or still manufacturing WMD. In fact, the failure to produce convincing evidence about the above-mentioned accusations was what made the Security Council declined the approval of the invasion of Iraq in 2003.

Days after the 9/11 attacks, arrangements and plans were in place to invade Iraq. Part of these arrangements was to fully adapt, manipulate and exploit all the Iraqi external opposition groups to use them to destabilise and topple the Baath regime, even though they had no major support inside Iraq.

The United States, backed mainly by Britain and Israel, with symbolic participation of other countries, formed an international coalition that invaded Iraq in March 2003. This decision caused massive international popular protests. It was said that between January and April 2003, 36 million people across the globe took part in almost 3000 protests against the war on Iraq. Europe saw the biggest mobilization of protesters, including a rally of three million people in Rome alone. However, these activities didn't deter President G.W. Bush and Premier Tony Blair from their decision. The most important conclusion one could draw from these facts is that all the US governments' claims about the role and influence of public opinion on shaping decision-making were a mere farce.

To justify the occupation, the USA, Britain and Israel invented several lies and fabricated allegations. On top of the false claim that Iraq possessed WMD, the United States also claimed that the deteriorating human rights situation, absence of democracy and lack of freedom, especially for women in Iraq were issues raising international concern. All of these allegations can only be described as right words to prove wrong implications, or as they say in English (a wolf in sheep clothing). More than eighteen years of occupation and rule of governments imposed by the United States, the human rights situation in Iraq has deteriorated further due to insecurity, complete chaos, mass killings, torture, humiliating treatment to prisoners and disrespect to human rights were what characterized the Iraqi situation after the occupation. These negative phenomena, together with the spreading and mushrooming of illegally armed militias and private foreign and local security companies as well as the widespread corruption, made a large percentage of simple Iraqis yearn for the Baath regime and its former president. A fair number of former dissidents or members of the external opposition of the Baath regime wrote and spoke with remorse about the mistakes made by them that caused misery to the Iraqi people. Indeed, many leading members of the post-occupation regime even regretted that they had taken part in the process of removing the Baath one or assisting the occupying forces. As for the democracy established by the occupation, it was nothing but a (legitimize) massive corruption, that emptied the Iraqi treasury, squandered its resources and caused the starvation of the majority of the population. It was also a sterile process to recycle and protect corrupt politicians. Yet the freedom boasted about was nothing but freedom for armed militias to assassinate and kidnap whoever criticizes them and loot as much as possible from public funds. Not a single murder was seriously investigated nor a single assassin taken to account, and not a single big official was sentenced for his or her corruption, even though most of them were penniless before the occupation, and within a short period became millionaires.

Thus, Iraq was soon rated as a failed state par excellence. It was also considered one of the most dangerous countries to live in and one of the most corrupt countries in the world. Illiteracy became widespread, after it was eradicated in the seventies of the last century. Iraq was also described as the state of widows and orphans, as well as the country that displaced a quarter of its population, living in camps, or migrated (internally and externally).

Following the occupation, Iraq became the only country in the world that does not have a proper army, police forces, or any Iraqi security or military services that maintained law and order. This was due to Bremer deciding to disband the old army and security forces, replacing them with one based on the militias of the parties that came with the occupation. The occupation forces did not fulfil their duty, as stipulated in international conventions, to maintain law and security to prevent chaos, looting and random killing. Indeed, the occupation forces were also accused of having participated in the assassination attempts that took place after 2003.

The main negative result of the designs to invade and occupy Iraq was that they were based on the idea that there was nothing called Iraq or Iraqi identity. For the occupying administration, Iraq was merely a collection of different sects, religions and racial groups. This harmful way of thinking did not remain as a viewpoint; it was embodied in the new permanent constitution that was drafted by a junior US law lecturer.

The problem with the constitution (like the Transitional Administrative Law that preceded it, and of which the Constitution was, in fact, a copy), was not only it being written originally in English by non-Iraqi, or that its translation into Arabic was weak, the more serious problem was that it did not give any importance to the issue of citizenship, belonging to Iraq and the preservation of territorial integrity. In other words, many of its contradictory clauses were encouraging indirectly, and even directly, the sense of multiple identities in the country that in turn encouraged the possibility of fragmentation. It in reality laid the foundations for tearing and fragmenting Iraq, or keeping it weak and dispersed at best. For this purposes, it intentionally kept some articles vague and shrouded with ambiguity.

Finally and most importantly in reality this constitution is an illegal or forged document. This was because after its draft was supposed to have been accepted through a general referendum (with serious claims of rigging and forgery), five new articles that affected the unity of the state were added secretly without even informing the committee that was supposed to have drafted the constitution, or the general public.

Treating Iraq as an entity composed of different sects and nationalities by the occupying administration, as well as appointing officials according to the sectarian and racial quota system, and insisting on incarnating all these ideas in a divisive constitution that ignited the fuse of sectarianism and racial differences. As a result, this deepened the division inside the Iraqi society. The ruling clique was not interested in healing this division merely because it believed, almost rightly, that keeping and boosting it was the best way for their survival and remaining in power. National reconciliation thus became another problem. Sectarian, religious and racial division was widespread and caused area cleansing, armed confrontations and mass killings, either on the hands of the militias supporting such a policy or on the many terrorist groups that infiltrated Iraq following the occupation, such al-Qaeda or ISIS (Daesh). Every religious sect or nationality in Iraq began to depend on its militia and on a foreign power to support it. On top of the US influence, Iran, Turkey, Israel and the Gulf Arab states became major and influential players in Iraqi politics.

As the successive governments and ruling political parties showed no real interest in carrying out general, comprehensive, and national reconciliation, it is essential that other civil society organization accept this vital task. Professional unions, Universities, artists, tribal leaders, religious leaders (clergymen) of all religions and sects, as well as independent media should take upon themselves the duty of bridging the gap created by the new politicians and parochial religious and racial leaders.

In the end, remembering that the many problems facing Iraq today are in essence part of the region's chronicle problems, especially the Arab–Israeli dispute, the war in Syria, and the Iranian–US dispute. The suffering of the Iraqis will not end without finding a solution to these problems, especially the war in Syria, which is fostering terrorism in the area and spilling it into Iraq, and the rising US–Iranian tension and confrontation, which are culminated by the two sides attempting to make Iraq their battleground.

To conclude, one cannot but blame the ill-thought-out and misguided decision taken by the United States and Britain to invade and occupy Iraq. Iraq has since its US-led invasion in 2003 descended into a labyrinth of sectarian conflict and has fallen under the ubiquitous influence of the heavy Iranian infiltration. Widespread corruption and the mushrooming of terrorist organizations have compounded matters and worsened the already fraught situation. On the other hand, the hastily compiled constitution has etched even deeper the mutual suspicion between the central government and the KRG. The systematic destruction of Iraq, the state, cannot be stopped unless its people find their own way to genuine democracy and freedom. Only then can they start rebuilding their country.

The international community (especially the UN) which has stood by watching disaster after disaster unfold, should also rise to the challenge of their responsibility. The notion which some international and regional powers entertain which purports that a strong Iraq is a threat to world and regional peace and even to their own national security has proved to be wrong. Events have clearly demonstrated that a weak and disunited Iraq, dominated by uncontrollable militias and terrorist groups is beyond any doubt the real threat to its own people as well as to the region and international peace and security.

NOTES

1. Direct conversation with H. Jamil, October 1973, Baghdad.
2. The Gulf's historical name was the Gulf of Basra; there are many old Ottoman maps to prove that. It was only in the sixteenth century that the Safawid Shah has changed its name to the Persian Gulf. For the last five decades, many sources refer to it simply as The Gulf.
3. It was said that following the failure of Aytollah Khomeinis strategy to instigate the Iraqi Shiites, he said (this is not something strange for the Iraqis, aren't they the ones who abandoned and killed Imam Ali and his Son Imam Hussein?).
4. As an example of the fear that the Iraqi president might do the same during the invasion of 2003, the USA dispatched some special forces to the western Sahara of Iraq to make sure that there were no long-range missiles launchers directed at Israel.

INDEX

CPSIA information can be obtained
at www.ICGtesting.com
Printed in the USA
LVHW080326220722
724147LV00003B/33

9 783030 721053